THE REFORMATION

THE REFORMATION

Roots and Ramifications

Heiko A. Oberman

Translated by Andrew Colin Gow

William B. Eerdmans Publishing Company
Grand Rapids, Michigan

Published in Great Britain by T&T Clark Ltd,
59 George Street, Edinburgh EH2 2LQ, Scotland

This edition published under license from T&T Clark Ltd by

Wm. B. Eerdmans Publishing Co.,
255 Jefferson Ave. S.E., Grand Rapids, Michigan 49503

First published 1994

ISBN 0 8028 0825 5

Typeset by Buccleuch Printers Ltd, Hawick
Printed and bound in Great Britain by Redwood Books, Wiltshire

'Palma sub pondere crescit'

Gerrit Willem
Ida
Hester Elsa
Raoul Foppe Maarten Luther

Bora
Ruben
Simon
Wouter
Darijn

'Fama crescit eundo'

CONTENTS

PREFACE

All of the essays in this volume share a common goal, in that each investigates the unity and the expansion of the Reformation movement. The book's title announces both a program and an urgent question: What effect did the original reformer, Martin Luther, have on the Reformation of the sixteenth century? What was religiously changed; what was politically 're-formed' – in the cities and principalities, inside and outside the Empire, in the fast-changing social constellations – on the journey from the Protestant breakthrough to the Protestant diaspora? In my view the questions raised here are crucial to the central quest in Reformation scholarship today.

In the past I have concentrated primarily on the transition from medieval to early modern Europe, and on the unmistakable identity of the Reformation when it is seen from the perspective of the later Middle Ages. This volume, however, follows the winding path of the Reformation from Wittenberg through the southern German cities, south to Zurich, and then on to Geneva. These essays, first published between 1966 and 1984, during my tenure at Tübingen, are not organized here by the dates of their publication or conception, but according to historical and chronological criteria. Nearly all of them were originally written to honor specific Reformation commemorations – not surprising, since I enjoyed the privilege of being able to help to plan and carry out a decade of recollective celebrations in Europe: the Peasants' War (1975), the Confessio Augustana (1980), the Luther-Year (1983) and the Zwingli Memorial (1984). These 'external' duties provided unique opportunities for interpreting history, both within and outside the lecture-hall, addressing specialists as well as a broader public – opportunities for making history relevant for today. One cannot reach this sort of goal by following the well-worn paths of contemporary trends and methods of thinking. Goethe's description of the Devil, 'Er is der Geist, der stets verneint', may not, in fact, fit *him;* but in three respects, in the face of three challenges, it must fit the historian – he must be the one who says 'No!'

First, Reformation scholars tend to be moved by an ecumenical desire – by no means contemptible in itself – to blame the division of western Christendom on dogmatic disputes, which we today, from our enlightened perspective, are said to recognize as 'misunderstandings'. It is as if scholars breathe a sigh of long-overdue relief, and want to abandon our past in the dustbin of history. Reformation studies are exploited as a promising field in which they may test and prove their modern, optimistic theories. They hail the Catholic 'recognition' of the Augsburg Confession, and applaud the 'ecumenical breadth' of the *Confutatio.* And ecumenical rapprochement can indeed be brought about in this fashion – but only if the doctrine of justification, central to the Reformation, is truncated to fit the pronouncements of the Council of Trent, or rephrased in terms of its being the forerunner of psychological 'self-fulfillment'. In either case, the cost is exorbitant: the doctrine of justification itself.

Secondly, in our day social history is in its ascendancy; its impatience with traditional historiography is so well-founded that we cannot afford to ignore it. Social historians have presented Reformation scholars with a whopping bill for their withdrawal into the comfortable, exclusive, and safe world of ideas. The history of theology becomes powerless – senseless – when it is removed from the rough-and-ready conditions of 'real', everyday life. Hence the suspicion that the entire exercise of intellectual history is nothing but an artificial construct, built on literary sources drawn mainly from the pens of an educated élite, is quite understandable. It is true that historians have subjected the theology of the reformers to a probing and minute analysis for far too long, without seeking even a partial answer to the one inescapable question: How did a system so difficult and so refined spread so far and obtain such far-reaching results? It is not only the writings and sermons of the reformers that were significant; what was heard 'at the bottom' or 'on the highest rungs' –

what eventually changed in people's beliefs, in their political and social mentality – was also of great importance. But now the anti-theological reaction has gone so far that it is time to return once more to the sources of the Reformation, to re-emphasize the 'spade work' that is necessary to arrive at any understanding of these sources – to listen and to watch, with an eye bent keenly upon reality – in order to follow the Reformation from its theological inception to its religious impact.

The third battleground is just as important as the first two, and is peculiarly connected with them: On both sides of the Atlantic a new 'orthodoxy' is emerging. The twentieth-century Luther renaissance freed the reformer from the fetters of the Lutheran Confessions (thanks primarily to the work of Karl Holl and his students). Since the Second World War, however, a new Luther has been molded along lines that only *seem* to have followed the path laid out by Holl. This new Luther is presented as the 'first modern man', who overcame the Middle Ages and cleared the way for modernity. Nothing could be farther from the truth. Luther went against the grain of both the Middle Ages *and* the modern world. From our perspective, he is a man between the times, not a man of any one particular era; but from his own perspective, his life and calling existed at the very end of time itself. The modern 'Lutheran' Luther must be completely reworked – an unexpected, and therefore expensive and painful, 'Reformation'.

The title pages bear two classical proverbs, strangely appropriate to the roots and ramifications of the Reformation. The first, 'Palma sub pondere crescit', the motto of Queen Emma of the Netherlands, applies fully to the Reformation: the movement grew under pressure and under persecution, by which it developed in spiritual depth. 'Fama crescit eundo', also draws upon human experience; that is, not only misleading rumor, but the reforming message itself, 'grows as it spreads'. In its growth and spreading, this message spawned descendants of its own, quite different from the original, which deserve to be appreciated in their own right, and to be evaluated with insight and respect.

The index of names and modern authors was compiled by Dr Sabine Holtz; Dr Sigrun Haude carefully gathered the *Index Verborum Latinorum*. Mr Scott Manetsch made many helpful comments and suggestions during the drafting of the penultimate version of the translation. Mr Peter Dykema applied his gift of precision to the proofs. Undoubtedly, the most difficult work was the English translation, undertaken by Dr Andrew Gow, who proved to be an able intermediary, not merely in rendering conventional words, but in bridging the unconventional worlds separated by the Atlantic.

Finally, I must reveal my indebtedness to two people: to Ms Suse Rau, who has typed at least once the German versions of each of these essays, always under considerable pressure to beat yet another deadline; and to Mr Manfred Schulze, who thought through the architecture of the German edition with me, and who suggested – in places even demanded – revisions to the original texts.

Heiko A. Oberman
Tucson, Arizona

LIST OF ABBREVIATIONS

AWA	*Archiv zur Weimarer Lutherausgabe*
C	Centuria; see John Eck, *Chrysopassus*, Augsburg 1514
CC	*Corpus Catholicorum*
CChr	*Corpus Christianorum*
Conf.	Confutatio; in Herbert Immenkötter, *Die Confutatio der Confessio Augustana vom 3. August 1530*, *CC* 33, Münster 1979, 74–207
CR	*Corpus Reformatorum*
EA var. arg.	*D. Martini Lutheri opera Latina varii argumenti*, Erlangen 1865
MGH.SS	*Monumenta Germaniae Historica:* Scriptores
PL	*Patrologiae cursus completus: Series Latina*
RE	*Realencyklopädie für protestantische Theologie und Kirche*
RGG	*Die Religion in Geschichte und Gegenwart*
SVRG	Schriften des Vereins für Reformationsgeschichte
WA	*D. Martin Luthers Werke: Kritische Gesamtausgabe, Schriften*
WAB	*D. Martin Luthers Werke: Kritische Gesamtausgabe, Briefwechsel*
WADB	*D. Martin Luthers Werke: Kritische Gesamtausgabe, Die Deutsche Bibel*
WAT	*D. Martin Luthers Werke: Kritische Gesamtausgabe, Tischreden*
ZKG	*Zeitschrift für Kirchengeschichte*
ZThK	*Zeitschrift für Theologie und Kirche*
ZW	*Huldreich Zwinglis sämtliche Werke*

Chapter 1

THE REFORMATION: THE QUEST FOR THE HISTORICAL LUTHER

1. The Growth of a Reformer

Intellectual history is under heavy fire. Its ambitious project of uncovering the idea 'ultimately' determinative of an era, 'the spirit of the age', has encountered vigorous opposition. Research in late medieval, Renaissance and Reformation history, with its deeply-layered intellectual traditions, is particularly susceptible to this sort of attack. Detailed work on Italian humanism and the history of its dissemination in the world of ideas is more and more frequently described as élitist scholarship, although book reviews are still the preferred forum for such ideas. Yet studies on the beginnings of the Reformation – for example, in the imperial cities – written without the slightest knowledge of theological history are no longer confined to the realm of nightmare. Historians who think nothing of applying psychosomatic insights to their everyday lives work hard in their professional writing and teaching to tear mind from matter, often without any clear ideological motivation for doing so.

Yet this concentrated critical attack is justified only in so far as it concerns the history of ideas. The history of thought, however, is in my view something else altogether. It tells the story of how people come to grips, both intellectually and emotionally, with the circumstances and conditions of their life. Understood in this way, the history of thought is in no danger of being condemned as irrelevant and élitist. Individuals and groups struggle to make sense of life through what they think and what they do; this struggle in turn contributes to the environment and living conditions of both contemporaries and posterity. If history claims to do more than record data and statistics, it must address the question of how people come to grips with the conditions that govern their life. Yet it would be impossible to undertake such an analysis

1

without a clear understanding of specific circumstances. The history of thought works best when it sticks to its topic – ever mindful of the goals set by its synthetic method – and searches the primary sources to discover the story of how people come to grips with the conditions that govern their life.

For Luther scholarship this rules out any retreat to the 'ideal space' of the reformer's study. Such a retreat permits the knowledge and recognition of one theme only: Luther, the interpreter of Scripture, outside time and space, on a lonely voyage of exploration through the Word of God, left to himself by the traditional authorities and soon abandoned by succeeding generations. The history of thought, on the other hand, gives the reformer back his historical position. It takes seriously the conditions in which he lived, and therefore takes root in concrete reality. It discovers Luther's schooling in the *via moderna,* then his life in an observant Augustinian monastery, with its ordered daily round of prayer, meditation and scholarly study. Decisive in the development of Luther's thought were his acceptance in 1512 of the Augustinian professorship at Wittenberg and, starting in 1515, political responsibility for the two Augustinian *studia* ('seminaries') in Saxony, as well as the maintenance of correct observance in a large district covering eleven religious houses. On this stage, he appears as an administrator and an organizer, led from the very beginning by a strong sense of the direct challenge of heresy and the danger it poses to the unity of the Church.[1] From the Augustinian tradition he inherited the belief that theology is the guardian of the true Church, but this traditional truth became real and practical to him only during years of fierce controversy about the realization of the true Church within his own order. In what follows we will concentrate on the *via moderna,* because nominalism has been either discounted as a transitional phase or vilified as a lasting un-Catholic poison, and used to attack the Reformation.

Luther, at age 25, took with him from Erfurt to Wittenberg a fund of scholarly ground-work and religious convictions as well as the greatest respect for both faith and scholarship. But Luther's unmistakable traits first come into view in Wittenberg, as he learned to sift through the maelstrom of experiences that poured in on him. As he liked to put it, he strode forward through public disputation

[1] Cf. Ulrich Mauser, *Der junge Luther und die Häresie,* SVRG 184, Gütersloh 1968, 91ff.

and quiet study, through teaching, preaching and the necessity to express himself in writing.[2] The historical Luther cannot be located and pinned down once and for all – as his development shows. His historical significance must not be allowed to work as a selective filter that automatically answers, in a pious and predetermined way, the question of how Luther digested and molded the tradition handed down to him. Luther's historical position does, however, compel us to set the reforming upheaval and breakthrough within the framework of the medieval inheritance that Luther brought with him to Wittenberg, a system and style of thinking and believing that continued, for the time being, to flourish at that university. This line of reasoning has certain consequences. In his commentary on Romans, Luther for the first time castigated the leaders of his own school and his teachers in the *via moderna*. His attack of 1515/16 on 'those stinking, swinish theologians [*Sautheologen*]' does not mean that he had 'sloughed off the [Roman] snakeskin'. His new beginning has been interpreted as a sharp break or a refounding of scholarship, theology, the Christian faith and the Catholic church, free of presuppositions and premises. Nothing could be farther from the truth. Coming to grips with the past, even when the attempt succeeds, will never obliterate the archetypes that provide our perceptual and conceptual models. Even the reformer has obligations; he too is bound by ties of kin.

2. The Reformation: Conflicts and Controversies

These last statements carry us into the midst of the scholarly cross-fire. The quest for the historical Luther compels us to take a stand on the broader question of just what the Reformation was. One choice has forced itself on generations of historians: either the Reformation was the last outlying foothills of the Middle Ages, or it was a new departure, the beginning of the modern era. According to an announcement made by two German secular historians in 1978, the assumption of a breach between the Middle Ages and the Reformation was caused by an optical illusion. Modern scholars have only recently discovered how to see through this illusion. The inner unity between the late medieval and early modern periods is now established as a

---

[2] *WAB* 1, 389.21–390.24; May 1519.

proven result of research, and the quest for a watershed is dismissed as antiquated:

> For quite some time now, the traditional frontier between the 'Middle Ages' and 'modern times' (a frontier generally placed about 1500) has posed a vexed question in historical research. The revolution involving the Renaissance, the Reformation, discoveries and inventions, changes in society, economic life, church and state between the fifteenth century and the sixteenth evidently [sic!] lacks the profound significance ascribed to it for centuries. Compared to the fundamental changes introduced starting in the mid-eighteenth century by industrialization and revolution, the supposed chasm around 1500, which allegedly divides two whole eons from one another, looks rather small. That which connects before and after, what they have in common, and that which survived into the eighteenth century – the elements of social order and ways of life, and above all the values that sustain daily life and determine the conflicts of countries and religious denominations – is more and more evident, despite the changing times.[3]

The experiences of the post-Reformation era, from the beginning of the Enlightenment down to today's ecological crisis, make earlier periods look like an undifferentiated continuum. We may expect that in the next century, our own time will appear similarly 'medieval' to many a historian without firm ideological commitments. And yet this viewpoint, as a *historical* judgement, must be challenged: not primarily because it underestimates Luther's importance, although it does. Indeed, Luther would have been the first to insist that the Reformation had been unable to realize the hoped-for 'revaluation of all values' in the Church and among the 'common folk', in theology

---

[3] 'Schon seit langem ist der Forschung die traditionelle, gewöhnlich um das Jahr 1500 angesetzte Grenzscheide zwischen "Mittelalter" und "Neuzeit" problematisch geworden. Der Umbruch, der durch Renaissance, Reformation, Entdeckungen, durch Erfindungen und Wandlungen in Gesellschaft, Wirtschaft, Kirche und Staat zwischen dem 15. und 16. Jahrhundert geschehen ist, hat offensichtlich [!] nicht die Tiefendimension, die ihm seit Jahrhunderten beigelegt worden ist. Angesichts der fundamentalen Veränderungen, die seit der Mitte des 18. Jahrhunderts durch Industrialisierung und Revolutionen eingeleitet worden sind, schrumpft der vermeintliche Graben um 1500, der gar zwei Weltalter voneinander trennen soll, zusammen: das Verbindende, Gemeinsame zwischen Vorher und Nachher und das bis ins 18. Jahrhundert hinein Überdauernde gerade in den Grundzügen der Gesellschafts- und Lebensordnung und vor allem den Wertvorstellungen, die das tägliche Leben tragen und die Auseinandersetzungen der Staaten und Konfessionen bestimmten, tritt durch alle Veränderungen der Zeiten hindurch immer stärker zutage' (Joseph Engel and Ernst Walter Zeeden, introduction to the series 'Spätmittelalter und Frühe Neuzeit. Tübinger Beiträge zur Geschichtsforschung', in: Karl Trüdinger, *Stadt und Kirche in spätmittelalterlichen Würzburg*, Stuttgart 1978, 7).

and in society. He grappled repeatedly with the abuse of 'Christian freedom' not only by the peasants, but also by the 'big shots'. His realistic perception of the true situation led to visitations and the Lutheran Catechism.

The view that no dividing line is to be found here must be refuted. To hold this view, from the detached scholarly heights of great historical distance, is to judge by the standards of our modern, secular twentieth-century perspective, thus overlooking the way in which that earlier 'modern era' saw and understood itself. Part of our task as historians is to make judgements based on our own 'modern' perspective, and thus to pursue historical investigation as the *pre*-history to our own times. But this is only one part of a larger task. It is equally important – and this is what makes the writing of history a scientific undertaking – for us as historians to be directed by an understanding of our own time as *post*-history. The modern era, by no means the inevitable outcome of earlier epochs, has fulfilled, adopted and pursued no more than a gleaning of the many possibilities offered by the past. The 'present' is the result of a selection process: we have left behind many forces and ideas, many false starts, but also many discoveries of earlier times. The way our ancestors saw and understood themselves must not, as a matter of principle, be overlooked. Their view of themselves finds eloquent expression precisely in sixteenth-century sources. Everywhere in these sources we find the awareness that what men and women are experiencing and suffering is an abrupt change in the times. This applies not only within the sphere of influence of the Reformation, but also in humanistically enlightened circles and in the opposing camp of the old Church.

The canonization of whatever happens to be the most modern perspective at any given time has particularly serious consequences in the study of history. An indispensable tool in the hands of the historian, the historical scalpel is thus misused as a levelling scythe. The scalpel as a historical tool can be used specifically to expose both continuity *and* discontinuity between the late Middle Ages and the Reformation. The task at hand is as far as possible to present the Reformation as a medieval phenomenon – in order to work out what is new about it. The assumption of an inner unity between the late Middle Ages and the early modern period is not in question here.

What is questionable is the decision to be content with asserting this unity without reference to the new understanding, characteristic for the early modern period, of God, human beings, the Church, hierarchical structures and the secular order. It is both peculiar and darkly significant that this position can find support in certain trends of the Luther renaissance, which has portrayed Luther's theology as so subtle that the reformer would have been understood by no single one of his contemporaries and by very few of those who came after him. It would be impossible to proclaim a change of epochs based on so solitary a figure, particularly if theology, spirituality and religion are conceded no part in shaping the course of history – which is supposed to have been determined 'in the final analysis' only by politics and economics.

If we are to stick to the historian's task of interrogating a particular epoch, of searching for the protean aspects of how it viewed itself, then we must track down the multifarious factors that contribute to the profile of the time, or even determine it. This means surveying the late Middle Ages, the Renaissance and the Reformation as a whole; this three-fold division, familiar to us though it is, also belongs to a view of the past as *pre*-history. What is in fact a single era is thus carved up into three.

This epochal survey must be supplemented by respect for theological, political and social forces as determining factors if we are to gain access to the age of the Reformation. Constant change in the central viewpoint of the eighteenth, nineteenth and twentieth centuries decreed that in each case one of these three factors would be judged to be entirely determinative; a comprehensive explanation was expected from each one in turn. We ought to treat such all-encompassing claims with a healthy dose of skepticism. All three factors will have to be pressed into service to illuminate this epoch, each in its own way. All three will have to be pondered carefully and balanced each against the others on the level of what I regard as a new history of thought. For this history of thought is not the Hegelian history of ideas, but rather the history of how people have come to grips with the changing conditions that govern their lives. Understood in this way, the history of thought concerns the attempt by individuals or groups to cope with life. In so far as these attempts have been successful, they in their turn contribute to the environment and living conditions of contemporaries and posterity. Whenever either social structures, political events or polemical theological writings are required to carry alone the complete explanatory burden of this epoch and are invested with absolute hegemony, only *one* layer is exposed. We see only a fraction of the conditions that determined how life was lived. Even if we are forced to conclude that as specialists we can generally bring light to only one of these areas, such work must be understood as a contribution toward a complete portrait of the Reformation.

We hardly need to worry whether the role of political and social factors has been accorded sufficient recognition. However, the theological dimension, the due regard for faith as a potent force in history, is clearly in danger of being forgotten. Reformation historians have reacted in very different ways to the enormous challenge of recent social history. Some have withdrawn to Luther's beginnings, clinging to him as the original figure of the Reformation, primal and unique. Others have jumped onto recent psychological and psychoanalytic bandwagons. They explain Luther's Reformation as the liberation of the conscience from the yoke of the confessional.[4] A third group remains under the spell of the nineteenth century. Here, theological factors are barely touched on. The Reformation is absorbed into the course of German political history.[5] The importance these historians ascribe to the Diet of Worms is reminiscent of the confident belief that publishing the documents concerning the imperial diets had finally made accessible the sources necessary to study the 'real' history of the Reformation.

In all these approaches – Luther renaissance, psychohistory and political history – one great and obstinately irreducible sixteenth-century dimension has been suppressed, though in a different way in each case. This dimension is that of faith and choices concerning faith, the dimension of theology, the dispute about the form of the Church, and the beginnings of a new spirituality. Scholars of the

---

[4] Steven E. Ozment, *The Reformation in the Cities. The Appeal of Protestantism to Sixteenth Century Germany and Switzerland,* New Haven 1975. Cf. Hans-Christoph Rublack, 'Forschungsbericht Stadt und Reformation', in: *Stadt und Kirche im 16. Jahrhundert,* ed. B. Moeller, SVRG 190, Gütersloh 1978, 9–26; 23.

[5] Bernd Moeller, *Deutschland im Zeitalter der Reformation,* Deutsche Geschichte 4, Göttingen 1977. Cf. here Robert Scribner's review in: *The Journal of Ecclesiastical History* 29 (1978), 374ff.

Luther renaissance have restricted themselves to the in-house debate. The psychohistorical viewpoint reduces the early sixteenth century to the phenomenon of anti-clericalism, understood as the driving force of psychological liberation. Political history skips Luther's concerns to concentrate on the Lutheran cause and its constitutional consequences for the Empire. To sum up in simplified form, in each case the events of the Reformation are coupled with a different *sola* (exclusive criterion), and subordinated to a different postulate:

– without the Empire and the princes, no Reformation;

– without the social crisis, no Reformation;

– without the cities, no Reformation.

On the other hand, we must recognize as fundamental to our understanding the following truism:

– without the reformers, no Reformation.

Social and political factors guided, accelerated and likewise hindered the spread and public effects of Protestant preaching. However, in a survey of the age as a whole they must not be overestimated and seen as causes of the Reformation, nor as its fundamental preconditions.

3. Serfs and Citizens: The Reformation of the Princes Versus the City Reformation

The drive for a comprehensive survey of the Reformation that will be true to the sources now compels us to re-open files that have long been closed. Recent research has consolidated questions concerning various types of Reformation under the pair of opposites formed by 'the Reformation of the Princes' versus 'the City Reformation'. Traditional Catholic accounts deal with the entire consolidation phase of the Reformation from this perspective, as a contrast to the new beginning of Trent when 'the sixteenth-century church, so corrupt within and so hard-pressed from without, was indeed able to renew itself under its own power and from within'[6] – apparently

---

[6] '[D]ie von innen her so korrupte und von außen her so schwer angeschlagene Kirche des 16. Jahrhunderts sich doch aus eigener Kraft und von der eigenen Mitte her erneuert hat . . .', Erwin Iserloh, *Luther und die Reformation. Beiträge zu einem ökumenischen Lutherverständnis*, Der Christ in der Welt XI, 4, Aschaffenburg 1974, 27. For the Catholic

without any help from the princes! An analogous thesis, no longer confined to Anglo-American scholarship, and without a clear denominational thrust, is that the 'real' Reformation was the City Reformation, which was later paralysed and sterilized by self-interested princes.

The very terms and concepts used betray that these categories belong to the sphere of political and social history. The history of theology, which formerly was in advance of all other scholarship in this area, now commands no attention at all, and has not made any significant impression on this topic for quite some time. As a result, it has a good deal of catching up to do. Attempts to wring an all-encompassing explanatory framework for historical research from theology have been discredited. This discipline – no longer strained beyond its capacity – can now make a much more precise and appropriate contribution of its own.

The attempt to accord equal importance to the theological perspective in illuminating the history of the Reformation has demonstrated that the late medieval dispute between the *via antiqua* and the *via moderna* continued to exert a vital influence in the Reformation era, even in places where we would not initially expect to find it. Once our eyes are opened to possibilities other than the opposition 'prince versus city' – namely for the antithesis between *via antiqua* and *via moderna* – we discover how much more this opposition contributes to an understanding of Luther's theology than has hitherto been realized. The fierce hostility Luther felt toward the *via moderna* is sufficiently well known as a step on his way to becoming a reformer. Nonetheless, this opposition has been interpreted in widely varying ways: either as a tragically un-Catholic overreaction, or as part of a dramatically Protestant process of emancipation.

Any attempt to grasp Luther's development in terms of his opposition to Gabriel Biel will produce a one-sided and therefore distorted picture. For one, Wittenberg theology solidly opposed the ecclesiastically-sanctioned scholasticism of both *viae*. For another, the

---

'Princes' Reform' and its extirpation of Protestantism, cf. for southern Europe Peter F. Barton, 'Schickt die protestantischen Prediger auf die Galeeren!', in: *Kirche im Osten. Studien zur osteuropäischen Kirchengeschichte und Kirchenkunde* 20 (1977), 57–71.

influence of Luther's education cannot be seen in purely negative terms.[7] Here we find the historically pertinent key to his thinking in 'sectors' measured out by God himself. Luther's use of the dialectic between God's absolute power *(potentia dei absoluta)* and God's actual use of power *(potentia dei ordinata)* as a foundation for worldly order is exemplary and revealing. This order is based not on natural law or the requirements of our rationality, but on God's inscrutable wisdom: 'Absoluta potentia sua posset Deus alia ratione prohibere inoboedientes filios, sed utitur ordinata, scilicet magistratu.'[8] – that is, in his absolute power God could have restrained his disobedient children by other means, but he chose the worldly powers he ordained.

This situates the power to constitute the worldly authority of the *paterfamilias* or of the civil powers outside the realm of changeable human designs and motives. Therefore, this constitutive power is not deduced from changeable theories of society based on natural law or philosophical concepts. However, because authority and its responsibilities are decreed by God, they are particularly vulnerable to the assaults of the Devil. All appearances in scholarship to the contrary, Luther does not blindly support the established authorities in the role of a princely vassal: when circumstances require it, he castigates the princes' 'diabolical perversion' with a free and forceful candor audacious not only to feudal ears.[9]

This is furthermore how Luther justified his triple progression: where domestic authority comes to grief, higher authority must intervene, albeit only *in loco parentis*;[10] where higher authority fails, all Hell breaks loose – beyond established authority lies not Utopia, but merely the end of human civilization. There is surely no state

---

[7] The assumption concerning Luther's un-Catholic nominalist foundations has remained unshaken in recent research. See for example Vinzenz Pfnür, *Einig in der Rechtfertigungslehre? Die Rechtfertigungslehre der Confessio Augustana (1530) und die Stellungnahme der katholischen Kontroverstheologen zwischen 1530 und 1535,* Wiesbaden 1970, 386.

[8] *WAT* 1, no. 415; 181.42f.

[9] On Luther's political influence and his relationship to the princely authorities, cf. Hermann Kunst, *Evangelischer Glaube und politische Verantwortung. Martin Luther als politischer Berater seines Landesherren und seine Teilnahme an den Fragen des öffentlichen Lebens,* Stuttgart 1976, 400f.

[10] *WAT* 1, no. 415; 182.4.

today, whatever its ideological stance, that would deny the truth of this assertion.

If we use a scythe in place of the historian's scalpel, we will see nothing but the Middle Ages. Yet it is the very link between the two medieval elements – the dialectic between God's *potentiae* (possible powers) and the apocalyptic struggle of God and the Devil – that sheds new light on authority: installed in their office directly subordinate to God, the established authorities are freed from medieval papal domination. This also means that they are made pure, that is, made internally responsible to God. Their disobedience is not, however, excused on the grounds of internal jurisdiction over themselves, but branded as diabolical apostasy.

This inscrutable divine decree comes to bear on a second point of concentration – and later of separation – peculiar to the reform era: the doctrine of the sacraments. The efficacy and effectiveness of the sacramental elements is ascribed to the *pactum dei,* that is, to God's unchangeable decree: this view is already expressed in the *Dictata* (1513–15); it is expounded in detail in the sermons on the sacraments of 1519, and can be traced right through to the *Table Talk*.[11] Reason, even the reason of the theologians, depends on the divine decision that precedes all our thinking. The doctrines of transubstantiation and signification are both attempts to solve the puzzle of God's decrees without taking Christ's intervention into account.

For the urban Reformation, the height of reason is the height of access to revelation. The Mass, denounced with disgust as 'eating God' and 'drinking God', is too gross to correspond to the spiritual meaning of revelation. And it is quite certainly not reasonable to allow this question to become a matter of political dispute as well. For *pactum* refers at most to a clever policy of alliance, not to a divine decree that is beyond reason. In this way the urban drive for emancipation could be fused seamlessly with the Gospel: the common good *(bonum commune)* still embraces Church and society, as previously in the papal bull *Unam sanctam,* and therefore finds its

---

[11] 'Thomas dixit, quod in baptismate im wasser soll ein heimliche kraft sein; ibi coepta est disputatio, et deinde imprimitur character. Sed Scotus dixit: Non, sed ex pacto divino quando sacerdos baptisat, tunc adest Deus suo pacto; et recte dixit, und ist ein seher feiner mensch gewesen' (*WAT* 2, no. 1745; 202.21–5, 18 August 1532).

significance, purpose and fulfilment in the cause of God – just as do all forms of learning in theology, according to the *via antiqua*.[12]

Concerning both the interpretation of authority and the sacraments, Luther was bound to remain incomprehensible to all urban theologians whose background was the *via antiqua*. This theological clash was a Catholic inheritance hidden in the seemingly closed ranks of the Protestant camp from the very beginning. To the profound disappointment of many supporters of the Reformation, it proved impossible to heal this rupture by way of the new 'reasonable' exegesis beholden to Erasmus. The breach between the confessional parties did not begin immediately before or after the outbreak of the Peasants' War with the so-called sacramentarian controversy. We should, however, be wary of putting our faith in closed 'chains of events' or of hypostatizing 'inevitable practical pressures and forces', be they theological, political or social. If we lose our intuitive sense that contingency is the basic structure of historical events, we will lose all access to history.

4. *The Punctum Protestantissimum: Worldly Reason and Faith in Christ*

The city reformers, all of them educated at Latin schools and elevated to city preacherships, must nearly all be assigned to the *via antiqua* and to the circle of Erasmus' pupils. Zwingli is no exception. They all believed that Scripture and the common good mesh seamlessly with faith and learning, or at the very least, that the two sides could be combined in a harmonious way. Against this backdrop, one characteristic of Luther's theology stands out very clearly: justification by faith alone not only excludes human merit; 'faith alone' is another spearhead aimed at the claims of reason (*ratio*).

If we take this to be one of the established cornerstones of Luther research, then an old controversial point becomes red-hot once again: Luther's famous address to the Imperial Diet at Worms.[13] The double

---

[12] Cf. Heiko A. Oberman, *Werden und Wertung der Reformation. Vom Wegestreit zum Glaubenskampf,* Tübingen 1979,[2] 377; English trans.: *Masters of the Reformation. The emergence of a new intellectual climate in Europe,* revised and abridged trans. by D. Martin, Cambridge 1981, 294–5.

[13] Joachim Rogge has provided an excellent volume of sources, while the Worms Festschrift offers important aids to the interpretation of this Diet. See Rogge, *1521–1971. Luther in Worms. Ein Quellenbuch,* Witten 1971; Fritz Reuter (ed.), *Der Reichstag zu*

appeal Luther makes to Scripture and to pure reason in this address seems to me to have been sufficiently appreciated neither in its theological nor in its secular implications.

Kurt-Victor Selge has presented a balanced account of the state of research. We are bound to agree with him completely when he says:

> In his famous concluding words Luther puts forward as the counter-argument to which he is prepared to submit, in addition to the testimony of Scripture, the evidence of clear reason *(ratio evidens)*. Luther himself continually used arguments based on reason to show his opponents that their proofs from Scripture were unsound. He knew that a pure Biblicism content to rely on quotation to solve all problems was insufficient.[14]

But Selge's next statement requires more reflection: 'Luther does not here place *ratio* beside scriptural evidence as an independent, autonomous authority.'[15]

This solution to the problem would be entirely in accord with the Protestant principle of 'Scripture alone'. However, it is still unclear why Luther insisted so firmly on distinguishing between two authorities.[16] Emanuel Hirsch chose a different way out, anchoring this twofold, external authority immanently and anthropologically in the conscience. I would like to call to mind his apt formulation: Luther's confession of 18 April 1521

Worms von 1521. Reichspolitik und Luthersache, Worms 1971. As exegetical and existential (= tropological) background for the *punctum protestantissimum* cf. Luther's interpretation of Ps. 9.5 (God is *iudex iustitiae)* in the *Operationes in Psalmos,* the extensive commentary which Luther was forced to break off because he had been ordered to Worms (*AWA* 2, 520.6–18, and 28–37; *WA* 5, 292.11–23, and 32–41).

[14] 'In seinen berühmten Schlußworten führt Luther als Gegenargument, dem er sich beugen will, neben den Schriftzeugnissen auch den "klaren Grund" (*ratio evidens*) an. Luther hat selbst immer wieder mit Vernunftargumenten gearbeitet, um seinen Gegnern die Unstimmigkeit ihrer Schriftbeweise zu zeigen. Er hat gewußt, daß man mit einem reinen Biblizismus, der sich mit Zitaten begnügt, um alle Fragen zu lösen, nicht auskommt'; 'Capta conscientiae in verbis Dei, Luthers Widerrufsverweigerung in Worms', in: *Der Reichstag zu Worms,* 180–207; esp. 200.

[15] ibid.; cf. Bernhard Lohse, *Ratio und Fides,* Göttingen 1958, 134.

[16] For help in interpreting the idea of 'double authority', see the passage which Luther himself cites, though not until 1530, from Augustine (*Epistola* 82, *PL* 33, col. 277; *WA* 30II, 385.4f.). Biel appeals to Gerson in the matter of a threefold certainty, although the third is of no use to the extent that it rests on 'probabilibus coniectures'. The first is based on the truths contained in Holy Scripture (*certitudo supernaturalis*); the second (*certitudo naturalis*), on internal experience 'ut sol orietur'. *Canonis Misse expositio resolutissima Gabrielis Biel,* Lectio 8 B, ed. H. A. Oberman, W. J. Courtenay, I, Wiesbaden 1963, 59.

became the beacon that has continued to shine through the history of the collective European spirit down to the present day, and that gave the word 'conscience' its essential significance concerning the ultimate questions of human existence.[17]

Hirsch comes to the conclusion – and here we sense that we are in the presence of a grateful pupil of Karl Holl – that 'for Luther the conscience is both the fountainhead of every human search for truth and the locus where all the certainty of truth received by mankind is to be found'.[18]

Indeed; for Luther, the conscience is the place where all the certainty of truth received by human beings can be found. However, did he really think at Worms that the conscience was also the source of every human search for truth, the anthropological bulwark of faith, proof against the incursion of sin? This might make sense to us as modern observers, but does not accord with Luther's own experience of conscience. He is all too aware that the human conscience is moveable and restless, a focus of unrest in human existence, capable of error and open to influence. The misery of mankind can even be identified with restless human conscience. The Augustinian principle that the heart finds rest only in God was transferred by Luther from the heart (*cor*) to the conscience (*conscientia*), specifically in the sense that the conscience finds a firm hold only in Scripture.

The allegorical method can no longer be of help in finding out what the Word of God really means. The wall of the Babylonian captivity has been demolished with the rejection of the claim that the inerrant Church interprets Scripture without check or hindrance. So how is Holy Scripture to be interpreted properly? Up to now we have had recourse to Luther's epistemological principle: *was Christum treibet* – whatever furthers Christ. This certainly clarifies the interpretive goal or purpose, but sheds light neither on the authority for the interpretation nor on the interpretive process. Rational insight (*ratio evidens*), understood as immanent to theology, begins to

[17] '[I]st das Fanal geworden, das durch die Geschichte des gesamten europäischen Geistes weiter leuchtet bis heute und von dem das Wort Gewissen seine entscheidende Bedeutung für die letzten Fragen des menschlichen Daseins empfangen hat' (*Lutherstudien I,* Gütersloh 1954, 175).

[18] '[Daß] für Luther das Gewissen sowohl der Quell alles menschlichen Wahrheitssuchens wie der Ort aller vom Menschen empfangenen Wahrheitsgewißheit ist' (ibid., 179).

function here. 'Was Christum treibet' is not left merely to the *eruditi* and the *experti,* the scholarly exegetes of the Old and New Testaments. Scripture is clear inasmuch as any given interpretation must be acceptable in terms of the worldly reason shared by all human beings.

The interpretation of Scripture thus becomes a worldly affair, exposed to the chilly winds of critical reason, subject to the demand that its process and conclusions be comprehensible, and that it stand up to testing. Here Luther adopts a conclusion from the medieval dispute between academic and monastic theology. Academic theology had won the day: catholic truths were supposed to be based on authority (*auctoritas*) and reason (*ratio*), that is, on Scripture or tradition *and* on the conclusions drawn from these with the help of philosophy.[19]

For Luther, the tradition of the Church is not an autonomous court of appeal responsible for determining truth. Scripture is the only authority in matters of truth, since Scripture alone is the Word of God. But parallel to scriptural authority is the persuasive power of clear reason available to all. As authorities, Scripture and clear reason can clash strongly, for example if human reason threatens, in its foolishness, to smother divine truth, or when reason, quibbling over the clear sense of God's word, bends that sense according to its own standards, which are external to the text and therefore speculative.

It is a different matter, however, when reason listens for the decisions of divine authority and seeks the conclusions that can be drawn in a clear, necessary and irrefutable manner from the Word of Scripture according to all the rules of logical procedure. Reason may make the same claim to truth as the Word of Scripture itself, a claim it need not put forward for discussion as an *opinio* but may formulate as an assertion that will give way only in the face of conclusive evidence to the contrary. That a counter-proof can still be demanded demonstrates the continuing distinction between the *assertio* and the Word of God; but as long as clear evidence to the contrary has not

---

[19] Cf. the treatise by John Brevicoxa (+1423 as Bishop of Geneva), 'De Fide, et Ecclesia, Romano Pontifice, et Concilio Generali', in: *Joannis Gersonii Opera Omnia,* ed. L. E. Du Pin, I, Antwerp 1706, col. 805–904. Cf. here also Hermann-Josef Sieben, 'Die "quaestio de infallibilitate concilii generalis" (Ockhamexzerpte) des Pariser Theologen Jean Courtecuisse (+1423)', in: *Annuarium Historia Concilium* 8 (1976), 176–99.

been provided, the unconditionally obligatory power of the evident exegesis still stands.

In his treatise *De votis monasticis* (*On Monastic Vows*), finished in November 1521 – that is, before the end of the year in which the Diet of Worms took place – Luther once again takes up his statement at Worms, maintaining in his conclusion that his concerns are justified by Scripture and by clear arguments understandable to everyone.[20]

If we examine more carefully the method of argument that Luther employed in this work, we see that he is working out his concept of 'Christian freedom' on the basis of Holy Scripture. But with the help of clear reason, he now extends this concern to mean it is 'as clear as day' (*omnium evidentissimum*) that vows plague the conscience uselessly with sins that are not true sins at all. Rather than freeing us, vows enslave those who take them and alienate them from true piety. Such vows are, therefore, nefarious, impious and contrary to the teachings of the Gospel.[21]

The second sphere of activity where clear reason (*ratio evidens*) exerts its influence is within the world and worldly experience. Just as worldly reason cannot invade the sphere of revelation without becoming a whore, so in her own worldly sphere, reason is that original source of life which, undiminished by the fall and disbelief, belongs even to the godless. Indeed, reason is the discoverer and guide of all things and people (*inventrix et gubernatrix omnium*),[22] disclosing, illuminating and ordering the world. Luther broadens the discussion, moving from the frequently ridiculed and fiercely criticized 'logic-chopping' of the *moderni* to experience as the central reference point for a nominalist understanding of the world.

Luther, the alleged fideist, formulates the independent force of worldly reason more radically than anyone had ever dared to do before him. Reason has not been destroyed by the Fall – it has not even been impaired. On the contrary, it has been confirmed and strengthened in its position, able both to resist the assaults mounted by the world and to shape Creation, which has become hostile.[23]

---

[20] '[A]rbitror omnia scripturis et rationibus evidentibus munita . . .' (*WA* 8, 668.24f.).

[21] '[I]llicita, impia et Evangelio pugnantia' (*WA* 8, 668.16).

[22] *WA* 39I, 175.11.

[23] 'Nec eam Maiestatem Deus post lapsum Adae ademit rationi, sed potius confirmavit' (*De homine,* Thesis 9; *WA* 39I, 175.20f.). Cf. Gerhard Ebeling, *Lutherstudien II: Disputatio de homine* 1, Tübingen 1977, 17.

To sum up: when Luther is prepared at Worms to submit only to Scripture and reasonable proof, he is not striking a rhetorical blow on behalf of the appellate authority of Scripture. Nor is this a manifesto for the conscience as an inerrant source of truth.[24] Conscience on its own is never wholly solid, but must be anchored in Holy Scripture. It must stand on the rock of the Word, *super petram,* in the firm knowledge that the God who speaks in Holy Scripture does not lie.[25] Otherwise, conscience has fallen victim to the world, the flesh and the Devil, the entire realm that is hostile to God.

At the same time, if the conscience is to stand fast it must face up to clear reason in the form of worldly experience. We must not interpret clear reason (*ratio evidens*) as reason in the philosophical sense, be it Thomist or post-Kantian. Rather, it means empirical knowledge of the world, based on the demonstrable facts of experience. Reason appeals to experience and must stand the test of experience. Its evidence can be verified by that secular experience which is stored up and passed down in proverbs and popular adages. Experience shares another characteristic with reason: in the sphere of faith (unlike in the worldly sphere), it can be assigned no constitutive function without, like reason, leading to 'whoredom' – that is, to arbitrary and unauthorized enthusiasm. When confined to the secular dimension, however, clear reason (*ratio evidens*) has the power to defend itself against attacks by ecclesiastical authority, even without Scripture: 'And that crazed ass of a pope has done things so badly, that [his behavior] would be felt [indefensible] even if judged by reason alone, even if we did not have Scripture'.[26]

With this secular dimension of clear reason, or everyday experience, Luther introduces elements of the nominalist inheritance into the Reformation. This experience is not reserved for mystics or experts, but is available to the man or woman in the street. Indebted as he was to the *via moderna,* at the end of 1532 Luther defined with succinct precision the differing place of experience in the two spheres we have discussed:

---

[24] Cf. also Michael G. Baylor's apt criticism on this point in his book *Action and Person. Conscience in late scholasticism and the young Luther,* Leiden 1977, 265f.

[25] *WA* 8, 669.2–4.

[26] 'Et ille insensatus asinus papa hats so grob gemacht, ut etiam palparetur iudicio rationis, etiamsi non haberemus scripturam' (*WAT* 2, no. 1346; 60.16f.).

In the sphere of the world, experience makes our perception possible, sharpens it and provides the foundation for our understanding. In the sphere of theology the reverse is true: listening in faith to God's Word and firm trust in his Word precede all experience.[27]

5. The Protestant Breakthrough and the Nominalist 'Principle'

The document central to any understanding of the Protestant breakthrough is still (despite repeated objections and misgivings) the retrospective in the preface to the first edition of Luther's *Opera Omnia*, published at Wittenberg in 1545. This autobiographical piece is rather puzzling, especially because we generally assume that the text is a self-contained whole, without noticing that it is really the final product of a lengthy series of gradually expanding retrospective meditations. If we do not confine ourselves to the well-known parallels to this piece of autobiography, but seek also for its predecessors,[28] we come upon the *Table Talk*. Its value as a source has up to now been unjustly underestimated. It also provides evidence that this text is the result of a process that began as early as 1532.

One of these earlier forms now helps us to grasp the point at which the Wittenberg friar and doctor of philosophy became the reformer:

> Since I first read and sang [!] in the psalm: 'In your righteousness [*iustitia*], set me free!' I shrank back and was an enemy to the words: 'the righteousness of God', 'the judgement of God', 'the work of God'; for I knew nothing other but that the righteousness of God meant his stern judgement. And should I now be saved according to this his stern

[27] 'In natura experientia est causa, cur audiamus, et praecedit assensum; in theologia autem experientia sequitur assensum, non praecedit' (*WAT* 1, no. 423; 183.25–7; cf. *WAT* 4, no. 4091; 129.23f: 'experientia, rerum magistra, omnia moderari deberet').

[28] The degree to which Luther's reminiscences were bound up with the idea of a collected edition of his works is shown, for example, by a conversation with Georg Maior, the later co-editor of the Wittenberg Luther edition: 'Cum aliqui libri haberentur in mensa ex primis, quos edidit, inquit: O, ich wolt gern, das ich sie alle bei einander hett! – Responsio Maioris: So kunde man sehen, Domine Doctor, quam haec doctrina accrevisset. – Respondit Doctor: Ja es ist war! Ergo eram primo valde imbecillis. Ich war in vilen dingen sehr schwach.' (Since certain books, among the first that he published, were on the table, he said: Oh, how glad I would be if I had them all together! – Maior's answer: In this way one could see, Dominie Doctor, how this doctrine grew. – Doctor Luther responded: Indeed, that is right! I was, after all, very infirm at the beginning. I was very weak in many things.) (*WAT* 5, no. 5471; 172.1–6; cf. no. 5511; 204.30–32). *Tischrede* (*Table Talk*) no. 5346 (75f.) is important because it testifies to Staupitz's intervention (according to my own view, in 1512 (75.20) and 1515 (76.6)), as well as because of the affirmation 'ego disputavi de indulgentiis' (I debated on the topic of indulgences) – 76.16.

judgement? If so I should be eternally lost! But 'God's mercy' and 'God's help' – those words pleased me better. God be praised that I understood the substance and knew that the righteousness of God meant justice, by which we are justified through the righteousness given in Christ Jesus. Then did I understand the grammar [*grammatica*], and only then was the psalter sweet to me.[29]

The essential point marking the breakthrough which made Luther a reformer now proves to be entirely comprehensible in the context of the nominalist tradition with which Luther was so familiar: 'God be praised that I understood the substance ... Then did I understand the grammar, and only then was the psalter sweet to me.' At first glance, this assertion would seem to contradict our thesis that Luther remained a nominalist even as a reformer. He could even say: 'Things are teachers. Anyone who does not understand the substance will be unable to tease meaning out of words'.[30]

Luther is undoubtedly following that classical tradition we can trace back to Tacitus and Cato: 'Rem tene, verba sequuntur'[31] – hold fast to the substance, the words will follow. And who could fail to hear at the same time the battle cry of the *via antiqua:* 'We are concerned with the substance and leave the dispute over words to the nominalists'?[32]

Yet simply to make this the guiding principle of the *via Lutheri* would be to disregard the nominalist distinction between the two spheres that was a special concern of the reformer. In theology, contrary to the worldly sphere, the *assensus* – that is, submission to God's revelation – is paramount; it precedes all experience. The Word

[29] 'Da ich erstlich im psalmen laß und sang: In iustitia tua libera me!, da erschrak ich alle mal und war den worten feindt: Iustitia Dei, iudicium Dei, opus Dei, denn ich wust nichts anders, iustitia Dei hies sein gestreng gericht. Nuhn solt er mich noch [nach] sein gestrengen gericht erretten? So wer ich ewig verloren! Aber misericordia Dei, adiutorium Dei, die wortt hett ich lieber. Gott lob, da ich die res verstunde und wiste, das iustitia Dei hieß iustitia, qua nos iustificat per donatam iustitiam in Christo Ihesu, da verstunde ich die grammatica, und schmeckt mir erst der Psalter.' *WAT* 5, no. 5247; 26.18–26; cf. *WAT* 4, no. 4769; 479.29–31: 'Multo maxime necessarium est in sacris literis, quid nominis primum et certissimum habere, quia de rebus incognitis et tantum fide perceptis agitur.'

[30] 'Res sunt praeceptores. Qui non intellegit res, non potest ex verbis sensum elicere' (*WAT* 5, no. 5246; 26.11f.).

[31] Cf. *WADB*, 3, 121, n. 2.

[32] Cf. Gerhard Ritter, 'Via antiqua und via moderna auf den deutschen Universitäten des XV. Jahrhunderts', in: *Studien zur Spätscholastik II,* Sitzungsberichte der Heidelberger Akademie der Wissenschaften, Phil.-hist. Klasse, Jahrgang 1922, 7. Abhandlung, Heidelberg 1922 (Darmstadt 1975), 133.

of God is revealed in its *grammatica* only at a second stage. This second stage acquires its underlying meaning in the biblical disclosure of the righteousness of God. The 'reforming' discovery becomes the joyful reforming experience – the much-discussed turning point – only when Luther succeeds in connecting his 'assent' (*assensus*) to God's word with the 'grammar' (*grammatica*) of God's word. In general terms: the principle *sola fide* (by faith alone) became the 'reforming breakthrough' at the moment it could stand the test of Scripture alone.

This observation is of considerable importance for the dating of the upheaval. It makes no sense to see the 'reforming breakthrough' wherever Luther mentions or even postulates freely given (unearned) justification in a reforming vein. The real breakthrough required both justification by faith and its exegetically verifiable foundation in the Word.

The irreversible sequence leading from assent (that is, the living obedience of faith) to 'grammar' (faithfulness to Scripture) made Luther a reformer. But as a reformer he is at the same time obliged to the *via moderna* in that he distinguishes the two spheres from one another: the reverse sequence of thought – which is the rule in the worldly sphere – is, in the realm of Scripture, rigorously denounced as 'whoredom' and the Devil's own work. In theology there is no generally binding prior understanding, neither philological nor philosophical – in short, no understanding that can be attained by scientific means – that by-passes assent and is able to make Scripture so transparent that we can see right through it to the true God.[33] Luther does not reduce Scripture to the bare letter, as he charges the spiritual enthusiasts with doing. Assent to the Word of God becomes the rock of personal conscience, the source of joy in faith, the basis of doctrinal assertions, and the foundation on which the Church is built only when assent is made fast to Scripture, and therefore is able to withstand and does withstand inner and outer contradiction.

Our concern would be misunderstood if it were interpreted as an attempt to carve Luther up into his sources and his constituent parts.

---

[33] This guiding principle is persuasively developed as a program for New Testament exegesis in Peter Stuhlmacher, *Vom Verstehen des Neuen Testaments. Eine Hermeneutik,* Das Neue Testament Deutsch, Ergänzungsreihe 6, Göttingen 1979, 206ff.

Placing him historically allows us to make distinctions between what is traditional and what is novel, to grasp the revaluation of the old and to discover and evaluate the new. To return to our point of departure: we asked about the relationship between the late Middle Ages and the Reformation. Based on the *punctum protestantissimum* – the confession of Worms – and that *cause célèbre,* the 'Reformation breakthrough', we have seen that the distinction between 'continuity' and 'discontinuity' distorts the reformers' own view of themselves and obscures the characteristics of the period. As a result, modern observers are denied access to decisive episodes and aspects of the Reformation; hence, the ill-conceived assertion that 'The Reformation of the sixteenth century failed'.[34]

---

[34] 'Die Reformation im 16. Jahrhundert ist gescheitert'; Erwin Iserloh, *Luther und die Reformation* (see n. 6), 7.

Chapter 2

MARTIN LUTHER:
FORERUNNER OF THE REFORMATION

1. The Reformation as a Failed Transformation

The school of social history that views the religious motives behind the
Reformation as marginal phenomena specific to the period has, not
surprisingly, found the thesis that the Reformation failed to be very
attractive. According to this school of thought, new sources have led
research away from the traditional fixation on the élite as the bearers of
culture and have provided insight into the culture of the 'common
man', who complied with the Europe-wide missionary activity of the
reform only externally and temporarily, as Gerald Strauss argues.[1] In
other words, 'official Christianity' throughout the centuries was able
to capture only a very narrow élite layer of the population, not the
'underground' constituted by popular culture. The 'Christian West' is
therefore reduced to a hagiographic projection and a moral illusion.

Given such a stubborn, vigorous 'subculture', the main goal of the
Reformation is construed as a programmatic attempt finally to
penetrate all of society in order to bring about the transformation[2]

[1] G. Strauss, *Luther's House of Learning. Indoctrination of the Young in the German
Reformation,* Baltimore/London 1978. Strauss writes of a 'vigorous subculture' (303). 'The
deep current of popular life nourishing this subterranean religion was beyond the
theologian's grasp, the preacher's appeal, or the visitor's power to compel' (ibid.). To
Strauss, the stubbornness of popular superstition is both a symptom and proof of the failure
of the Reformation: 'Success and Failure in the German Reformation', in: *Past and Present*
19 (1975), 30–63; 62f. Lionel Rothkrug has pursued the same issue independently of
Strauss. 'Popular Religion and Holy Shrines. Their influence on the Origins of the German
Reformation and Their Role in German Cultural Development', in: *Religion and the
People, 800–1700,* ed. J. Obelkevich, Chapel Hill, N.C. 1979, 20–86.

[2] '[I]f its central purpose was to make people – all people – think, feel and act as Christians,
to imbue them with a Christian mind-set, motivational drive, and way of life, it failed' (Strauss,
Luther's House of Learning, 307). The conditional 'if' should not be understood to introduce
an open question. The author is quite sure of his position. As far as he is concerned, the burden
of proof is no longer in his camp but among those who think 'that the Reformation in
Germany aroused a widespread, meaningful and lasting response to its message' (ibid., 307f.).

dreamed of by medieval missionaries and which the Inquisition tried in vain to produce. Martin Luther seems to be the ideal representative of such a vision,[3] since he considered the common man to be a priest as well, and wanted to remodel his practical faith in a lasting and thorough way by means of visitations. We are obliged, however, to check the sources carefully with this fundamental question in mind: did Luther ever want or attempt to realize 'Reformation' in the terms of such a transformation?[4]

2. Desperate Times at the End of Time

The image of Luther the heroic and fearless reformer, the confident advance guard of the 'transformation', evokes not only his performance at the Imperial Diet of Worms (April 1521) and his public refusal to renounce his writing. There is no doubt that 'Luther before the Emperor at Worms' became a symbol of reforming courage to confess and defend one's faith[5] that reached many of those who could not read.[6] The reforming 'deed' made a deep impression on the people, preparing them for the reforming Word. Even people of letters – right up to our own time – have read Luther's works in the

[3] However, Strauss in no way feels obliged to 'interrogate' Luther on this topic: 'Luther himself blurred the division between secular and ecclesiastical competences, and – in any case – events soon passed him by' (ibid., 313, n. 50).

[4] I see Steven Ozment's closing remarks as an affirmative answer to this question, as he also uses the concept 'transformation' and includes Luther in his general critique: 'The great shortcoming of the Reformation was its naïve expectation that the majority of people were capable of radical religious enlightenment and moral transformation, whether by persuasion or by coercion' (The Age of Reform 1250–1550. An Intellectual and Religious History of Late Medieval and Reformation Europe, New Haven/London 1980, 437). Although Bernd Moeller is concerned to distinguish between Luther ('the Christian stands as an individual before God') and the urban Reformation ('the common good' – Gemeinwohl), he also opines that Luther 'in his optimistic early years' actually held 'the gradual victory of the Word' to be possible; 'he was still deeply-enough embedded in the intellectual world of the Middle Ages that he could see such a victory as an attainable goal' (Reichsstadt und Reformation, Gütersloh 1962, 37). I am not persuaded by Moeller's attempt to support this thesis by appealing to Luther's De instituendis ministris Ecclesiae (1523; WA 12, 169–96), a work addressed to the Bohemians, as 'characteristic of Luther's thoughts on this matter'.

[5] See Luther's own retrospective interpretation of this event in a letter to Melanchthon dated 9 June 1530. (WAB 5, 456.3–9).

[6] The cultural élite was also deeply impressed by the symbolic power of this action, as Albrecht Dürer's lament concerning Luther shows. Cf. Albrecht Dürer, 'Tagebuch der Reise in die Niederlande', in: Dürer, Schriftlicher Nachlaß, ed. H. Rupprich, Berlin 1956, vol. I, 170–2.

light of this act. The reforming Word had continually to direct and correct this early tendency to cast Luther as a hero, to personalize his message, in order to push forward the real agenda of the Reformation. Read in this light, the works of 1520 are indeed a reforming program and the triumphant conclusion of Luther's early development. Even if the Edict of Worms had been able to stop Luther from writing anything more,[7] the basic traits of his theology would nonetheless be clear to us today.

To be fascinated by the 'act of Reformation' is to run the risk of confusing the person with the office in a Donatistic way. Luther himself was able to avoid this confusion. He understood his program of reform as a scientifically verifiable discovery that could exist only as an entity separate from his person. Such a distinction between person and office or function is in no way easy, particularly because it must disappear when the person becomes a figure of great historical significance. From the perspective of an enthusiastic contemporary, it makes perfect sense to see the years from 1519–21 as the 'hey-day' of the charismatic Luther: 'It was the marvelous time when Luther . . . charged on, as certain of himself as a sleepwalker, as though obsessed by the inevitability of his fate, abandoned to the will of his God.'[8]

However, what appeared in 1520 (a boom year for publishing) as Luther's own effervescent innovation was not 'the certainty of a sleepwalker' in the sense of a dream, but the fruits of his intellectual and literary labors, gathered during seven years of biblical exegesis. His polemical topics are firmly anchored in the exegetical results of work on the Hebrew text of the Psalms, results that were broadly developed, after years of painstakingly skillful interpretation of the

---

[7] Cf. *WAB* 2, 336.10f.

[8] 'Es ist jene wunderbare Zeit, da Luther . . . in nachtwandlerischer Sicherheit vorwärts stürmt, wie besessen von der Unausweichlichkeit seines Geschicks und preisgegeben dem Willen seines Gottes' (H. Freiherr von Campenhausen, 'Reformatorisches Selbstbewußtsein und reformatorisches Geschichtsbewußtsein bei Luther, 1517–1522' (1940), in: *Tradition und Leben. Kräfte der Kirchengeschichte. Aufsätze und Vorträge,* Tübingen 1960, 318–42; 330). Here (331, n. 67) von Campenhausen criticizes H. Preuß (*Martin Luther. Der Prophet,* Gütersloh 1933, 112–19), and corrects (329, n. 58; 339, n. 125) Karl Holl ('Luthers Urteile über sich selbst', in: *Gesammelte Aufsätze zur Kirchengeschichte* I, Tübingen 1932, 381–419). Von Campenhausen's clear and persuasive description is correct in all its parts, but nonetheless does not manage to bring the overall picture into focus: Luther's own conception of 'reformatio' and the 'expectations of success' determined by this concept are not given their due.

Bible, in his *Operationes in Psalmos,* his Psalms commentary, which he was forced to break off abruptly by the summons to Worms. He elucidates the reforming message in a clear and concentrated way in the detailed exegesis of Psalm 10 (9b), which he had presented to his students in university lectures.[9] Here he develops the basic ideas of his *An den christlichen Adel deutscher Nation* (*To the Christian Nobility of the German Nation*), which he would write in mid-August. He also establishes the textual foundation for his view of 'captivity' (*captivitas*), seen in the context of the 'history of salvation' (the Passion story). The *De captivitate Babylonica* (*On the Babylonian Captivity of the Church*) must be interpreted within this framework. Here Luther reveals his own understanding of *reformatio,* thus clarifying the duty of a reformer and the way in which he interpreted his own mission.

This 'Reformation psalm' is both a portrayal and an announcement of the apocalyptic menace. It provided him, in its staccato verses, with a psychological, in fact a spiritual portrait of the Church in his times: 'For if the government of the clergy and of the powers of the Church were mine today, [and I were to] deal with it in prayer properly, appropriately, agreeably, fully and perfectly, I would recite this psalm . . .'.[10] The leaders of the Church do not want to hear the Gospel, because it would make 'reformation' inevitable for them: 'the Church and the clergy must be reformed'.[11] But reformation means turning away from power and pomp, as well as turning to preaching and prayer. It insists on apostolic poverty, and leads to the dangerous necessity of having to defend the Truth without any protection.[12] This theme is not new. We find in an early sermon and in the *Dictata* Luther's conviction that the Church can be reformed

---

[9] W. Maurer has dated the exegesis of Psalm 13 (14) to March 1520. Cf. *Von der Freiheit eines Christenmenschen. Zwei Untersuchungen zu Luthers Reformationsschriften 1520/21,* Göttingen 1949, 78.

[10] 'Nam si mihi ecclesiasticorum et dominantium in ecclesia administratio hodierna esset oratione propria, apta, commoda, plena perfectaque disserenda, hunc psalmum recitarem . . .' (Psalm 10.7; *AWA* 2, 588.8–10; *WA* 5, 336.37–337.1).

[11] 'ecclesiam et ecclesiasticos oportere reformari' (*AWA* 2, 588.14; *WA* 5, 337.4f.).

[12] '. . . positis pompa, fastu, regnis et mundi negotiis, ministerio verbi et orationi instandum sit et apostolorum exemplo in penuria et periculo vitae pro veritate vivendum; quod ne fiat, potius omnia praedicemus, sive hinc populorum animae maledictionem capiant sive quid peius' (*AWA* 2, 588.14–18; *WA* 5, 337.5–8).

only by preaching the Word.[13] The age of church reform is now over, no more reformers can be expected, God himself must[14] and will carry out the 'reformation'.[15] Only he merits the title 'reformer', because he will consummate the reformation at the end of time, on Judgement Day.[16]

What function, what task can there be for Luther in *this* vision of reformation? How did he make sense of his own role? The interpretive possibilities that have been popular are those of 'hero' or of 'the German prophet', even 'the successful reformer of the Church'. These all originate in a belief in progress that no longer recognizes 'eschatology' as an integral element of Luther's way of thinking and living. We will get no closer to Luther's mission if we do not enter

[13] See *WA* 1, 13.24–40 (1512?). In reference to the papalistic theses of Prierias, Luther says in his Commentary on Galatians 6.6 ('catechisatur verbo'): 'Et, ut dicam libere, impossibile est, scripturas posse elucidari et alias ecclesias reformari, nisi universale illud reale, Romana curia, quam primum reforetur. Haec enim verbum dei audire non potest nec sustinere ut pure tractetur: verbo autem dei non tractato neque caeteris ecclesiis succurri potest' (*WA* 2, 609.10–14 (1519)). 'Succurri' refers to the command to Peter in Luke 22.32: '. . . strengthen thy brethren'. The 'irreformability' of Rome blocks all 'reformation' this side of the Last Day.

[14] 'Ecclesia indiget reformatione, quod non est unius hominis Pontificis nec multorum Cardinalium officium, sicut probavit utrumque novissimum concilium, sed tocius orbis, immo solius dei. Tempus autem huius reformationis novit solus ille, qui condidit tempora. Interim vitia tam manifesta negare non possumus. Claves sunt in abusu et servitute avaritiae et ambitionis, et gurges accepit impetum: *non est nostrum remorari eum.* Iniquitates nostrae respondent nobis, et onus unicuique sermo suus' (*Resolutiones disputationum de indulgentiarum virtute*, 1518: *WA* 1, 627.27–34). I have italicized Luther's conclusion so that his view of the 'desperate times at the end of time' is clear, since this could have prevented errors in the interpretation of what has been said (see n. 16).

[15] 'Non vincitur Satanas et Christianorum hostis nobis operantibus, sed dumtaxat patientibus et clamantibus' (*AWA* 2, 571.28f.; *WA* 5, 327.13–15).

[16] 'Ita vides psalmum hunc finem suum in finem mundi et iudicii diem constituere' (*AWA* 2, 619.19f.; *WA* 5, 352.25f.). The statement 'immo solius dei' (see n. 14) has not been overlooked in the literature, but as far as I can see, it is without exception interpreted within the framework of the doctrine of justification, and its ecclesiological aspects are ignored. W.-E. Peuckert concludes: Luther 'feels that he is called to be a reformer, to be the one who must accomplish the task set by God'; in *Die große Wende II: Geistesgeschichte und Volkskunde*, Darmstadt 1966, 568. W. Maurer sees Luther's refusal of the title 'Reformer' in moral terms as a 'humble attitude' and his expectation of what is yet to come – 'free of all apocalyptic expectations' – as resignation; see his article 'Was verstand Luther unter der Reformation der Kirche?', in: *Luther* 28 (1957), 49–62; 54f. R. Stupperich interprets the passage 'immo solius dei' in the strict sense of justification: 'Luther weiß, daß Menschen Entscheidendes nicht zu leisten vermögen' – 'Luther und die Reform der Kirche', in: *Reformatio Ecclesiae. Festgabe für Erwin Iserloh*, ed. R. Bäumer, Paderborn 1980, 521–34; 524.

into his graphic, dramatic eschatology. It cannot simply be brushed
aside in order to get to his permanent, henceforth obligatory,
theological view of history.[17] For the purposes of our discussion, we
cannot be content to posit late medieval apocalyptic fears specific to
the period, fears that needed merely to be shaken off and disposed of.
What is apocalyptic about Luther cannot be ascribed to the 'waning
of the Middle Ages', characterized as an epoch weighed down by
fantastic fears, a time whose only hope lay in feverish anticipation of
the end of time. Certainly this belonged to the general tenor of the
times.[18] The expectation of a general renewal, fed by the Joachimite,
Lollard and Hussite traditions, took root in the farthest-flung (and
most central) parts of Europe, losing much of its heretical
'scandalousness' in the process. The main characteristic of this
phenomenon is the inauguration of the third *Reich* or age, the epoch
of the outpouring of the Holy Spirit: this is when the general
transformation is supposed to happen, when the Body of Christians
(*Corpus Christianorum*) will finally coincide with the Body of Christ
(*Corpus Christi*).

Luther, however, energetically rejected this understanding of
'reformation' all through his life. In fact, it is surprising how closely
his eschatology corresponds to that of Augustine in the *City of God*,[19]

[17] The relevant material has already been collected and reviewed, though for varying
reasons and with varying emphasis. There is general agreement concerning the thesis that
apocalypticism did not play a primordial role in Luther's development. Peuckert claims to
find it only in 1531, and considers it to be a function of the 'peasant thinking' which he
feels constrains and continually reasserts control over Luther (Peuckert, see n. 16, 544).
Compared to Peuckert's work, that of M. Greschat ('Luthers Haltung im Bauernkrieg', in:
ARG 56 (1965), 31–47) is an important step in the right direction. Greschat rightly
emphasizes the apocalyptic context of Luther's treatises on the Peasants' War, though he
too errs on the side of caution (p. 32) in dating this to November 20th, 1514 (Luther's
sermon on the Synoptic Apocalypse, Matt. 24, 15ff.; *WA* 15, 738–58). As we will
demonstrate, Greschat does not accord sufficient weight to Luther's teaching on the Two
Kingdoms in his conclusion (35): 'Angesichts der Schrecken des kommenden Gerichts
wird alles Ringen und Feilschen um irdische Vorteile und Rechte bedeutungslos.' J.
Wallmann's conclusive new dating of the Treaty of Weingarten in his article 'Luthers
letztes Wort im Bauernkrieg' (*Der Wirklichkeitsanspruch von Theologie und Religion,
Festschrift Ernst Steinbach*, ed. D. Henke et al., Tübingen 1976, 57–75) rather underlines
Luther's hopes for a general and secular peace settlement.
[18] See the literature already cited and the work of H. Gülzow, 'Eschatologie und Politik.
Zum religiösen Pluralismus im 16. Jahrhundert', in: *Das 'Augsburger Bekenntnis' von 1530
damals und heute*, ed. B. Lohse and O. H. Pesch, Munich 1980, 32–63.
[19] See Augustine, *De civitate Dei* XX, 7–13; *CChr* 48, 708–23.

while also looking back, beyond the Church Fathers, to draw on and rekindle the imminentist expectations of the early Christians. Like Augustine,[20] he keeps his distance from any form of chiliasm. The parousia of Christ is *not* prepared by a transformation of society or by a theocracy initiated by 'prophets', 'judges' or 'apostolic messengers'. Militant apocalypticism of the kind represented by Thomas Müntzer, Hans Hut, Melchior Hoffmann or Jan Matthijs, which predicted the extermination of the godless before the last Judgement, is therefore excluded from the very beginning.[21]

Luther also agrees with Augustine in interpreting Revelation 20.3 – 'and after that he [Satan] must be loosed a little season' – as the last phase of history, when God will allow the Antichrist to tempt the elect and to attack the true Church with all his might. But Augustine stresses that this period will be shortened by God's mercy, and will last only three years and six months.[22] Luther, on the other hand, does not pretend to know how long it will last. He counts on a prelude of three to four hundred years, and allows his calculations concerning the End Time to be influenced repeatedly by 'signs of the times'; but the signs remain signs and never become revelation. The hidden God (*Deus absconditus*) is by no means a mere negative place-holder opposed to the revealed God (*Deus revelatus*).[23] God the judge and lawgiver is no less real because we cannot make an accounting to him; his time is very close.

Augustine concentrates on the great 'interim', the thousand-year interval between the first and second coming of Christ.[24] He foretells the ordeals of the last days and confesses he is still unsure whether the

---

[20] Cf. Augustine, ibid., XX.7; *CChr* 48, 708–12.

[21] Cf. H.-W. Krumwiede, *Glaube und Geschichte in der Theologie Luthers. Zur Entstehung des geschichtlichen Denkens in Deutschland,* Berlin 1952; J. M. Headley, *Luther's View of Church History,* New Haven/London 1963; U. Asendorf, *Eschatologie bei Luther,* Göttingen 1967; K. Deppermann, *Melchior Hoffman. Soziale Unruhen und apokalyptischen Visionen im Zeitalter der Reformation,* Göttingen 1979; M. Reeves, *The Influence of Prophecy in the Later Middle Ages. A Study in Joachimism,* Oxford 1969. On the background to late medieval apocalypticism, see H. D. Rauh, *Das Bild des Antichrist im Mittelalter: Von Tyconius bis zum Deutschen Symbolismus,* Münster 1979.²

[22] Cf. Augustine, *De civitate Dei* XX.8, 13; *CChr* 48, 713.37–40; 722.1f.; 723.47f.

[23] See G. Ebeling, 'Existenz zwischen Gott und Gott. Ein Beitrag zur Frage nach der Existenz Gottes' (1965), in: *Wort und Glaube II,* Tübingen 1969, 257–86, esp. 282.

[24] Augustine, *De civitate Dei* XX.13; *CChr* 48, 722.13–17; cf. XX.8; *CChr* 48, 712.21–713.27.

Antichrist will appear within the Church itself, or outside it as an anti-church (2 Thess. 2.1–4).[25]

Luther considers Augustine's interval to be nearly over. He feels that he is living at the end of the 'interim', as he terms the time between the unchaining of Satan and the return of Christ: 'The only thing that comforts you in this interim is the coming Judgement and the belief that the Lord is King for ever and ever – finally all the godless will perish.'[26] At the beginning of 1520, Luther is certain that the Antichrist – now, at the end of time – has infiltrated the Church from within, from its center, the Holy See at Rome. Although Augustine had mentioned this last and most cunning manifestation of Satan as one possible ending of history, Luther adds a new element: that God must renew his Gospel –already eclipsed for the past three or four hundred years – to gather the elect and protect them against this demonic imposture. Augustine counts on the baptized Christians who have been instructed in the faith, who can hold out for the final three and a half years without gospel preaching, buoyed by secret baptism and meditation on Scripture,[27] while Luther believes that God openly intervenes by means of his Word to protect the 'poor in spirit' (*pauperes*), the chosen 'remainder of Israel' against the deceptions of the Antichrist. In his *Dictata* (1513), Luther had interpreted Psalm 10 (9b) as the call of the 'original congregation' for God's intervention against the Jews,[28] but here he explicitly expands his field of vision to include the apocalyptic menace now presented by the Antichrist.[29] Luther's only reservation at the beginning of 1520 is that he is not yet entirely certain whether or not the Antichrist has appeared in the flesh, which would mean that the End Time would

[25] Augustine, ibid., XX.19; *CChr* 48, 731.26–52.

[26] 'Quare una interim consolatio tua erit futuri iudicii dies et fides, qua credis, dominum tuum regnare imperpetuum, et perituros esse tandem omnes impios' (Ps. 10(9b).16; *AWA* 2, 615.1–3; *WA* 5, 350.7–9).

[27] '[A]diuvante Dei gratia per considerationem scripturarum . . .' (*De civitate Dei* XX.8; *CChr* 48, 715.117f.).

[28] 'Contra Iudeos, qui apostolos et discipulos Christi persequebantur, hic Psalmus proprie loquitur et respicit in tempus apostolorum et discipulorum Christi, licet aliqui de Antichristo exponant' (*WA* 55I, 76.16–18; cf. *WA* 4, 478.20f.).

[29] *AWA* 2, 567.13ff.; *WA* 5, 324.23f. Given the medieval collective understanding of Jews, heretics, Turks and 'antichristiani', this is in no way a shifting or blurring of the battle lines, but rather the prophesied and expected intensification of the End Times. Cf. *AWA* 2, 571.19–29; *WA* 5, 327.5–15.

be over very soon. But it cannot be denied that everything the exegetes have unanimously ascribed to the Antichrist 'has now been fulfilled down to the last jot and tittle.'[30] It is hardly credible that yet another Antichrist is to be expected who could cause worse damage (*peiora*).[31] The oppression of the Gospel in the Church and in theology, which had been increasing for centuries, is without a doubt the prologue, the immediate preliminary act signaling his arrival: the last forerunners of the Antichrist – and this is certain – have already arrived.[32] In this sense, a counter-reformation preceded the Reformation.

Approximately six months before the publication of the bull threatening his excommunication (15 June 1520), Luther interpreted the psalm's opening words 'Arise, O Lord' ('Exsurge Domine'; Psalm 10(9b).12) as the last gasp of the Church of Christ hard-pressed by the Antichrist: 'Arise, O Lord; O God, lift up thine hand.' No one else will ever again intervene to correct the situation, no other reformer will ever come other than Christ himself, at the Last Judgement. During the intervening period before the reform, the godless will make great gains: 'In the meanwhile the godless make constant advances from bad to worse, until the end.'[33] The majority of the Church, especially its leadership (*pars nobilior et melior*), has already been led into Babylonian captivity.[34] To Luther, it is certain that everything foretold in this psalm about the End Time is happening today (*nostro saeculo*), and in fact some of it has already happened.[35]

So this question becomes more and more germane: what office, what mission remains for Luther? The answer is: the office of the 'pre-

[30] 'hodie impletum esse usque ad minimum apicem et iota' (*AWA* 2, 589.2f.; *WA* 5, 337.13f.).

[31] See *AWA* 2, 590.13f.; *WA* 5, 337.36f.

[32] '[F]ortiter tamen Antichristo praeludunt . . .' (*AWA* 2, 593.7; *WA* 5, 339.12). For the originally typological, then eschatological meaning of *praeludere* and *praeludium,* see *WA* 4, 200.29–38 (the *confractio* of the Jews); 605.26; *WA* 9, 461.11; *WA* 13, 646.35; *WA* 25, 282.7; *WA* 31II, 337.12 and 28. On *WA* 4, 605, the sermon of 6 November 1519, see E. Vogelsang, 'Zur Datierung der frühesten Lutherpredigten', in: *ZKG* 50 (1931), 112–45; 127.

[33] 'Interim proficient impii in peius semper usque in finem' (*AWA* 2, 605.12f.; *WA* 5, 345.19f.). Cf. *AWA* 2, 609.10f.; *WA* 5, 347.18f.

[34] Cf. *AWA* 2, 600.9f.; *WA* 5, 343.7f.

[35] 'non sit dubium nostro saeculo, immo iam plusquam tribus saeculis huius psalmi rem pleno cursu geri et gestam esse' (*AWA* 2, 606.2–4; *WA* 5, 345.28–30).

reformation' interpreter of Scripture, charged with the mission of giving voice once again, far beyond the walls of the lecture hall, to the call of the prophet – a call that had been drowned out, denounced, even accused of heresy.[36] The children of God will be able to escape the clutches of Satan only if they are prepared by this voice for the tricks of the Antichrist, and thus firmly grounded in the Gospel of justification.[37] Since the Antichrist also usurps worldly power, those who confess Christ openly are in danger of their life.[38] Two years later he will write to the Prince-Elector: 'No sword can be of any use in this affair, God must take care of it on his own, without any human efforts or contributions. Therefore: he who believes the most will provide the most protection in this matter.'[39] No human being will be able to offer the evangelist protection at the time of the Antichrist, 'except God alone'.[40] This *evangelista* is Luther,[41] called in his capacity as a Doctor of Holy Writ to proclaim[42] 'the spirit of the prophet'. He considers himself to have been entrusted with the double job of arming the elect[43] with

[36] Cf. *AWA* 2, 580.17–19; *WA* 5, 332.34–6.

[37] '[Q]uae [the truth] quam primum revelata fuerit, omnium animos in se rapit et fraudem nudam et ignominiosam relinquit' (*AWA* 2, 597.9f.; *WA* 5, 341.10f.). The 'optimistic thesis' (see n. 4) could use as evidence the conviction expressed here that even Satan knows that the truth will drag *omnium animos* in its wake – if the word *pauperum* were omitted. The truth of the Gospel will not gather 'everyone' without distinction, but 'all the elect'. Cf. also *AWA* 2, 610.16–611.5; *WA* 5, 348.6–15.

[38] Cf. *AWA* 2, 599.32f.; *WA* 5, 342.37–9.

[39] 'Dieser Sachen soll noch kann kein Schwert raten oder helfen, Gott muß hie allein schaffen, ohn alles menschlich Sorgen und Zutun. Darumb: wer am meisten gläubt, der wird hie am meisten schützen' (*WAB* 2, 455.80–456.2; 5 March 1522 from Luther to Prince-Elector Frederick on the way home from the Wartburg).

[40] '[N]isi solus Deus' (*AWA* 2, 611.8f.; *WA* 5, 348.18f.). The connection between 'pre-reformation' and Reformation is expressed once more in a letter to Staupitz, dated 17 June 1522: 'Destruendum est mihi, mi Pater, regnum illud abominationis et perditionis Papae, cum toto corpore suo. Atque id agit iam sine nobis, sine manu, solo verbo: finis eius venit coram Domino' (*WAB* 2, 567.19–21).

[41] Von Campenhausen (see n. 8), 331, dates this self-description to 1522 at the earliest. But as early as the beginning of 1520, Luther describes the office of *evangelista* in such a way as to include precisely what he was already doing as an interpreter of Scripture.

[42] Luther also calls himself the 'German Prophet' (*WA* 30II, 290.28) or a second Jeremiah (*WAT* 5, 24.5). Cf. Holl, (see n. 8), 392. The central point is that *evangelista* is not, for Luther, a formal title, but an 'interim office' held in anticipation of the God's reformation.

[43] 'Sed Antichristus nostris episcopis et ecclesiaticis rectoribus utetur, sicut in hereticis coepit, quibus cum in omnibus oboediendum sit vice Christi, periculosissimum erit non oboedisse, rursum idem periculum oboedisse, cum et electi hic in errorem duci queant' (*AWA* 2, 610.16–19; *WA* 5, 348.6–9).

Scripture against being led astray, and of begging God to intervene[44] and, at the close of the 'history of salvation', to end the (human) 'history of damnation': thus he prays 'Arise, O Lord!' The Pope would soon beg God with these very words to step in against the Reformation.

Luther's fearless behavior in the godless End Time certainly lends him an 'heroic aura'. However, he is not a Promethean torch-bearer or a Germanic war-leader; he is not an Old Testament judge who fearlessly, trusting only in God, 'introduces' the Reformation; he is not even a theocrat arisen to effect a 'transformation'. The only transformation that will occur before Judgement Day is Satan's rapidly advancing triumphal march. His worldly radiance and his power guarantee that 'the entire globe will slide into obedience to the Antichrist'.[45] Far from wanting to achieve a 'reformation', the evangelist Luther knows that by proclaiming the Word of God, he is accelerating the satanic rape and enslavement of the world: 'It is not our job to hold it back.'[46]

3. Praeludium Lutheri: Prologue to the 'Reformation'

What grounds are there to call Luther's writings of 1520 –which were now appearing in quick succession – a program designed to realize a 'reformation' over against the inroads made by satanic forces into the ecclesiastical and secular worlds? If these writings do in fact constitute

[44] 'Non quod deus his indigeat, ut moveatur, sed nos, ne in fide et spe succumbamus, his artibus nos armemus et roboremus' (*AWA* 2, 607.5–7; *WA* 5, 346.16–18). God must be called on, but so long as he allows evil – as Luther writes to Staupitz on 31 March 1518, concerning the errors of scholastic theology – there can be no holding it back: 'Sed, si Deus operatur, nemo est, qui avertet. Si quiescit, nemo suscitabit' (*WAB* 1, 160.25f.). Cf. his position three years later: 'Sed non est, qui surgat et teneat Deum, aut opponat sese murum pro domo Israel, in hoc die novissimo irae eius. O dignum regnum Papae fine et faece saeculorum! Deus misereatur nostri!' (*WAB* 2, 333.15–17; 12 May 1521 to Melanchthon).

[45] *AWA* 2, 611.3f.; *WA* 5, 348.12f.

[46] 'Non est nostrum remorari eum' (*WA* 1, 627.33; see n. 14). See also the revealing comments concerning Electoral Saxony, tending in the same direction, in a sermon of 1531: 'persequimur eius ministros, quos mittit, ut nos mit gnaden visitir. Ideo sol die scharhansen [the nobility] komen und die Cives et rusticos auffressen, post ipsi seipsos. Sed non hilfft: quando dicitur, non creditur, es wil sich erfarn. Rustici et Cives colligunt pecuniam, stelen, hat kein not, und Scharhansen habent arma. Quicquid dicitur, ut timeamus et deum in ehren halten, nihil fit, wir konnens nicht auffhalten' (*WA* 34II, 87.10–88.5; 13 August 1531, on Luke 19.41–4 (the destruction of Jerusalem)). On the thieving 'Scharren' (scraping, scrabbling) of the nobility, see *WA* 22, 192.35f. (1532).

a reformation program, certain questions are unavoidable. In January of 1520, Luther completed his interpretation of *Exsurge Domine* (Psalm 10.12). One question is whether, in the few months that followed, Luther decided that the 'interim' had been extended long enough for reformation – however local or symbolic – to become a historical possibility, in anticipation of the Last Judgement.

There is, however, no evidence for such an about-face. His sermon on good works (March 1520) and the treatise *On the Freedom of a Christian* (late October 1520), which begin and end, respectively, the great series of works Luther wrote in that year, are not only contemporaneous with his psalms interpretation, but both are rooted in the *Operationes in Psalmos*.[47] Both these programmatic works are concerned with the gospel of liberation and the Christian life of those freed in this way, to whom the 'comforting words of God's justice' and union with Christ in faith can now be preached openly. Both works correspond to Luther's description of the treatise on freedom: 'It's just a little booklet when you look at the amount of paper in it, but it contains the entire sum of a Christian life, if you grasp its meaning.'[48] These words are not merely ornamental, but constitute, in the tension between the letter (paper) and the spirit (meaning), an important reservation: only the *pauperes,* the chosen children of God, will understand the evangelist.

Luther does speak in both works as a 'public' pastor, but only in order to gather in the 'remnant of Israel' that groans under the moral law of scholastic theology and is tyrannized by the canon law of the papal Church. Luther wants to reanimate the *spiritus prophetae* (the prophetic spirit) for the sake of this 'remnant' and make the Gospel shine forth once again: because those who have been freed can escape Satan's toils and stand firm in faith only within the in-gathered congregation. Without this soteriological background, the 'Sermon' would appear to be nothing but an apology against the charge of laxity, and the treatise, the source of a new evangelical mysticism, the springboard for a modern anthropology or a Protestant ethic. All four perspectives have a certain validity, based on momentous passages,

---

[47] See Maurer (see n. 9), 78.

[48] 'Es ist eyn kleyn büchle, ßo das papyr wirt angesehen, aber doch die gantz summa eyniß Christlichen leben drynnen begriffen, ßo der synn vorstandenn wirt' (*WA* 7, 11.8–10.)

and are finally fused in the conclusion of the treatise: 'From all of this comes the conclusion that a Christian lives not in himself but in Christ by faith and in his neighbor by love: by faith he rises above himself into God, and from God he comes back down to humanity by love, and remains nonetheless in God and in God's love forever.'[49]

Luther is neither a passive nor an active proponent of the apocalypse. Rather, he develops an 'interim ethic' as the consequence of his view of freedom. This ethic is actually directed toward maintaining the world, not toward its approaching end: 'Therefore just as God helped us gratis through Christ, so we should help our neighbor with our body and its accomplishments and actions', 'to serve him and to amend him'.[50] This amendment is not intended to apply only to individuals. It entails institutional and legal reforms, as announced in the title of the treatise to the nobility – 'concerning the amendment of the Christian estate' ('Von des christlichen Standes Besserung', mid-August 1520). Since papal encroachment has practically neutralized the proper execution of episcopal duties (preaching the Word!) and has damaged the poor in spirit (*pauperes!*), 'the Emperor and his nobility are obliged to beat back and punish such tyranny'.[51]

Luther does indeed take hold of the current polemical term 'reformation', but uses it as an equivalent for secular amendment or improvement, *not* for 'apocalyptic transformation'. Thus he can, as a historian, describe and evaluate medieval reform movements as failed attempts to achieve 'amendment'. Using the vocabulary of the late medieval councils, he argues that Rome propagated the mendicant orders for the sole purpose of preventing, by means of these auxiliary troops, an episcopal reformation.[52] The powers of the End Time had

---

[49] 'Aus dem allenn folget der beschluß, das eyn Christen mensch lebt nit ynn yhm selb, sondern ynn Christo und seynem nehstenn, ynn Christo durch den glauben, ym nehsten durch die liebe: durch den glauben feret er uber sich yn gott, auß gott feret er widder unter sich durch die liebe, und bleybt doch ymmer ynn gott und gottlicher liebe' (*WA* 7, 38.6–10).

[50] 'Darumb wie uns gott hatt durch Christum umbsonst geholffen, alßo sollen wir durch den leyp und seyne werck nit anders den dem nehsten helffen' [ihm] 'zu willen und besserung' (*WA* 7, 36.6–8 and 30).

[51] '[D]er keyszer [ist] mit seynem adel schuldig, solch tyranney zuweeren und straffen' (*WA* 6, 433.24f.).

[52] Cf. *WA* 6, 438.30–34.

already established themselves at Rome in the fifteenth century so firmly that a reformation as self-reform in the spiritual sphere was no longer possible.

Luther can draw on the academic, secular institution of the *reformatores*,[53] enshrined in the university statutes at Wittenberg when he writes: 'The universities also need a good hard reformation.'[54] Reformation understood as amendment is therefore not to be confused with the historically powerful medieval dream of a complete transformation brought about by an angelic pope and an emperor of peace (*Friedenskaiser*).[55] Secular amendment is nonetheless possible and needed. It is a rearguard defensive action[56] against a satanic tidal wave that will be followed only by worse and more wicked times (*peiora*). He is advocating, then, not a transformation, but a worldly enterprise, amendment as the protection of a threatened creation, a 'needful order, especially in our perilous times.'[57] One element added since the beginning of the year

[53] 'Magistri deputentur ad lecciones ordinarias per reformatores' (*Urkundenbuch der Universität Wittenberg*, vol. I, ed. W. Friedensburg, Magdeburg 1926, 56). See also *Geschichtsquellen der Provinz Sachsen und angrenzender Gebiete,* ed. K. Pallas, vol. 41: *Die Registraturen der Kirchenvisitationen im ehemals sächsischen Kurkreise* II/2, Halle 1907, 1. On the reformation of the *series lectionum* see Luther's letter to Spalatin of 11 March 1518. Here Luther reports his discussion with Karlstadt 'de lectionibus studii nostri initiandis vel instituendis' (*WAB* 1, 153.5) and opines that the enclosed plan offers a 'vera occasio omnium universitatum reformandarum' (line 11f.). The detailed proposal of 23 February 1519, directed to the Prince-Elector, was signed by both Luther and Karlstadt, among others (*WAB* 1, 350.43f.).

[54] 'Die universiteten dorfften auch wol eyner gutten starken reformation' (*WA* 6, 457.28f.).

[55] For background, see G. B. Ladner, *The Idea of Reform. Its Impact on Christian Thought and Action in the Age of the Fathers,* Cambridge, MA 1959, esp. 284ff. and 402ff. Cf. L. Graf zu Dohna, *Reformatio Sigismundi. Beiträge zum Verständnis einer Reformschrift des fünfzehnten Jahrhunderts,* Veröffentlichungen des Max-Planck-Instituts für Geschichte 4, Göttingen 1960, esp. 68, 82 and 135f.

[56] Cf. '[I]ch hofft, es solt schier besser werden' (*WA* 6, 457.12).

[57] '[E]in nottige ordnung, beszondern zu unsern ferlichen zeytten'; *WA* 6, 439.33f. Hans Kotter, a reform-minded poet (+1541 at Berne), read the epistle to the nobility as a call for *reformatz*. His letter to Bonifatius Amerbach, dated 22 October 1520, offers an unique testimony to the immediate effects of Luther's message: 'Deßglichen hab ich nie gelesen noch gehört; alle mönschen verwonderen sich dorab, etzlich meinen, der tufel redt vß im oder der heilig geist. Er riert den boden [= filth], dz dem heiligen vatter vnd der römer wesen nit wol schmecken wirt . . . Also kumbt herfurrer die boßheit, so zü Rom furgath.

Eß mag in die leng nit bestan,
ein reformatz missen si han,
Carolus wurdt dz fahen an.'

Die Amerbachkorrespondenz, ed. A. Hartmann, vol. II: *Die Briefe aus den Jahren 1514–24,* Basel 1943, 260.36–9 and 51–3.

is the thought that Satan's confusion of the two 'kingdoms' will destroy both, by causing diabolical chaos in God's creation.[58] Wherever the Gospel is restored, secular amendment will banish this chaos, because the confusion of the kingdoms is thereby ended and the secular kingdom can function as it should. The Gospel will bring amendment to the country that defends it, because the divinely-willed dignity and power of the worldly kingdom will thereby be recognized and restored. Now the cloisters and other ecclesiastical foundations are given the task of serving, as in the past, as schools 'where writing and "discipline" [public order] are taught in a Christian manner, and people are raised to govern and preach'.[59] This public order is by no means a delayed product of creeping fossilization, or an unforeseen consequence of the newly-introduced principle according to which territorial princes determined the religious affiliation of their dominions.[60]

Secular 'amendment' or improvement has traditionally been interpreted in Reformation scholarship, contrary to what Luther meant, as meaning an apocalyptic turning-point in the world and the Church. On the other hand, the genuinely apocalyptic *Praeludium Lutheri* in the title of the *Captivitas Babylonica* has been denatured and secularized, and turned into a polemic satirical song. It is

[58] As an example of a potential amendment or improvement, Luther suggests a policy of reconciliation with the Bohemians that would renounce military intervention intended to force them to accept papal jurisdiction. Cf. *WA* 6, 454.17–457.27. Luther also hopes for 'improvement' from the renewal of secular law, which is 'better, better-made, more honest than canon law' ('besser, kunstlicher, redlicher . . . den das geystlich') (*WA* 6, 459.31). In 1530, he sees in Electoral Saxony the exemplar of a just government, a renewal of original goodness: 'ein großes Teil des Himmelreichs Christi in E. K. F. G. Land ist durch das heilsam Wort erbauet ohn Unterlaß; das weiß er [Satan] und siehet seinen Unwillen dran' (*WAB* 5, 327.102–3). Cf. Luther's lecture on the Song of Songs (4.13), dating to the same period: *WA* 31II, 697.4–16.

[59] *WA* 6, 439.38f.; cf. 461.11–23.

[60] It appears that there is no textual evidence for what some scholars have seen as a contrast between a 'spontaneous' younger Luther and an older Luther concerned with the 'control and supervision of morals'. His word *Zucht* cannot be translated by 'discipline' in the sense of how individuals lead their (moral) lives. *Zucht* concerns public order as a whole, and includes public measures against luxury (*ubirflusz*), commerce (*specirey*), usury (*zynsz kauff*), monopolies (*Fuckern*) and prostitution (*frawenheuszer*): *WA* 6, 465.25–467.26. But Luther also has 'discipline' in mind when he attacks gluttony and hard drinking as the particular vices (*szondern laster*) of the Germans. These vices cannot be stopped by preaching; the secular authorities must do something ('Es mag das weltlich scwert hie etwas weren . . .') (*WA* 6, 467.8 and 12).

commonly translated as 'Luther's Prelude', as a satire on the papists.[61]
But this entirely overlooks the eschatological dimension, the
interpretive framework within which this work must be read. The
Praeludium Lutheri is the opening act to divine judgement, a
preliminary glimpse of the Apocalypse on the Last Day, when the
malignant oppression of the true Christians will be revealed abruptly
by God's universal reformation, and simultaneously overturned.

The ludic element of this 'prelude' lies in our own limited ability to
play God's 'game': divine wisdom seen with worldly eyes can appear
only to be folly. Erasmus had already developed this theme eloquently
in his *In Praise of Folly* (*Moriae Encomium*) (1511–14).[62] However,
the abuses Erasmus pillories with satiric gusto and thereby 'sees
through' in a spiritual sense – i.e., which he leaves behind – Luther
applies to the End Time, gravely announcing it as a final warning.[63]
This warning is not directed at 'Babylon', the ruling Church, the
papacy or the Curia, but rather is intended to summon, convert and
gather in the faithful – who would otherwise remain in captivity,
confused and misled in the absence of the Word of Truth and
hopelessly weak without the sacraments instituted to impart comfort
and strength.[64]

The *Sendbrief* (epistle) to Pope Leo X (end of October, 1520),
written at about the same time as the treatise on freedom and
intended to accompany the latter, does not originate in apprehension
caused by his own daring, nor in a clever distortion or even in an

---

[61] Cf. the introduction to *De Captivitate*, *WA* 6, 486.

[62] M. A. Screech has convincingly shown this 'enlightenment' to be both ecstasy and
raptus in his *Ecstasy and the Praise of Folly*, London 1980, esp. 218–22 and 248f.

[63] This eschatological reference in the 'prelude' does not exclude, but rather includes –
in accordance with the foregoing interpretation – the singing of satirical songs that taunt
the enemy: 'Huttenus et multi alii fortiter scribunt pro me, et parantur indies cantica, quae
Babylonem istam parum delectabunt' (*WAB* 2, 264.51f.; 9 February 1521, to Staupitz).
See also the conclusion of Luther's treatise addressed to the nobility: *WA* 6, 469.1–4. Yet
this game is in deadly earnest, because Christ is made a laughing-stock in the Babylonian
captivity: 'Verum seria res est . . . quando per totum orbem ipse optimus salvator, qui sese
pro nobis dedit, ludibrium iactatur . . .' (*WAB* 2, 263.27–9).

[64] As does Augustine, Luther emphasizes the centrality of Scripture, which becomes a
public event, opened up in the preaching of the Word. However, Augustine finally
decided, after some hesitation as to whether anyone would be converted to Christianity in
the ordeals of the End Times, that the children of confessing Christians would be saved, in
the last days, by *secret* baptism, and adults by *private* meditation. Cf. *De civitate Dei* XX.8;
CChr 48, 715.115–18.

ironic non-sequitur.[65] Rather, it illustrates how Luther attempts to minister to the Pope as a person, to wrench him away from the Antichrist, distinguishing all the while between the Pope and the Babylonian institution of the papacy: Your Holiness 'is praised in all the world'; 'against your person' I have nothing to object.[66] The manners and morals of Rome, under universal attack, play absolutely no role in this matter. But in the name of the Pope and of the Roman Church the 'poor people of the whole world'[67] are deceived and harmed:

> The papal throne is done for, God's wrath has come over it ceaselessly. It is an enemy of the General Councils, it will not allow itself to be corrected or reformed, and yet it cannot stop its raging unChristian essence from fulfilling what is said of its mother, old Babylon in Jeremiah [Jeremiah 51.9]: 'We would have healed Babylon, but she is not healed: forsake her . . .'.[68]

Jeremiah's advice will accompany Luther to the end of his days. At the same time, he formulates his call for preaching, as well as the expectation that the reformation will not be successful.[69]

Luther forces us to go yet one step farther. Far from starting this reformation full of optimism that it will initiate a 'transformation', the rediscovery and renewed preaching of the gospel as a *praeludium* has the opposite effect: it provokes Satan to a counter-offensive, it practically challenges him, and forces him – in the service of God – to step up his diabolical operations against the world. In this way the duration of his unchained freedom is shortened by God's grace, and the Last Judgement is brought closer.[70]

---

[65] For the opposite view, see R. Bäumer, *Martin Luther und der Papst,* Münster 1970[2], 61f.

[66] '[Y]n aller welt beruffen'; 'widder deyne person' (*WA* 7, 4.8f. and 38).

[67] '[D]as arm volck ynn aller welt' (*WA* 7, 5.14f).

[68] 'Es ist auß mit dem Romischen stuel. gottis tzorn hat yhn ubirfallen on auffhoren. Er ist feynd den gemeynen Conciliis, er will sich nit unterweyßen noch reformieren lassen, und vormag doch seyn wuttends unchristlichs weßen nit hindernn, damit er erfullet, das gesagt ist von seyner mutter, der alten Babylonen, Hiere.: 'Wyr haben viel geheylett an der Babylonen, noch ist sie nit gesund wordenn, wyr wollen sie faren lassenn' (*WA* 7, 5.37–6.3). See M. Brecht, 'Curavimus enim Babylonem et non est sanata', in: *Reformatio Ecclesiae* (see n. 16), 581–95.

[69] '[D]ixi Prophetam loqui hoc psalmo de his, qui extremo iudicio apprehendentur in fine mundi, postquam impietas eorum praevaluerit per orbem in desperatam usque emendationem' (*AWA* 2, 609.9–11; *WA* 5, 347.17–19). Cf. for the year 1533 *WA* 38,73.28f. and 38–40.

[70] '[A]t ego indies magis provoco Satanam et suas squamas, ut acceleretur dies ille Christi destructurus Antichristum istum' (*WAB* 2, 567.35f.; to Staupitz, dated 27 June 1522).

The apocalyptic notions Luther uses here are employed not merely to make himself understood by contemporaries, but also in the context of his own intellectual and personal experience. Satan directs his attention to the center of resistance to himself, and tries to hem Martin Luther in, physically and psychically. The final battle, therefore, is a very personal business for Luther; this stands out in nearly every letter. His stay at the Wartburg is a time of particularly strong diabolical attack – like his stint some nine years later as an observer at the fortress of Coburg – because it seems that Luther, having been removed from the battle-front, is no longer worthy of the final battle: 'There is nothing that I desire more fervently than to throw myself against the enemy.'[71] This in no way means that Luther was tired of life and therefore desired martyrdom for psychological reasons,[72] but is the logical result of his expectation that the destruction of the 'evangelist' would signal Satan's last assault, and therefore accelerate the end of his fury: the Last Judgement.[73]

Starting in May of 1521, Luther is constantly kept informed in his 'exile' at the Wartburg of the widespread approval among the people. Not the end of time, but the beginning of a new era seems to be in the works. Three factors can be distinguished in the Luther of the twenties which allowed him, despite his apocalyptic expectations, to come to terms with precisely what he did not expect: 'success'.

The first is his refusal of any violent course of action undertaken in the name of the Gospel. His success and popularity as a 'freedom

---

[71] 'Nihil magis opto, quam furoribus adversariorum occurrere obiecto iugulo . . . Sed non est, qui surgat et teneat Deum, aut opponat sese murum pro domo Israel, in hoc die novissimo irae eius. O dignum regnum Papae fine et faece saeculorum! Deus misereatur nostri! Quare tu verbi minister interim insta, et munito muros et turres Hierusalem, *donec et te invadant'* (*WAB* 2, 332.8f.; 333.15–19; to Melanchthon, dated 12 May 1521). Cf. the letter of the same day to Agricola: 'optem in publico stare pro verbo, sed dignus nondum fui' (*WAB* 2, 336.10f.).

[72] At least this is how a psycho-historical interpreter might understand Luther's desire, if seen in isolation: 'Iam in christiana libertate ago, absolutus ab omnibus tyranni istius legibus, quamquam mallem, ut ille porcus Dresdensis publice praedicantem dignus esset interficere, si Deo placeret, ut pro verbo eius paterer; fiat voluntas Domini' (*WAB* 2, 338.62–6; to Spalatin, dated 14 May 1521).

[73] I also interpret Luther's expectation that he will die sooner rather than later, when he rejects the thought of marriage six months before his wedding: 'animus alienus est a coniugio, cum expectem quotidie mortem, et meritum haeretici supplicium. Itaque nec Deo figam terminum operis in me, nec in corde meo nitar. Spero autem, quod non sinet me diu vivere' (*WAB* 2, 367.16).

fighter' is a sarcastic joke of the Devil: 'I am extremely displeased that men approve of me . . .'.[74] With this, he renounces anything that tends toward militant apocalypticism, not in regard to the peasants in 1525, but four years earlier, in relation to entirely different social groups: the rapacious knights and the greedy, unscrupulous officials of Electoral Saxony.

Another consideration relates to the traditional definition of faith from the Epistle to the Hebrews that had occupied Luther since the very beginning: faith has to do with 'things not seen' (Hebrews 11.1). This had always signified for him the qualitative difference between heaven and earth;[75] the hope of faith refers to that which is invisible, hidden in the future. Now, at the end of time, it is a characteristic of Christian faith to expect the unexpected, the seemingly impossible.[76] This might mean that he had already played his role as evangelist, and that someone else, perhaps Melanchthon, will be called to fill his place: 'Even if I die, the gospel – in which you now surpass me – will in no way perish . . .'.[77] But the Antichrist might also have to give up his plan to garrotte his opposition secretly – 'it's all under the table'[78] – given Luther's fast-growing following, in favor of an open exchange of blows. Then violence will no longer be avoidable: 'Germany has a great many strong farm boys.'[79] Despite Luther's vehement insistence that he started 'the affair',[80] he would, in time, learn to deal with the growing numbers of evangelical preachers – though during his Wartburg exile only he and Melanchthon stand in the first rank, at

---

[74] 'Vehementer enim me offendit ista gratia hominum in nos, ex qua liquido videmus, nondum esse nos dignos coram Deo verbi sui ministros, et Sathanam in nostra studia ludere et ridere' (*WAB* 2, 332.5–7; to Melanchthon, approx. 8 May 1521). Cf. his comments to Spalatin in June of 1521: 'Sed nihil proficiet; non sunt nostri, qui haec faciunt' (*WAB* 2, 367.16).

[75] See G. Ebeling, *Luther. Einführung in sein Denken,* Tübingen 1964, 272f.

[76] 'Toties de fide et spe rerum non apparentium locuti sumus; age, semel vel in modico eius doctrinae periculum faciamus, quando id vocante Deo, non nobis tentantibus ita contingit' (*WAB* 2, 348.45–8; to Melanchthon, dated 26 May 1521). Cf. *WA* 4, 322.16–24; 324.1–4; scholion on Ps. 119.31 and 34.

[77] 'Ego etiam si peream, nihil peribit euangelio, in quo tu nunc me superas . . .' (*WAB* 2, 348.48). In the next letter to Melanchthon, Luther describes his colleague as (Wittembergensis Ecclesiae) 'Evangelista': *WAB* 2, 356.1f.

[78] '[E]s geht unter dem hudlin zu' (*AWA* 2, 597.1; 595.25; *WA* 5, 341.1f.; 340.20).

[79] 'Habet Germania valde multos Karsthansen' (*WAB* 2, 348.64f.; to Melanchthon, dated 26 May 1521).

[80] Cf. von Campenhausen (see n. 8), 328.

the battlefront.[81] Luther writes to Archbishop Albrecht of Mainz at the end of 1521, sure that he no longer stands alone: 'I will not keep quiet, and even if I am not successful, I do hope that you bishops don't get to finish your little song undisturbed. You have not yet destroyed everyone whom Christ has aroused against your idolatrous tyranny.'[82] Success therefore means progress in gathering the faithful together.

The third perspective on his unexpected success presupposes, starting in 1525, that the earlier questions have been resolved. The invincibility of the Truth is now limited to the image of the *farender platz regen*[83] (a wandering downpour that appears unexpectedly) and of the 'final extension granted by God's grace' (*Gnadenfrist*).[84] Truth has made the ground arable, the Gospel has been planted, now it needs to be tended and cared for. In this sense, we can speak of the successful dissemination of the Gospel as it 'ran its course'.[85] Looking back from the perspective of 1531, Luther can announce joyfully that God opened the door for the evangelical confession at the Imperial Diet of Augsburg.[86] The end of captivity and the cleansing of the papal Church that we generally call the 'Reformation' nonetheless refer, as far as Luther is concerned, to the temporally limited prelude to God's reformation. Only on the Last Day, when the Gospel has completed its task, will the *captivitas* be destroyed along with its walls and bulwarks.[87]

---

[81] 'Nos soli adhuc stamus in acie; te quaerent post me' (*WAB* 2, 333.21f.; to Melanchthon, dated 12 May 1521).

[82] 'Schweigen werde ich nicht, und ob mir's nicht würde gelingen, hoffe ich doch, ihr Bischoffe sollt euer Liedlin nicht mit Freuden hinaussingen. Ihr habt sie noch nicht alle vertilget, die Christus wider euer abgöttische Tyrannei erweckt hat' (*WAB* 2, 408.100–3; 1 December 1521).

[83] 'Auffs ander zeygt er die dahr an, das man die gnade nicht verseume. Damit er gewislich anzeygt, das die predigt des Evangelij nicht eyne ewige, werende, bleybende lere ist, sondern ist wie ein farender platz regen, der dahyn leufft, was er trifft, das trifft er, was feylet, das feylet' (*WA* 17II, 179.28–31).

[84] Cf. *WA* 41, 220.5f.

[85] Cf. *WA* 30III, 477.7–13; in general concerning the function of the Gospel: *WA* 49, 269.30f. (Gal. 5.7; Acts 20.23).

[86] Cf. *WAB* 5, 480.29f.; to Justus Jonas, Spalatin, Melanchthon and Agricola, dated 15 July 1530.

[87] 'Er hat, Gott lob, itzt auch angefangen, unsern Götzen und Larven, des Bapstumbs lesterlichen treudelmarck nider zu legen und seine Kirchen zu reinigen durch sein Euangelium, auch zum vorspiel, das man sehe, das er es mit jnen auch ein ende machen wil. Wie es fur augen schon angefangen zu fallen und teglich mehr und mehr fallen mus. Und

Luther claims that God's wrath has been put off for only a short time not because he is disappointed or in some nostalgic mood, remembering the promise of the early days, but at the time of the greatest visible 'success'. This wrath is about to break over an ungrateful Germany, where the Gospel is heard, but rejected: '. . . for I feel that the Lord will overrun Germany soon, just as its unbelieving nature, impiety and hatred of the gospel deserve.'[88] *What will later need to be explained is not resistance and failure, but breakthrough and success.* Luther's judgement of 1520 – 'non est nostrum remorari eum' – is translated, at the end of the most successful year of the Wittenberg Reformation, 1531, and repeated in the vernacular so as to be unmistakable: 'Wir konnens nicht auffhalten', we cannot hold it back.[89]

The unexpected turn taken by history – unexpected to Luther, at least – narrows the early questions of the Wartburg period down to one theme: the evangelical ingathering of the faithful will soon be complete. The opening act has already begun and can no longer be held back 'for the sake of a few pious folk'. The opening act will come to an end as soon as the 'tiny group that know Christ' have 'laid down their head'.[90]

4. Toward Visitations: Cito Visitet Dominus Germaniam

We might expect that Luther's eschatological expectations would shrink in proportion to the 'success' enjoyed by the evangelical movement. But this was not the case; in fact, the opposite is true. We

---

viel greulicher wird zu bodem gestossen werden und ewiglich zu grund gehen müssen, denn die Jüden zustört und vertilget sind. Dieweil es auch viel ein schendlicher grewel ist. Das sol sich erst recht anfahen, wenn nu das Euangelium hinweg ist, umb der schendlichen, greulichen lesterung willen. Aber zu letzt mit dem Jüngsten tag erst recht sein endliche und ewige zerstörung nemen' (*WA* 22, 193.12–21, Cruciger's postille of the sermon on Luke 19.41–48; 13 August 1531). Cf. *WA* 34II, 96.5–10.

[88] '[S]uspicor enim fore, ut cito visitet Dominus Germaniam, sicut meretur eius incredulitas, impietas et odium evangelii' (*WAB* 2, 372.75–6; to Melanchthon, dated 1 August 1521). There is no trace of 'optimism': 'At haec plaga tum nobis imputabitur, quod haeretici Deum provocaverimus, erimusque opprobrium hominum et abiectio plebis, illi vero apprehendent excusationes in peccatis suis, et iustificabunt semetipsos, ut probet, reprobos neque bonitate neque ira bonos fieri, et scandalisabuntur multi. Fiat, fiat voluntas Domini, Amen' (*WAB* 2, 372.76–81).

[89] *WA* 34II, 88.4f.; sermon preached 13 August 1531; see also nn. 46 and 71.

[90] [As soon as] 'der kleinest hauffe, so Christum kennen', 'das heubt legen': *WA* 22, 194.6; *WA* 21, 324.1f.; *WA* 22, 194.12.

encounter, in the years 1530–31, yet another intensification of Luther's certainty concerning the threatening 'furor finalis Dei'. The last wrath of God, the signs of God's anger, will allow the powers of the apocalypse to gather themselves together for one last assault on the Gospel and to overrun an ungrateful Germany.[91]

The question of the powers exercised by territorial princes to establish and direct their territorial Church becomes much more urgent at this time. What task can such a church government have in the Church of the last days? Were the visitations supposed to accomplish what the reformation could not? In order to chase down this suspicion, we will have to examine developments following Luther's stay at the Wartburg. He could accept the protection that 'Junker Jörg' received at the Wartburg as a secular action of the authorities, just as he later accepted visitations. The cause of the reformation, however, cannot be ensured or accelerated by worldly authorities. Called back from the protection of the Wartburg by the congregation at Wittenberg, the proscribed Luther boldly ventured back into the public eye, renouncing the protection of a territorial lord. Luther declared unequivocally and solemnly on 5 March 1522, 'that I have received the Gospel not from men, but from our Lord Jesus Christ, that I would have liked (as I wish to do from now on) to call myself and to write as [his] servant and evangelist . . . I come to Wittenberg under a much higher protection than that of the Prince-Elector . . . No sword can help in this affair, God must take care of it alone, without any human care or intervention.'[92] What Luther needs, what he asks from his friends in letter after letter, is not protection, but the prayers and solidarity of the ingathered. Protecting the evangelist is just as much God's business as accomplishing the great reformation.

[91] See my paper 'Luthers Beziehungen zu den Juden: Ahnen und Geahndete', in: *Leben und Werk Martin Luthers von 1526 bis 1546. Festgabe zu seinem 500. Geburtstag.* Im Auftrag des Theologischen Arbeitskreises für Reformationsgeschichtliche Forschung, ed. H. Junghans, Göttingen 1983, 519–30, 894–904; 525–7.

[92] [Luther proclaims] 'daß ich das Evangelium nicht von Menschen, sondern allein vom Himmel durch unsern Herrn Jesum Christum habe, daß ich mich wohl hätte mügen (wie ich denn hinfort tun will) einen Knecht und Evangelisten rühmen und schreiben. . . . ich komme gen Wittenberg in gar viel einem höhern Schutz denn des Kurfürsten . . . Dieser Sachen soll noch kann kein Schwert raten oder helfen, Gott muß hie allein schaffen, ohn alles menschlich Sorgen und Zutun' (*WAB* 2, 455.40–3; 455.76f.; 455.80–456.82; to Prince-Elector Frederick, dated 5 March 1522). Cf. Luther's letter written seven weeks later, on 27 June 1522, to Staupitz (see n. 40).

God does employ certain means, however, toward secular 'amendment': Christians and non-Christians in all offices, including and above all the Prince-Elector. The roots of the visitations are to be found here, in the secular realm.[93] Preliminary discussion and preparations for visitations started even before the Peasants' War, at the end of 1524.[94] Their realization, however, was hindered by the rebellions more than it was helped. On the eighth anniversary of the posting of the 95 Theses, 31 October 1525, Luther addressed an urgent request to the new Prince-Elector Johann, the brother of Frederick who died in the middle of the Peasants' War (5 May 1525). This supplication was also a reform program. Luther explicitly mentions the now-complete plan to 'put the university in order',[95] for which God used the Prince-Elector 'as his instrument'.[96] One month earlier, Luther spoke of reformation in the context of the confusion in the Church and its government, and could have called it in German *Besserung* (amendment) or *gute Ordnung* (good order), because he was talking about structural measures that had been for a long time in the hands of the secular authorities. The new order of divine service belongs in the same context. In his preface to the German Mass, Luther expressed his desire for divine service to be uniform throughout each territory.[97] After the liturgical reform, 'two things are

[93] See esp. n. 60.

[94] See H. Bornkamm, *Martin Luther in der Mitte seines Lebens. Das Jahrzehnt zwischen dem Wormser und dem Augsburger Reichstag,* Göttingen 1970, 425–42. Bornkamm cites and comments on H.-W. Krumwiede's book *Zur Entstehung des landesherrlichen Kirchenregimentes in Kursachsen und Braunschweig-Wolfenbüttel,* Göttingen 1967; there is also a paper of interest by I. Höß, 'The Lutheran Church of the Reformation: Problems of its Formation and Organization in the Middle and North German Territories', in: *The Social History of the Reformation,* ed. L. P. Bucks and J. Zophy, Columbus, OH 1972, 317–39. For the history of the early visitations, see I. Höß, 'Humanismus und Reformation', in: *Geschichte Thüringens,* ed. H. Patze and W. Schlesinger, vol. III: *Das Zeitalter des Humanismus und der Reformation,* Cologne 1967, 1–145; 71–84.

[95] 'die universitet zu ordiniren' (*WAB* 3, 594.11; cf. 595.36f.; 31 October 1525, addressed to Prince-Elector Johann). On the connection between *reformatio* and university reform, see n. 53.

[96] 'zum wergzeug gebraucht' (*WAB* 3, 595.33).

[97] Cf. *WA* 19, 73.6–8. Like university reform and the protection of parish churches, a uniform liturgy is a public concern and falls, therefore, within the Prince-Elector's competence: 'Scio reformatione parochiarum opus esse et institutis uniformibus ceremoniis, iamque hoc saxum volvo, et principem sollicitabo' (*WAB* 3, 582.5–7; addressed to Nikolaus Hausmann on 27 September 1525). The significant addition 'Satan est in medio' (582.11) is present here as well. The original hesitations concerning the structural constitution of an evangelical Church are often explained away by the claim that

left' (*noch zwey stuck furhanden*) that need 'inspection and ordering' (*eynsehen und ordenung*) by the Prince-Elector 'as the secular authority' (*als welltliche oberkeyt*).[98]

The first problem to be solved is that parishes, schools and preacherships are fading away through lack of money, 'and God's Word and service' are thereby allowed to fall into disuse.[99] The second problem is 'bad government, both in the cities and in the countryside'.[100] The Prince-Elector should also allow the secular government to be 'visited' (*visitirn*). There is no mention of calling on the territorial lord as an 'emergency bishop' (*Notbischof*). These duties all concern the common good, and therefore belong to the authorities. In medieval terms, these are *reformationes,* in modern terms, reforms that are designed to establish good order (*gut ordnung*) in the administration of the church and in the political order.

The connection between both realms in need of 'visitation' is clear: selfish functionaries, particularly the 'rapacious nobility' are helping themselves to the property of the Church, which is supposed to be used to pay for schools and the salaries of pastors.[101] The reforms are aimed at encouraging education and the next generation of civil servants, but above all at securing the economic basis of preaching.[102] They are also intended to gather the faithful,[103] although Luther does

---

Luther was not interested in organizational matters. This is expressed by Höß in his argument that Luther did not want to create a new Church, but renew the existing one ('Humanismus und Reformation', see n. 94), 71. The first, psychological explanation seems to me to be erroneous: Luther had a surprisingly good sense of what can be achieved within the triangle formed by political exigencies, financial dependency and what people are able to do and put up with. The second interpretation should be narrowed down to issues of ecclesiastical governance; moreover, it is incomplete without the important foreknowledge of God's powerful intervention 'in the last days'.

[98] *WAB* 3, 595.38f.

[99] '[U]nd also gotts wort und dienst zu boden gehen' (595.45).

[100] '[B]ose regiment, beyde ynn stedten und auff dem lande' (595.59f.).

[101] Cf. Luther's lament concerning the dwindling respect of the lower nobility for Prince-Elector Johann in the catastrophic wake of the *rapina monasteriorum* (rape of the monasteries): *WAB* 4, 150.33; 160.8–11.

[102] 'Ich tröste sie aber alle [the evangelical pastors lacking a salary] mit der zukünftigen Visitation.' There are 'etliche groß Hansen' (many 'big shots') who are actively opposed to the visitation: 'Wo dem so ist, so ist's aus mit Pfarren, Schulen und Evangelio in diesem Land; sie müssen entlaufen' (*WAB* 4, 168.6–9; letter to Prince-Elector Johann of 3 February 1527).

[103] By gathering (*Sammlung*), Luther means, as he always did, the separation of the elect and their ingathering to form the core of a truly Christian community that should be set up

not imagine there will be a big harvest. In each parish, only a few will cleave to Christ: 'How many, I ask, true followers of Christ are there among this great mass of people?'[104] The tenth anniversary of the posting of the 95 Theses was celebrated at Wittenberg with a drink and a clinking of glasses.[105] On the same day, the general visitation, for which Luther had long been asking the Prince-Elector, was finally inaugurated. Luther in no way expected the visitation to transform society, nor was he filled with 'the hope of better times'. On the contrary: 'We have one solace to put against the fury of the Devil, namely that we at least have the Word of God to save the souls of believers, even if he devours the Body.'[106]

5. The Antichrist: Myth or Mystery

Our portrait should by now have demonstrated that it was Luther – although not Luther alone, rather Luther as the speaker for a number of city pastors – who appealed to the Christian conscience of the originally hesitant Prince-Elector Johann and persuaded him to intervene with visitations to amend both the ecclesiastical and secular orders as a function of his secular office. The *ius circa sacra* ('rights concerning the sacred things' – that is, religious affairs) was

by the visitation (*WAB* 4, 181.10f.; addressed to Nikolaus Hausmann on 29 March 1527). This Christian community can practice Christian discipline (*Zucht*), which is not identical with the public supervision and control of morals for which secular government is responsible. See esp. *WAB* 4, 159.7f.; 181.20f; and even the preface to the German Mass: *WA* 19, 75.18–30 (1526).

[104] 'Quotos, quaeso, Christus in tanto suo populo proprio habuit adhaerentes?' (*WAB* 4, 167.18, dated 2 February 1527 and addressed to Johannes Draco (Drach, +1566), one of the signatories of the Schmalkaldic Articles). Cf. *Die Bekenntnisschriften der evangelisch-lutherischen Kirche*, Göttingen 1982⁹, 464, n. 6.

[105] According to the date given at the end of a letter to Amsdorf: 'Wittembergae die Omnium Sanctorum, anno decimo Indulgentiarum conculcatarum, quarum memoria hac hora bibimus utrinque consolati, 1527' (*WAB* 4, 275.25–27; 1 November 1527). E. Iserloh claims that this festive drink is sufficiently explained by the assumption that Luther sent the theses to the proper representatives of the church on 31 October: *Luther zwischen Reform und Reformation. Der Thesenanschlag fand nicht statt*, Münster 1968³, 57. See my arguments to the contrary in *Werden und Wertung der Reformation*, 190–2; English trans.: *Masters of the Reformation. The Emergence of a New Intellectual Climate in Europe*, trans. Dennis Martin, Cambridge 1981, 148–50.

[106] 'Sic sunt foris pugnae, intus pavores, satisque asperae, Christus nos visitat. Unum solatium est, quod Satanae furenti opponimus, scilicet verbum saltem Dei nos habere, pro servandis animabus credentium, utcunque corpora devoret. Proinde nos fratribus commendes et tibi ipsi, ut pro nobis oretis, ut feramus fortiter manum Domini, et Satanae vim et dolum vincamus, sive per mortem, sive per vitam, Amen' (*WAB* 4, 275.19–25).

interpreted by Luther to apply to the territorial prince in the sense of a *munus circa sacra* (a *duty* concerning the sacred things). The prince was responsible as a function of his office for the prosperity of his country and the amendment of the Church. This laid the foundation on which the territorial lords' responsibility for the governing of the Church was to be built, according to the varying circumstances of each territory.[107] The imperial solution of 1555 according to the principle *cuius regio eius religio* (the religion of a territory is to be that of its lord) presupposes that the territorial lord possesses a *ius reformandi* (the right to carry out reformation),[108] a right that Luther believed was confirmed in the Saxon treaty of partition (1484).[109] Luther and Melanchthon cooperated with Prince-Elector Johann in preparing visitations, and provided the basis for their accomplishment with instructions for the Visitors.

The agreement between the two Wittenberg reformers on this matter could not hide a far-reaching split between them, however. Luther's *Ur*-Christian expectation of the imminent end, based on his knowledge that the Gospel is threatened by the Antichrist (2 Thess. 2.4; Revelation 20.3) was not – unlike his strategy concerning visitations – adopted or supported by Melanchthon.[110] When Luther in the Schmalkaldic Articles (1537) says explicitly of the pope that he is 'the true Antichrist or Endchrist',[111] Melanchthon is willing to subscribe only under the condition that the pope, if he should accept and allow the preaching of the Gospel, will be recognized as the head of the Church, in order to

[107] Cf. G. Franz, *Die Kirchenleitung in Hohenlohe in den Jahrzehnten nach der Reformation*, Stuttgart 1971, 149f.

[108] On the *cura religionis* and the Religious Peace of Augsburg, see M. Heckel, 'Staat und Kirche nach den Lehren der evangelischen Juristen Deutschlands in der ersten Hälfte des 17. Jahrhunderts', in: *Jus ecclesiasticum* 6 (1968), 205–16, including an overview of the relevant literature.

[109] '[W]eil es geteilte Fürstentum wären, und Vertrag geschehen, daß ein jeglicher in seinem Fürstentum sollt gläuben lassen wie er möcht . . .' (*WAB* 4, 306.19f.; 28 December 1527 to the brothers von Einsiedel, whose possessions lay partly in Electoral and partly in Ducal Saxony). The extent to which the lords of Saxony took the *cura religionis* seriously can be judged from their policy on indulgences and their support for the Observant movement which produced Luther. See F. Gess' editorial introduction to the volume *Akten und Briefe zur Kirchenpolitik Herzog Georgs von Sachsen I: 1517–1524*, Leipzig 1905, xxi–lxxxviii. Cf. Luther's letter to Melanchthon of 21 July 1530, in which he laid bare his principles concerning the topic: 'sequitur, quod eadem persona non possit esse episcopus et princeps, nec simul pastor et paterfamilias' (*WAB* 5, 492.17f.).

[110] Cf. *WAB* 5, 496.7f.; addressed to Justus Jonas on 21 July 1530.

[111] *Bekenntnisschriften* (see n. 104), 430.14f.

ensure *pax et tranquillitas* (peace and security) in Christendom: peace with those who will hereafter (!) be under the papacy.[112]

In Melanchthon's *Tractatus de Potestate et Primatu papae* (1537), which was included along with the Schmalkaldic Articles in the Book of Concord, there is no hint of eschatological expectations, and the idea of the *Endechrist* is carefully but noticeably demythologized. It is true that 'all the vices prophesied concerning the Antichrist in the Scriptures correspond to the Kingdom of the Pope and its members',[113] but true Christians must beware of the Pope as though he were the Antichrist – 'rather it is necessary to oppose him *as though* [he were] the Antichrist'.[114] Here the papacy has become a cipher for 'opposition to God'. Behind the seemingly harmless word *tamquam* (as though) there is a radically different eschatology, namely the 'hope for better times'.[115]

---

[112] 'De pontifice autem statuo, si evangelium admitteret, posse ei propter pacem et communem tranquillitatem christianorum, qui jam sub ipso sunt et in posterum sub ipso erunt, superioritatem in episcopos, quam alioqui habet juro humano, etiam a nobis permitti.' ibid., 463.13–464.13–16.

[113] ibid., 484.19–22.

[114] ibid., 489.1f. Cf. 485.28f.

[115] Lucas Cranach's *Passional Christi et Antichristi* (March [?] 1521) was greeted by Luther as a 'bonus pro laicis liber' (*WAB* 2, 283.24f.) in a letter to Spalatin dated 7 March 1521. The caption for the twenty-sixth woodcut, which was commissioned along with the others by Melanchthon in cooperation with Johannes Schwertfeger (347.23f.), runs as follows: 'der herr Jesus . . . wirdt yn [the Antichrist] sturtzen durch die glori szeyner tzukunfft' (*WA* 9, 714.7f.). By this Luther means Christ's second coming. How easily the fall of the Antichrist could be identified with the rediscovery of the Gospel can be seen from the closing lines of the *Passional:* 'Nembt alszo vorgut: es wirdt baldt besser werden' (*WA* 9, 715.9f.) This last interpretation, which underwent further development all the way to Spener, was made accessible to the laity in the *Wunderliche Weissagung* (Nuremberg 1527), edited by Andreas Osiander and furnished with mnemonic verses by Hans Sachs: the hero Martin Luther began with the Gospel to make an end of papal government: 'Denn wirdt Gott selber setzen eyn/Getreue knechte seyner gemeyn/Und wirdt sie stercken durch seyn geyst,/Das sie die wayden machen feyst' (Andreas Osiander, Sr., *Gesamtausgabe*, ed. G. Müller, II, Gütersloh 1977, 403–84; 463 and 479). The hope connected with the Reformation is borne by the expectation that the Kingdom of Christ starts *right now* and comes into its full glory at the end of days: 'Die [servants of the Word] eeren wirdt die christlich schar,/Seyt das sie Christum leren klar,/Den edlen hymelischen schatz,/On menschenleer und all zusatz.' 'Das weren sol, biß Christus kum/Und richten wirdt bayd, pöß und frum./Dem wirdt der gwalt gantz ubergeben;/Mit dem wir ewig herschen werden. Amen' (ibid., 481 and 483). I consider K. Aland's queries to J. Wallmann to have been answered convincingly by the latter: K. Aland, 'Spener – Schütz – Labadie? Notwendige Bemerkungen zu den Voraussetzungen und der Entstehung des deutschen lutherischen Pietismus', in: *ZThK* 78 (1981), 206–34; J. Wallmann, 'Pietismus und Chiliasmus. Zur Kontroverse um Philipp Jakob Speners "Hoffnung besserer Zeiten"', ibid., 235–66. However, Wallmann's thesis concerning the 'new eschatology' in Spener ought to be examined in the light of the evidence just adduced.

Knowledge about Satan's fury in his last assault on the Gospel gives way to trust in evangelical enlightenment in sermons and schools. *For Melanchthon, the 'amendment' (that in Luther's eyes merely made possible the gathering of the faithful among the birth-pains of the End Time) could turn into the 'Reformation', in the sense that has determined our use of the word ever since.*[116] Erasmian erudition and reforming theology are fused here into a historical force that impressed its character deeply on the 'self-understanding' of early modern Protestantism, and left Luther behind as a 'pre-reformer'.

This synthesis was also basic to the urban Reformation, in its short hey-day. Huldrych Zwingli, the reformer of Zurich, held the same opinion as Melanchthon on this question.[117] Martin Bucer's

[116] This modern trait – by no means the only one in the thought of Melanchthon – is to be found in another genre, one with more historical influence, namely the oldest history of the Reformation, written by Melanchthon's young admirer Johannes Sleidanus. To Sleidan the pope was a dangerous and hypocritically pious world-political power opposed to all European attempts to make peace, but not the 'Endchrist'. See especially his two warning speeches to the Emperor and the German nation, written on the basis of the impressions he received at the Religious Colloquy of Hagenau (1540), in which he warns of the intervention of the 'römischer Nebenhaupt' (*Zwei Reden an Kaiser und Reich*, ed. E. Böhmer, Bibliothek des litterarischen Vereins in Stuttgart 145, Stuttgart 1879, esp. 122–35 and 249–52). At the end of the 'Oration an alle Stende des Reichs, Vom Römischen Nebenhaupt, im Keyserthumb erwachsen' (1541), he describes the public duty of the authorities to support religion, expanding considerably on Luther's justification for visitations: 'Gott der herr drewet gar ernstlich denjhenigen, so in vor den menschen verleugnen. Wie vil mehr will er dann von denen bekant sein, denen er land und leut bevolhen hat, dieselbigen, nit alleyn in zeit und burgerlichen sachen zu regieren, und vor gewalt zu beschützen, sonder auch im zwang zu halten. Und fürsehung zu thun, das sie eyn erbar leben füren, und mit keyner falschen lere verfüret werden?' (ibid., 133). Melanchthon's *tamquam* (as though) is transferred to the political realm in the continuation of the medieval contest between *sacerdotium* and *imperium:* 'Es sihet doch E.M. mehr dann augenscheinlich, das sie mit dem Bapstumb keinen nützlichen bestendigen raht noch anschlag annemen kan. Es wil ja kein glück dabei sein. Es hat ine und seine herrschung der prophet Daniel so hell und klar abgemalet, das einem billich grausamen solt, einige gemeinschafft mit ime zu haben.' 'Oration an Keiserliche Majestat. Von dem, das der jetzige Religionshandel kein menschlich, sondern Gottes werck und wunderthat seie . . .' (1544) (ibid., 250).

[117] G. W. Locher has noted that there is as yet no detailed study of Zwingli's eschatology, in *Die Zwinglische Reformation im Rahmen der europäischen Kirchengeschichte*, Göttingen 1979, 200. His own well-documented conclusion is that the Reformation movement that looked to Zurich for leadership was characterized less by the tension than by the link between divine and human justice. (618). Lefèvre d'Etaples was in contact with the city reformers. He felt that the unchaining of the Devil (Rev. 20.7) did indeed refer to the diabolical infiltration of the Church of his time, but he also trusted in the imminent coming of Christ *per suum verbum* –throughout Europe and the entire world. *Praefatio, Commentarii Initiatorii in quatuor Evangelia* (written before 2 April 1522); *Correspondance*

concessions in the religious colloquies at the beginning of the 1540s are based on his expectation of a successful and widespread German – and later English – Reformation, and in his description of the papacy as a worldly power. To Bucer, 'Rome' means a diabolically dangerous political power, not the phalanx of the Antichrist.[118] John Calvin and the tradition he founded emphasize rather Christ's gradual takeover and the growing visibility of his kingship,[119] less than the 're-evaluation of all values' via the spreading power of Satan in the last days. Aspects of Luther's eschatological theology flare up repeatedly in Lutheran orthodoxy, especially during the catastrophes of the Thirty Years' War.[120] One unanswered question for future research is to what extent the debate over the crypto-Calvinism of the Philippists hid (at that time) the fundamental disagreement over eschatology between Luther and Melanchthon, and therefore buried it.[121]

---

des Réformateurs dans les pays de langue française, ed. A. L. Herminjard, I, Geneva/Paris 1866 [Nieuwkoop 1965], 94.

[118] See C. Augustijn, 'Die Religionsgespräche der vierziger Jahre', in: *Die Religionsgespräche der Reformationszeit,* ed. G. Müller, Gütersloh 1980, 43–53; 47f. Caspar Hedio judged the papacy in much the same way. Cf. H. Keute, *Reformation und Geschichte. Kaspar Hedio als Historiograph,* Göttingen 1980, 239 and 384, n. 9.

[119] See Calvin's political testament, in: *Supplementa Calviniana I: Sermones de altero libro Regum,* ed. H. Rückert, Neukirchen 1936–1961, 104.42–105.10; 105.33–44. Cf. my article 'The "Extra" Dimension in the Theology of Calvin', in: *The Dawn of the Reformation. Essays in Late Medieval and Early Reformation Thought,* Edinburgh 1986, 234–58.

[120] Cf. Johannes Matthäus Meyfart, *Tuba novissima, das ist von den vier letzten Dingen des Menschen,* Coburg 1626, ed. E. Trunz, Tübingen 1980. Using a modern, boiled-down, individualistic or even 'gnostic' eschatology as a basis for comparison, H. E. Weber finds evidence that imminentist expectations survived and thrived on all sides: with Luther as well as Melanchthon and his school, and with the Gnesiolutherans and the Reformed party. *Reformation, Orthodoxie und Rationalismus I: Von der Reformation zur Orthodoxie,* second half-volume, Gütersloh [1940] 1960², 243.

[121] In Lutheran orthodoxy, chiliasm is rejected with Augustine, and the pope is called the *antichristus magnus* alongside a large number of *antichristi.* According to Johann Gerhard, in agreement with Luther, the pope has been 'loosed', with the Turk, since about the year 1300, that is, one thousand years after Constantine. Cf. H. Schmid, *Die Dogmatik der evangelisch-lutherischen Kirche. Dargestellt und aus den Quellen belegt,* newly edited by G. Pöhlmann, Gütersloh 1979⁹, 401–7; 405f. The universal conversion of the Jews as one of the last signs preceding Last Judgement is rejected by the majority, though accepted by Gerhard, who qualifies it by stating that not all, but many Jews would be converted (404). In Reformed orthodoxy, the theme of the Last Things is less developed and above all less clearly formulated. Polanus lists the unveiling of the Antichrist and the conversion of the Jews as the first two signs, but without in any way indicating that the two signs are already being fulfilled, and that the end is near (H. Heppe, *Die Dogmatik der evangelisch-reformierten Kirche. Dargestellt und aus den Quellen belegt,* newly edited by E. Bizer, Neukirchen 1958², 557–70; 562).

In his preface to the *Instructions for Visitors,* Luther names both the reason for visitations and their limitations as instruments of reformation. Reforming eschatology is clear on the topic of 'the Devil's and the Antichrist's mockeries and trickery'.[122] Visitations had already been transformed, during the Middle Ages, into a tyrannical institution. Even secular, evangelical visitation does not leave the Enemy behind in the Babylonian captivity as a mere piece of history: 'The Devil has not become pious or good this year, and never will.'[123]

Luther's reformation ended up in much worse straits than the thesis that it failed can possibly express. *Moral reformation as a transformation did not fail, it was not even expected.* Indeed, when ethical progress was equated with the kingdom of Christ, the Antichrist was believed to have a hand in it.[124] The doctrine of the two 'kingdoms', which Gerhard Ebeling has shown to be a sound bridge between Luther's legacy and a far-reaching new vision of modern theology, has, when understood correctly, helped to distinguish between reformation and visitation, between 'gathering' and 'amendment' (in the sense of improvement, which Luther did not share), between a battle in the name of a faith stripped of all illusions and a rational attempt to improve the world. Modern Protestantism has, with the modern era in general, demythologized the *Endechrist* in spiritual terms and applied the criteria of the Enlightenment to Luther. The price for this is very high indeed: an accumulation of mythological power that contributes to making an ideology out of secular improvement. Attempts to carry out this sort of improvement are invariably followed by bitter disappointments. Luther's understanding of worldly order dispenses altogether with this diabolical choice between transformation and resignation.

---

[122] 'des teufels und endechrists spott und gauckelwerck' (*WA* 26, 196.31; *Die evangelischen Kirchenordnungen des XVI. Jahrhunderts,* vol. I/1, ed. E. Sehling, Leipzig 1902, 150a).

[123] 'Der teufel ist nicht from noch gut worden dis jar, wirds auch nimer mehr' (*WA* 26, 2 01.4f.; *Kirchenordnungen,* 151b).

[124] W. Elert, *Morphologie des Luthertums I,* Munich 1965³, 451.

Chapter 3

MARTIN LUTHER: BETWEEN THE MIDDLE AGES AND MODERN TIMES

1. The Controversy

Fifty years ago, in November of 1933, the renowned German scholar of the Reformation Karl Barth addressed a warning to 'his dear Germans' in the face of the fateful events of that year:

> The man whose memory we are to honor on the 10th of November is harder to understand and nowhere near as accessible as he is currently thought to be. The symbolic figure that will soon appear in the churches and in the market-places to mark this festive occasion is not to be confused with Martin Luther. A sincere commemoration of Luther would have to blaze a new trail for itself, and repudiate the 'Luther' of most Luther festivals.[1]

In this passage Karl Barth clearly enters the lists against a certain view of Luther: Luther the national hero, the great German – Luther, prophet of the 'German hour' (*der deutschen Stunde*). Which Luther are we faced with today? What new trail needs to be blazed?

The answer seems at first, at least, to be easy and unequivocal: the 'brown' (National Socialist) Luther is dead and gone. Luther can no longer be harnessed as an archetype of the 'German Christian'. However, two other, equally seductive images of Luther beckon to us enticingly. One is 'Luther the Peacemaker', who has been hired by the ecumenical movement. His polemical teeth have been pulled; he has been dressed up nicely as an advocate of the One Holy Church, reconciled with a sanitized version of the papacy stripped of the glorious trappings of the Renaissance Church and imbued with a

---

[1] 'Der Mann, dessen Gedächtnis am 10. November gefeiert werden soll, ist schwerer verständlich und Wenigeren zugänglich, als man es in diesen Tagen wahrhaben wollen wird. Die Warnung ist am Platze, daß man ihn mit der symbolischen Gestalt, die jetzt in den Kirchen und auf dem Markt festlich sichtbar werden wird, nicht verwechseln soll. Ein ernstes Luthergedächtnis würde sich wohl vor allem an dem Luther der meisten Lutherfeiern vorbei freie Bahn brechen müssen.' Karl Barth, 'Lutherfeier 1933', in: *Theologische Existenz heute* 4, Munich 1933, 8.

factitious asceticism. The other modern Luther is a bogey-man representing everything we think we have grown out of and left behind: Luther the court lackey, stuck in the Middle Ages, deceiver of peasants, Jew-hater, rabid anti-papist, a retrograde figure that is of no use to 'us moderns' in the battle for peace and freedom.

This leads us right to the point, to the Luther whom it is so hard to assign to a given age. Where does he really belong on the continuum between the Middle Ages and the present? If we try to grant the historical figure – not the Luther of our imagination, but the Luther who lived and wrote – the freedom to 'blaze his own trail', where will he lead us?

This topic has an impressive scholarly past. Generations have fought over the place of the Reformation in the epochal structure of western culture. And a type of sphinx's riddle still vexes every new cohort of students of the Reformation: what *is* the Reformation? Do you agree with Karl Holl and see in Luther the founder of the 'modern era', or do you side with Ernst Troeltsch and place the Reformation squarely in the 'antiquated, outdated Middle Ages'? Working through the printed evidence of this debate, one has the persistent feeling that although we have indeed been torn away from our dream-images, we have been lured into a glass-bead game, the result of which is determined by the way the game is set up at the beginning. The Middle Ages or the modern era are defined in advance in such a way as to produce one of two results: Luther is passé, a mere fossil; or he is victorious, a prophet. The airy realms of this highly intellectual, history of ideas, however, are filled with 'universal' constructs, abstract definitions of epochs that ignore everyday experience and are *sine fundamento* (without grounding or basis); interesting, sometimes even impressive, intellectual structures have been built expressly for the purpose of interpreting Luther. However, when they are examined closely, they generally prove to be *sine fundamento in Luthero* – completely divorced from Luther's works and ideas.

It is not only the changing times, the succession of epochs, that have made Luther seem foreign to us – we Luther scholars have contributed our share as well. We have made him an élite figure, we have spiritualized his language, moved it to a higher level and stripped it of its bodily origins. The historical flesh-and-blood Luther, the cantankerous, food-stained, earthy Luther has been cleaned up in high-flown academic prose, made presentable in good society (*salonfähig*) – as well as in the lecture hall – then fitted to the Procrustean bed of a previously-defined modernity, freed from all temporal coordinates and immortalized.

If we recognize the fundamental danger posed by the rash modernization of Luther by over-eager apologists for one religious camp or another, or by ingenious philosophical categorizers, we are obliged to take a different tack, and start with the programmatic statement that a good historian must be 'bilingual'. Such a historian is an interpreter who knows the historical 'language' of the period in question just as well as the language of his or her own time. In our case, this means that the historian must be able to decipher and translate into contemporary terms the language(s) of the fourteenth, fifteenth and sixteenth centuries. This *is* possible, and it is a valid enterprise. For the same reason, it is not unreasonable to ask what Luther would say and do today if he were confronted with modern Catholicism, the ecumenical peace movement and feminism (in the wake of 'women's liberation') – that is, with the pope, Pershing missiles and patriarchy.

There is a second way to meet Luther: the path that leads backward, into the past, on which you are now invited to follow me. Instead of waiting for the past to be translated into contemporary terms, we can accept the challenge to travel to foreign places, to embark on a pilgrimage to the late Middle Ages. We will have to leave behind modern presuppositions, certainties and achievements that we think are established and secure in order to become contemporaries of Luther. Our task is to try to share his intellectual and experiential presuppositions,[2] to encounter him in such a way as to become his contemporary, to try to 'live' alongside him, instead of merely honoring him and constantly thinking about how we can

---

[2] In the preface to the German edition of my book *Luther. Man Between God and the Devil* (New Haven, 1989, tr. Eileen Walliser-Schwarzbart) I extended this invitation in unequivocal terms: 'Discovering Luther the man demands more than scholarship can ever expect to offer. We must be prepared to leave behind our own view of life and the world: to cross centuries of confessional and intellectual conflict in order to become his contemporary.' (translated as Preface to the First Edition; see Berlin edition, 1983[2], 7). This speech is deeply indebted to the methods and ideas that went into the Luther book – and I would like to hold fast to them. But here I would also like to continue along the path I chose then, sticking to the sources as the only reliable map to this uncharted territory, that is, using *everything* that 'scholarship can ever expect to offer'.

make him credible and digestible to an 'enlightened' modern audience.

One last remark before we attempt the journey back to the age of the Reformation: Luther, the writer who did not shy away from inventing the words he needed, the author of gripping treatises and stirring epistles and pamphlets both thorough and concise, knew much better than many later university professors that the speech or lecture is a very particular genre. He distinguished carefully between lively, flowing speech and the written word, which, published in print, leads a separate and narrower existence, waiting to be set free once again in living words.

Analysis of the differences between Luther's spoken lectures and sermons and their later printed form makes it very clear that he daringly renounced a pleasant and refined, carefully polished style in order to let the spoken word become genuine, living speech – *viva vox.*

Unlike the great urban reformers, such as Bucer, Capito and Zwingli, Luther was convinced that Holy Scripture was an 'emergency measure' of God, a form of the 'living Gospel' that exists and has been codified in this way only as a concession to our frailty. The Gospel confined between the pages must break out as the unrestrained Word once again in order to reach much more than the brain – namely the heart and the soul – of its audience. The Luther of the living Gospel cannot be fully plumbed in high-flown academic discussions, which often direct the readers' attention more to the erudition of the author than to the agenda of the reformer. Academic works run the danger of seeing Luther only as the scholar he undoubtedly was – among other things – by emphasizing his eminent precision and impressive intellectual discipline. When this happens, we lose sight of how much Luther the scholar was also a witness to the Gospel, and how much he ought to be understood as a prophet. Hidden beneath the dark robes and academic headgear of a distinguished scholar, the professor of Wittenberg loses his voice and the outlines of his body, and becomes a Saturn V rocket specially modified to launch select morsels of systematic theology into quotable orbit. The mighty theologian of the Word, the preacher and prophet, also disappears. Luther himself was able to connect both the living experience of faith and disciplined scholarly study of Holy

Scripture; his complex *oeuvre* is split by academic interpreters into pious preaching for the 'common man' and academic lectures, ready for press, that are comprehensible only to a tiny scholarly élite.

Just as Doctor Luther filled his gown to bursting with volcanic words of prophetic power, the modern historian will find it necessary to stretch academic good manners to the edge of indecency. On this journey back in time we will have to leave behind not only modern intellectual presuppositions and habits of thought, but also the 'academic' Luther whom we have house-broken and made presentable in good society and the lecture hall.

Enough, then, of this introduction, which is in no way intended as a *captatio benevolentiae,* but is rather a *praeparatio malevolentiae,* a warning about what we will be forced to confront when we meet Martin Luther.

2. Discoveries Along the Way

We must be prepared for three surprising corrections to the traditional image of Luther as constructed from the modern perspective.

1. If anyone were to ask today how Luther's function or office (*Amt*) might be described in a word, he would without a doubt receive a prompt, collective answer that cuts across all disagreement in Luther research: Martin Luther is 'the Reformer'; and the movement that started with him is 'the Reformation'. But if we free ourselves from modern (fore-)knowledge and prejudice, we discover that Luther never once called himself a reformer and that he never called the movement that started with him a 'Reformation'.[3]

Might this refusal to use terms employed ever since be due merely to modesty? Absolutely not. Of all the virtues, modesty is not one of which Luther can be accused. He did not hesitate to call himself a prophet and thus to place himself in the tradition of Old Testament prophecy. He wanted to be heard as an evangelist who has taken the

[3] Luther does speak of reformation as 'improvement' in the comparative sense, and he is able, within the framework of the conciliar tradition concerning this term, to characterize himself on occasion as a *reformator* – particularly when he mocks medieval-curial claims to be responsible for 'reformation': if the Curia professes to have jurisdiction over *reformationes,* then Luther has all the more right to make this claim! Therefore, Luther uses the term *reformator* not to describe himself or his office, but as a gesture of denial and disapproval. See chapter 2, 'Martin Luther: Forerunner of the Reformation', *supra.*

pure, unadulterated Gospel to the people as in the time of the apostles. And for this reason he is persuaded that he is himself an apostle, in direct succession from the Apostle Paul. However, he never called himself a reformer: it never occurred to him, not even for a moment, that a human being might be capable of accomplishing actual reformation. 'Reformation' will be brought about by God himself on the Last Day, when he renews everything, wipes away all tears, when he is all in all and every knee bends before him. Reformation is God's business alone. *God's* reformation, the only one that bears the name legitimately, will come over us soon, Luther feels, because the end of the world is at hand.

Another surprise follows the first. The rediscovery of the Gospel provokes the Devil, calling his constant presence powerfully to the fore. The 'repatriation' of the faithful to their true home in the Gospel rouses powerful hostile forces that prepare a mighty anti-reformation: 'when God's Word dawned, as it were, and his little group of followers gathered together, the Devil noticed the light and blew and raged against it from all corners with all the great winds and storms at his disposal to blow out so Godly a light.'[4]

The sequence of events that we commonly accept and repeat is the exact opposite of Luther's. He disagrees entirely with the order of events or epochs taught in the lecture halls of all universities all over the world: the 'Middle Ages' are followed by the 'Renaissance', 'Reformation' and 'Counter-Reformation'. But in Luther's view, it is clear that a counter-reformation *precedes* 'reformation': when this counter-reformation is at its appalling peak, God will make an end to its fury with *his reformation*. The counter-reformation rages on until the Last Day in Rome just as in Wittenberg, in Roman Catholicism just as in Protestantism, as long as the Devil still meets with any resistance. This is how Luther sees it, and our interpretation of each and every thing he says is fundamentally incorrect as long as we do not let him speak for himself, but steamroll him with our own ideas.

2. The second correction: Luther is aware of the presence and the force of the Devil. He believes in the Devil, and reckons constantly

---

[4] *WA* 50, 475.9–12. See also: 'Ja umb des frölichen seligen liechts willen, kan [the Church] nicht ruge haben, sondern mus jmer newe, und aber newe stürm winde des Teuffels gewarten, wie es von anfang geschehen ist . . .' (*WA* 50, 476.2–5).

with the menacing power of Satan, but this belief is in no way simply medieval. He was extremely critical of his contemporaries' superstitious beliefs concerning the Devil. In the Mass commentary of the great Tübingen theologian Gabriel Biel (+1495), Luther read in preparation for his first celebration of the Eucharist that to make the Devil into a God is a superstition worthy not of refutation, but only of laughter.[5] To Luther, it was superstitious to believe that the Devil could become a human being, disguised, perhaps, by ram's horns and horses's feet, but nonetheless a real and present human being. This is superstition, though in no way a laughable one, because the Devil is always present, bursting with envy and the hope of becoming a human being. And that is precisely what he cannot do. God alone is God and God alone can become a real human being. The Devil cannot.

This superstition is dangerous not because it reckons with the deadly peril posed by the Devil, but because it allows the Devil both actual physical presence and rights that he really does not have. We moderns are proud to have left medieval superstitions and the Devil behind us as 'enlightened' people; we have – in the Faustian tradition – anthropomorphized, psychologized and therefore denatured the Devil, such that he no longer seems to present any real threat. Not so Luther. His concept of the Devil is very real: the Devil can become neither God nor human being, he remains the Devil; but it is precisely as such that he endangers faith and Creation, and draws us away from God and our fellow human beings.

Luther's own reminiscences better illustrate his view of the Devil and make it truer-to-life than an accumulation of all the relevant passages can ever do. His remembrances lead us back to actual experience, which is itself, however, an episode of 'lived theology'.

It is winter of 1513/14, barely two years after Luther received his doctorate and thus, as was the custom at medieval universities, a professorship. The place is the Augustinian monastery. The monks have already gone to bed – they must sing matins early the next morning. But Luther is excused from this duty because he must prepare his lecture for the coming morning. He is working downstairs in the refectory, the only heated room, on the manuscript of his

[5] Lectio 67 A, *Canonis Misse expositio*, ed. H. A. Oberman, W. J. Courtenay, III, Wiesbaden 1966, 95f.

lecture. The monks are proud: our Brother Martinus here is a professor at the university. Tomorrow he will continue to lecture on the psalms, and is now writing his *Dictata super psalterium.*

The manuscript is still extant, in the library at Wolfenbüttel, and has been reproduced in a valuable facsimile edition for Luther's 500th birthday. Graphologists will be able to confirm that it is a record of someone writing down very quickly and yet with great precision a flood of ideas as they break over him: clearly a highly intelligent man! Experienced university teachers will take a more sober view: a young colleague is throwing together his lecture with enormous energy, under great pressure to have enough material prepared for the next day.

Luther is working on the 'Wolfenbüttel Psalter' close to the stove, behind which blocks of wood are piled. Suddenly there is a noise, a rustling among the logs. We modern, 'enlightened' folk would immediately guess it was made by rats, or woodworm. But Luther *knows:* it is the Devil.

This is a medieval reaction, that of a child of his time. Yet his commentary on the eerie noise he has ascribed to the Devil is not finished: it was the Devil, he says, 'so then I closed my manuscript and went to bed reassured'. This short addendum contains a reforming message. Under the protection of the Most High, implanted in Christ, I am followed and persecuted by the Devil, but not caught; I am tempted and attacked, but never overcome.

Looking back on this event, Luther even regrets that he did not 'sit the Devil out' and stay awake just to spite him. But his relaxed attitude is of more interest to posterity than curiosity would have been. When he is again bothered by the Devil, he once more reacts by going to sleep: 'Once I noticed it was him, I paid no heed and went back to sleep.'[6]

Whenever someone tries to illustrate the basic traits of Luther's theology, a certain Latin phrase is commonly and tellingly employed – whether or not the readers or listeners understand Latin, because a Latin phrase is lucid and brief. One Latin sentence requires three lines in Dutch, ten in English and three pages in German. This one is the soul of brevity and precision: 'simul iustus et peccator'.

[6] 'Da ich vermarkt, daß ers war, acht ichs nicht und schlief wieder ein' (*WAT* 6, 219.40; no. 6832).

No other phrase is capable of expressing Luther's theological 'reforming discovery' as clearly and as succinctly. It encompasses the broad differences between Luther's and pre-Reformation belief and, as one must add in a stage whisper, the contrast between Luther's faith and post-Reformation religiosity in both Catholic and Protestant churches. 'Simul iustus et peccator': a Christian is a sinner and righteous at one and the same time because the central celebration of the Christian calendar is Christmas Night – when God himself became a human being to seek out each sinner in the filth of this world and to make each sinner *iustus,* righteous. But someone who is not truly a sinner will be missed by God's dragnet; therefore: 'simul iustus et peccator' means that a person is both 'righteous and a sinner' at the same time.

Luther's memory of his meeting with the Devil in the winter of 1513/14 leads us to yet another *simul,* namely to the 'simultaneity' of the Middle Ages and the Reformation. Luther's medieval ideas concerning the presence of the Devil's demonic power help us to understand Luther's joy over our liberation in Christ. In place of the hasty choice so often demanded of us between the medieval and the modern Luther, a more leisurely appreciation of Luther as a medieval Christian and as a medieval theologian is necessary if we are to distinguish what is new in his reforming message.

3. The third discovery leads us to Luther's apocalypticism. By apocalypticism, which has become quite foreign to us, I mean first of all the certainty that the End Time, the last days, has already begun; and furthermore, that the End Time is a period of birth pangs, signalled by the alarms and terrors that precede God's New Time, his new creation of a new heaven and a new earth.

Finally, apocalypticism rests on the hopes that God will, in his mercy, not only shorten this terrifying End Time, but also call prophets who will keep watch on the walls of the Church in order to explain the signs of the times to the Christian faithful. Apocalyptic prophets announce the faithfulness of God and the fulfillment of his promises. They are *speculatores,* seers equipped with God's Word and Spirit – not builders of speculative philosophical and philosophical–theological systems, but those who scrutinize the mirror of the times for God's signs as foretold in Scripture.

The concept of apocalypticism is familiar to us from biblical exegesis, but we are encouraged by critical historical research to dismiss the apocalyptic elements of our sources as remnants of a bygone mode of thought and life, in order to discover the 'real meaning' of Malachi or Daniel in the Gospels or the Pauline epistles. Apocalypticism, according to this view, was merely the language of the time, and is no longer relevant for us. Leaving aside the question of how far this repression blocks access to the apocalyptic messages of the Bible, we can say with certainty of Luther that if we sweep away his apocalypticism, his theology will make no sense to us. And if we ignore the threatening dimension of the coming end in all its terror and hope, and 'demythologize' it in a typically modern and arrogant way, we will soon discover nothing is left that makes historical sense – only the self-referential notions of our contemporaries, as fickle as the trends and fashions of the moment.

In contemporary historical scholarship, apocalypticism is described as typical of the late Middle Ages; it is treated according to psychological categories, or as a 'class phenomenon', a belief specific to unsettled, insecure marginal groups. In terms of the history of dogmatic theology, it is dismissed as a heretical remnant of the influence exercised by Joachim of Fiore. Luther, however, learned his apocalypticism not from marginal groups, but from the greater and lesser prophets, from Paul and the Church Fathers, from Augustine and Bernard. He participated in the longstanding ecclesiastical tradition that placed the Word of Revelation at the center of its expectations:

> [The angel] laid hold of the dragon, that old serpent, which is the Devil, and bound him a thousand years . . . and when the thousand years are expired, Satan shall be loosed out of his prison, and shall go out to deceive the nations which are in the four quarters of the earth, Gog and Magog, to gather them together to battle: the number of whom is as the sand of the sea. (Rev. 20.2–3, 7–8)

Like Bernard of Clairvaux before him, Luther was also convinced that the last phase of history, the End Time, had already begun. The Gospel is proclaimed to gather the faithful together and to strengthen them against the raging attacks of Satan. Even as a young man, Luther knew that the Enemy would fall upon the Most Holy, namely the newly-freed Gospel, proclaimed by the Word and in the sacraments. Luther scholars have attempted to neutralize this apocalyptic vision by calling it a fantasy of the aged Luther that is not to be taken seriously, or even as immaterial and irrelevant, remarking that Luther never lectured on the Revelation of St. John. In fact, he did not need to, because the last book of the Christian Bible is present in all his lectures, sermons and hymns.

What relevance does this Luther, whom we discover when we venture back in time to the sixteenth century, with his ideas about reformation, the Devil, and the end of the world, have for us today? This is a question of the first magnitude. To answer it is to determine the state of the Reformation today – its status either as a curiosity foreign to our time or as a present-day challenge.

3. Luther's Reforming Discoveries

In the English-speaking countries, lecturers are only too glad to speak on the topic 'Luther discovers the Gospel'. Whenever I am invited to such a lecture, I find myself embarrassed by the Protestant triumphalism so manifest in this expression. Had no-one known the Gospel before Luther, and did Luther not refer to innumerable faithful prophets and evangelists? Did he not always speak of the medieval Church as our common Mother Church, that handed down the treasures of the Gospel with such great faithfulness? The medieval Church passed the Apostles' Creed, the Lord's Prayer, the sacraments and Holy Scripture down from one generation to the next. Without these treasures and without the faithful perseverance of the medieval Church no faith would be imaginable to later generations. It makes more sense, and gets us closer to Luther, to say 'Luther discovers Satan'. I would like to set forth the indispensable aspects of this discovery in four points.

1. Luther called the Devil *Doctor Consolatorius,* giving him the honorary title that the Christian tradition otherwise had accorded only to the Holy Spirit. Why did the reformer call the Unholy Spirit the Consoler? To pious ears the answer echoes clearly and sharply right down to the present day: if the Devil comes to you and can show you, based on the quality of your life, that you belong to him; if he discovers in your life that you are his, that your own sinfulness in word and deed threatens to erect a wall between you and God, then the demonic presence is precisely at that point proof of the presence of Christ and of his righteousness. For the Devil is not interested in the godless – he already has them. He attacks where he senses Christ, he seizes the opportunity when he 'smells' those righteous persons in whom Christ has taken up residence. He passes by the godless without touching them. The 'comfort' is as follows: if the Devil attacks you, you can be certain that you are implanted in Christ and are his property: 'Yet the fact that the Devil presses us so hard shows that we are on the right side.'[7]

This hitherto unheard-of view of the Devil is a revolution in the history of thought; a thousand years of Christian piety and western morality are abruptly overturned by this discovery. Satan is forced against his will, grumbling and cursing, into God's service and must, like Balaam's ass, bear witness to the Gospel. This is Luther's doctrine 'de servo arbitrio *diaboli*', concerning the unfree will of the Devil: against his will, he is forced to proclaim God's Word.

The significance of this role reversal can be measured against traditional depictions of the Last Judgement. Above the main entrance to medieval churches, for instance the Romanesque church at Conques in the Auvergne or at Autun in Burgundy, the Last Judgement is generally portrayed in the tympanum. The fateful scene of the last great decision, the separation of the sinners from the righteous, is carved in stone. The righteous stand or sit at the right hand of God quiet and immobile, obviously already enjoying the peace of Heaven. In order to exclude uncertainty about who belongs where, the Latin inscription is cut into the stone: *iusti* or *sancti* – the righteous, the holy.

However, not this side, the side of the just, but the left side with the *perversi* or *peccatores* (sinners) has attracted the full attention of the artist. Satan's gaping maw slavers greedily over his victims; the Devil's lackeys haul up the hordes of sinners quickly and unceasingly – these sinners are to receive their just deserts, the wages of sin: resisting and screaming, they are swallowed for ever by the jaws of Hell.

This fundamental view of the moral order of the universe (that goodness seeks out only the good, and evil consorts only with evil, and that the Devil by his very nature and by right corrals only the godless) determined the shape of medieval piety – and not only medieval piety, but also post-Reformation theology and religious

---

[7] 'Weil aber der Teuffel unß also zusetzt, so stets recht umb unß' (*WAT* 5, 44.8f.; no. 5284).

morality across confessional lines, indeed ecumenically, despite all changes in the understanding of Satan.

It is not difficult to imagine the results, had these artists been influenced by Luther, had the Devil and his lackeys raged not among the godless, but among the righteous: '*Diabolus non quiescet* [the Devil does not rest] when he is about to lose his kingdom: if you wish to and if you do honor God's name by your teaching and by the example you set, the Devil will attack you keenly in your person, your honor, your possessions, your wife and children.'[8] The only comfort is God's promise: those attacked in this way by Satan can fling Romans 8.38–39 at him with certainty 'that neither death, nor life, nor angels, nor any princedom, nor violence . . . shall be able to separate us from the love of God, which is in Christ Jesus our Lord'.

2. Luther's second discovery is even more surprising. He calls the Devil not only Doctor Comforter, but also *Magister conscientiae,* the past master of religious conscience. This seems even odder and more beside the point, given that the Luther-renaissance of the late nineteenth and early twentieth century marked Luther out with impressive emphasis as the great exponent of the religion of conscience: Luther, who is freed by and in his conscience, made possible – according to this view – the renewal of morality in the modern era. Many think in this connection of Luther at Worms, when he bravely refused, before the emperor, to renounce his beliefs. Thus, it is said, he introduced the modern age – by insisting on the power of his conscience in opposition to the powers of this world. But if Luther is allowed to speak for himself, he says something entirely different and insists not on his conscience, but on God's Word: 'My conscience is imprisoned by God's Word.'

The alternative to this 'prison in God' is not 'freedom of conscience' but 'conscience imprisoned by the Devil', because the conscience – and this is terrifying, even unbearable for the modern ear – is the natural kingdom of the Devil. He attacks us ceaselessly, not only from without, through fanatics and party spirit, but also from within – via the conscience.[9]

---

[8] 'Diabolus non quiescet, so er sein reich verlieren sol: wilt und soltu Gottes namen mit lere und leben ehren, so wird dich der Teufel gar getrost angreiffen an leib, ehr, gut, weib und kind' (*WA* 30I, 48.7–9).

[9] Cf. *WA* 30I, 49.30f.

We find not a trace in Luther of what is both a medieval and a secularized modern understanding of the conscience: that there is a spot in the human soul that remains untouched by sin, that is always directed toward God, just as a compass points north, immovable and infallible, the voice of God inside us. For Luther, the conscience is so clearly the Devil's prize that the Devil appears, boring into us and gnawing us when we go to bed at night and look back on the day's events. He cites the Ten Commandments, as he knows the Bible well, in order to condemn us and claim us as his own. The Devil is not only an exterior power, hidden under avarice and sexual lust. He reaches right into the *center* of the human soul and employs the voice of conscience for his own purposes. That is when the Christian can answer him: 'No! Satan, I appeal to a higher authority than my conscience, to Christ's righteous justice which I can hold on to despite all sins, firm in my faith; I am a child of God and belong to Christ, because I have been baptized.' There is no point in relying on our conscience, as the Devil has ensnared it already and turns it against God and against ourselves. In this sense, the Devil is the 'master of conscience'.

There can be no doubt that Luther surveyed and fathomed the broader significance of the conscience. But this is particularly true in the realm of secular rule. In the secular realm, Christians are able not only to make common cause with non-Christians, but are duty-bound to do so. For Luther, non-Christians are the vast majority of 'Christendom', in which true Christians are 'rare birds'. Christians are obliged to enter into such coalitions because they do not have access to any knowledge closed to non-Christians, knowledge which would allow them to rule the world according to some higher rationality or more reliable experience. This is conscience in professorial life and in office, among one's fellows – so far as God is concerned, a conscience free to deal with dirty business. In the realm of belief, however, *coram Deo* (before God) our conscience is the residence of the Devil; if it is not 'imprisoned in God's Word', it is a natural ally of the Devil, death and sin. The believer, caught in the battle between God and the Devil, may and indeed must appeal from his own conscience to the higher authority of righteousness through faith alone.

3. The Devil is the *princeps mundi* (the king of the world), God's adversary, his ceaselessly raging Enemy. Medieval ideas about the

Devil were not laughable to Luther, but wrong; wrong because they tend to cast the Devil as a relatively harmless character in a legend, and like legends, they catch us off guard and lull us into a false sense of security – and are therefore horribly dangerous. He recognized and exposed the Devil's power to an extent never equalled before or after. Without producing a metaphysical and speculative 'Satanology', Luther stood up against a central dogma that has become the final court of appeal for believers and atheists: the doctrine of God's omnipotence.

When the Christian faith was introduced to the Hellenistic world by Jewish Christians, the doctrine of divine omnipotence was one of the obvious, generally-understood attributes of God claimed by Christian apologists for the God of the Bible. This doctrine was fully developed – in the western tradition – by Jerome and Augustine; it became a classic dogmatic *locus* in scholastic theology. In the writings of Thomas Aquinas, John Calvin and later Protestant and Catholic systematic theologians, it became the fulcrum of doctrine concerning God: God is the *gubernator mundi* (the helmsman of the world), the irresistible ruler of the world. All cultures confirm the wisdom of the old spiritual concerning God: 'He's got the whole world in his hands'. This article of faith was expressed and interpreted repeatedly by Luther himself, but as a promise made by a faithful God, in confident trust of his eschatological truth. William of Ockham went some way toward formulating it, but with Luther it became an article of reforming faith: that God is omnipotent is proved by faith alone.[10]

In discovering the Devil, Luther pushed the doctrine of omnipotence almost to the breaking-point, then filled it with a completely different content: 'But the Devil is Lord in this world, and I was myself never able to believe that the Devil was Lord and God of the world, until I had finally learned, as is true and fitting, that it is also an article of faith: Princeps mundi, Deus huius seculi [Prince of the world, God of this age]'.[11] God is now, here and today, fully

---

[10] *Quodl.* 1 q.1; *Guillelmi de Ockham, Opera Theologica*, vol. IX: *Quodlibeta septem*, St. Bonaventure 1980, 11.230f.; on Luther's conclusions see chapter 9, 'Zwingli's Reformation Between Success and Failure', section 3, 'Luther and Zwingli'.

[11] 'Aber der Teuffel ist herr jnn der welt, und ich have es selbs nie können gleuben, das der Teuffel solt Herr und Gott der welt sein, bis ichs nu mals zimlich erfahren, das es auch ein artickel des glaubens sey: Princeps mundi, Deus huius seculi' (*WA* 50, 473.34–7).

occupied in the attempt to win back his creation; he will fight with Satan until the Last Day. Only then, on the day of the great *reformatio,* will his omnipotence be fully deployed and visible, when he is all in all, in heaven and on earth.

The terrifying consequences attendant on the unbroken medieval tradition of the doctrine of divine omnipotence are well known to everyone who has learned from the study of history or experienced as a pastor how it has become impossible for millions of people to call themselves believers any longer in the light, say, of 'Voltaire's' earthquake at Lisbon, or two world wars, or after Auschwitz – or when confronted by the no less mysterious blows dealt us in everyday life in the form of disease, destitution and death.

It is impossible to believe in this kind of all-powerful God, this ruler of the world; what seems to be the solid core of Christian teaching concerning God serves atheists as a fundamental pillar as well. They adhere to it with a certainty as untroubled by doubt as that of the most fervent pietists; and in an ironic twist it serves as both appellate authority *and* main evidence in the case against God.

Martin Luther – like the author of the Book of Job – did not create a 'Satanology'. In the Book of Job, Satan is simply present, without any explanation, as the Enemy of the righteous, even at God's deliberations. There is no point in speculating about the Devil; the battle leaves no time or leisure for it, and the battle itself is proof enough. He simply exists, the Enemy of God and of humanity. Surveying the battle against the Devil, Luther was able to speak about God's work in Christ in a way that distinguished his voice from all the myriad others in the tradition of western Christianity. The God revealed to us is no omnipotent God – that much is proven by Christ's birth and death.

The Devil is therefore not only 'Doctor Comforter' and 'Master of the Conscience'. He is also the great negator, and a sickeningly powerful adversary. He will be forced to end his raging fury only at the end of time. Then he will drop to his knees, when all knees bend. Today we are eagerly pursuing a new social and political theology designed to make the Church 'credible' to a secularized world. What we can learn from Luther is to start at the center of things – namely with the insight that the doctrine of God's omnipotence is not biblical.

4. The Devil is the very spirit of misery. He is the origin of depression and the 'sickness unto death'. Luther himself suffered frequently and for extended periods from depression, and thus had occasion to develop a thorough knowledge of psychology. He describes depression in language so firmly based in experience that it bridges the centuries and makes us forget the gulf that separates us from him. When he speaks of getting up in the morning only to have the day stretch out endlessly before him, when he says the pleasures of life have lost their spice and that nothing entices him but the solitude of his bedroom, he is talking about depression. Such depressed states are not pathological, not a neurotic exception, but rather belong to the fundamental characteristics of humanity since the fall from grace.

Depressive states are like birds, Luther writes from the Coburg: you can't stop them from circling around your head, but you can stop them from nesting in your hair. Behind depression is the Devil, who wants to isolate us and lock us up in solitude.

Luther discovers in this 'Mirror of the Devil' that the Christian must resist by seeking out fellowship, by breaking through the isolation of the 'ego'. The proud Protestant ideal of individualism is nowhere to be seen. The self-sufficient individual is on the side of the Devil, opposed to Luther. Human beings are social creatures, and ought to seek out company as a gift of God, to make music – because according to Holy Scripture, the Devil hates nothing as much as he hates music. It is the believer above all who attracts the Devil; the believer, therefore, more than all others, should play cards, sing and drink wine and beer.

Wherever he travels, Luther keeps his wife Katharina informed about the quality of the beer and wine. Here, he writes, the beer is excellent, but the next day and in the next town he complains that the beer is horrible: the Devil got there before him and poured tar into the kegs.

Playing music, singing, playing cards, dancing and drinking: *all to spite the Devil.* For the Devil is a morose spirit, but the believer is not: he enjoys the pleasures of creation, which include what Luther has to say about sexuality – although this cannot be included in a portrayal of Luther that has been house-broken, removed from the realm of the body and made presentable in polite company, and suitable for the lecture hall.

In considering the characteristics of the Devil, Luther discovered God's gift of the senses, which had before his time been decried as the way to perdition, and would be again afterwards. For Luther, a woman's desire for a man and a man's for a woman are not only an original gift of God to creation, but the active presence of God's creative Word among us. Marriage is the right thing to do, but this 'hunger' is already a divine gift all on its own, lovingly implanted in human beings. For this reason, Luther says as early as 1525: I am marrying to spite the Devil. He imagines that this will cause the Devil considerable distress: 'I have made myself so despicable and worthless by marrying that I hope all the angels will laugh and all the devils will cry. The world and its wise men do not understand this divine gift, in fact they claim that for me it is godless and devilish.'[12]

Reformation history of the sanitized, powdered and perfumed variety has made Luther's marriage into a lovely idyll, the founding of the German pastor's household. Luther knew better: it was a moral revolution. The world likes to revere its spiritual leaders as ascetics who have escaped the snares and deceptions of the Devil and the flesh. But Luther learned to distinguish between these two, the Devil and the flesh. Marrying Katharina was his version of iconoclasm – and it had a much more revolutionary effect than the smashing of saints' images when the Reformation swept through the cities.

A few months after his wedding, Luther wrote to his friend Georg Spalatin, former secretary and privy councillor of the Prince-Elector of Saxony, Frederick the Wise. Spalatin also took this controversial step and married. It has been possible to reconstruct this letter in its entirety only in the modern critical edition, after a passage offensive to bourgeois morality had been suppressed for hundreds of years. The stumbling-block is one of the most revealing and most engaging pieces of evidence for Luther's delight in the senses.

He writes that he could not be present to take part in Spalatin's wedding festivities because the winter rains could cause the rivers to rise so quickly that he would not be able to get back to Wittenberg on time to give his lecture. This is why Luther only wrote a letter: Do not let yourself, my dear Spalatin, be confused by evil tongues. You do no

---

[12] 'Sic me vilem et contemptum his nuptiis feci, vt angelos ridere et omnes daemones flere sperem. Necdum mundus et sapientes agnoscunt opus Dei pium et sacrum, Et in me vno faciunt id impium et diabolicum' (*WAB* 3, 533.8–10; 16 June 1525).

damage to your priestly duties by marrying, because marriage is a gift of God. 'When you sleep with your Katharina and take her in your arms, you should think to yourself: this human being, this marvelous creature of God has been given me by Christ, all honor and glory be unto him.' Then comes the passage that had to be eliminated: 'On the evening of the day on which you will receive my letter, according to my calculations, I will at the same time make love with my wife in the same manner and thus be united with you in love.'[13]

We have house-broken Luther, made him presentable for the living-room and the lecture hall. The historical Luther has disappeared, shrouded in a refined and well-tailored academic gown. His insights or 'discoveries' concerning the Devil and the flesh have been eroded from both sides. The Devil of Luther's theology has been contaminated by the fatal attraction exercised by the anthropomorphic features of the Devil in the Faust legend, or demythologized to the point of innocuousness. On the literary side, we have taken Luther's bodily, fleshly language – a language to which scholarship has devoted entire erudite tomes as the language of his Bible translation, 'to which we owe modern German' – and sublimated it from its bodily origins, from the senses and from all material grounding in everyday, concrete reality. We 'Hegelianize' Luther's language in those passages and works, of all places, where we discuss the importance of the *word* in Luther's work! One can write a dissertation on Hegel and receive a doctorate in Hegel studies, but it is impossible to communicate with him *extra muros,* informally, transcending linguistic barriers. Communication was Luther's concern – language as a weapon in the service of clarity, language that breaks down all barriers of education.

How was it possible, the historian is forced to ask, to hush up and suppress Luther in this way? The question can be answered only if we are more precise about the Reformation of the sixteenth century and distinguish Luther's reformation sufficiently from that of the city reformers. These, whether Bucer in Strasbourg, Zwingli at Zurich or the young Calvin of Geneva, wanted and achieved a Reformation in the modern sense of the word. They did not believe that true

[13] 'Ego quoque, cum diuinauero diem, qua has acceperis, mox ea nocte simili opere meam amabo in tui memoriam et tibi par pari referam' (*WAB* 3, 635.26–8; 6 December 1525).

reformation would happen only at the end of time. The Devil is still present to them, but only as a code-word for political resistance to God's triumphal march, and most feared as an instigator of moral offences. He is no longer the great Antagonist against whom God must actually struggle and finally defeat not by everyday means, but out of his unlimited omnipotence.

The moral instructor of this Reformation was not Luther, but Erasmus of Rotterdam. Erasmus had published his *Enchiridion militis christiani* in 1503 – a 'manual for the Christian soldier'. It is the most boring book in the history of piety – at least that was the judgement of his contemporaries, because it was a publishing failure. It finally became a bestseller in a new edition of 1518, and then later a classic that is still numbered among Erasmus' main works. Nothing was changed in the second edition, only one word added. Erasmus in this work comes as close to Luther, in terms of content, as he ever did. He almost says that indulgences are unworthy of the Gospel – but in typical Dutch fashion, he always maintains his balance, without stepping on anyone's toes or offending anyone.

Then comes the decisive passage in which Erasmus calls for the reformation the monks had aspired to in their monasteries to be carried out in the cities by the burghers. The city is a big monastery and within its walls, the 'Body of Christians' takes on reality: 'What else is the city but a big monastery?'[14] What we are doing in the city is in truth nothing less than what monks have sworn themselves to accomplish. The three vows of chastity, poverty and obedience produce no greater holiness than that which baptism gives to all Christians. Chastity is put to the test in Christian marriage within the city; poverty becomes a 'common possession' when everyone pays something of his income into the community chest and thus helps the truly poor. The false poor, however, are to be driven from the city. Erasmus is thinking primarily of the mendicants. And finally on the topic of obedience: we burghers respect our bishop or city preacher just as monks respect their abbot. In another passage, Erasmus draws a political conclusion from this idea of obedience: if the city council makes political decisions that are contrary to one's own convictions,

---

[14] Erasmus of Rotterdam, *Enchiridion militis christiani*, ed. V. Welzig, in: *Erasmus von Rotterdam, Ausgewählte Schriften* 1, Darmstadt 1968, 48f.

one ought to yield to the majority. These are the hesitant beginnings of something we might, for lack of a better word, call 'proto-democracy'. Virtues and even values are indubitably being discovered here and put into practice.

But it is precisely in these cities that card-playing, dancing and drinking are forbidden and prostitution is suppressed and described in such terms that human sexuality takes on a disgusting taint under the opprobrious designation *fornicatio*. The morality of the sixteenth-century city Reformation won out, and pulled a gray veil over all of Europe – a veil that spread from Switzerland and France to the Netherlands, England and finally the United States. Protestantism all over the world is still hemmed in to a very great extent by this veil; even liberal Protestants are affected by it much more than they would like to admit. Modern Protestantism has not broken with the moral consensus still preached by the modern papacy as Christian ethics in unbroken continuity with medieval monastic values and morality: against the emancipation of women, abortion and family planning.

The city Reformation can be summed up as follows: The new laymen were really only old monks. Martin Luther, however, the former monk, became truly a new layman. He looked into the Devil's mirror and recaptured a Christian zest for life. This is a portion of his legacy that is still waiting for us, not between the epochs, but beyond medieval and modern times.

4. A Prophet for Today

We have come to the end of our pilgrimage back to the Middle Ages. We have found Luther where he really lived and come across a surprising confusion of epochs. What was once thought to be safely behind us suddenly beckons us into the future. But what use do we have today for the Devil and the end of the world? Our proud and enlightened culture has smashed the Devil's mirror – how can we find our way back to the Gospel of comfort and to God's battle for us, that is, to an evangelical delight in God and the world?

Concerning the Devil I have only one thing more to say: enlightened cosmopolitans have abandoned him, demythologized and forgotten him. If asked, they would respond that the Devil is dead. Psychiatrists have rediscovered him, however, finding him wherever human beings are fettered by their own isolation and locked *inside* the prison of their own conscience. We must allow ourselves to learn a great deal more from Luther the spiritual researcher. The Devil is not a laughable, humanized figure with horns and horse's hoofs, but a superindividual, demonic force that threatens both the world of faith and the created world, and strives to infiltrate God's work in both areas.

What about the apocalyptic Luther? Was he not completely wrong in prophesying that the world was coming to an end? As it turns out, he was wrong, just like the Apostle Paul. The end of the world has not come yet. But we still ought to listen to what Luther had to say: the world is old and will come to an end. Just as God created the world in the beginning, so he will have to put an end to it. This end, however, is only the beginning of the great, the true reformation.

All learned treatises on Luther's faith will fail to hit their mark if they are not grounded in this 'Lutheran' principle: living faith is oriented toward the end and therefore toward the beginning of the actual revelation of God's omnipotence in heaven and on earth. When Luther interpreted the Lord's Prayer for his Wittenberg congregation in the summer of 1532, he remarked on the decisive significance of the main request: 'thy Kingdom come'. This prayer is the sign of the true Christian; the true Church assembles around this request. The rest, however, make this appeal only *sub condicione,* with conditions attached.

True faith does not allow prayer with conditions. Even if apocalyptic faith is wrong about the exact date, it nonetheless orients itself, full of hope, toward the end of the world as a new beginning. Until then the task and the challenge is not to fall prey to crippling fear, but to maintain the old world as God's creation, without conditions. This is a good place for the celebrated apocalyptic *bon mot:* Even if the Kingdom of God were coming tomorrow, I would still plant an apple tree today.

Although this is vintage Luther, it cannot be found in his surviving writings. It is worth noting that it has a direct rabbinical parallel. This version is ascribed to Rabbi Yohannan ben Zakkai (c. 1–80 CE): 'If you are planting a seedling and you hear that the Messiah has arrived, finish planting it before you go to welcome him.'[15]

---

[15] Jacob Neusner, *A Life of Yohannan ben Zakkai. Ca. 1–80 C.E.,* Leiden 1970, 183.

Luther could have learned a great deal from the Jewish tradition, and found a great deal to approve of – but this leads us to a dark chapter of history. Here Luther was unable to break through his own medieval limitations.[16] Yet the reformer has also been made frighteningly, horribly modern in our own century. This example is a powerful reminder of just how dangerous it is to concoct an 'updated' Luther for our own purposes. We need to meet the historical Luther once again, on the other side of the mountains 'progress' has thrown up in the path leading back into the past. We are still far from being able to recognize in full and appreciate Luther's role as an evangelical prophet for today.

---

[16] See Oberman, *The Roots of Antisemitism in the Age of Renaissance and Reformation*, trans. James I. Porter, Philadelphia 1984, orig. pub. in German as *Wurzeln des Antisemitismus. Christenangst und Judenplage im Zeitalter von Humanismus und Renaissance*, Berlin 1981.

Chapter 4

THE MEANING OF MYSTICISM FROM MEISTER ECKHART TO MARTIN LUTHER

1. Disputed Experience

The disputed and therefore vague concept 'mysticism' covers a number of religious phenomena and attitudes. Before we can perceive these with any clarity, we must establish two important distinctions.

For one, within the concept of faith there are two 'dimensions': the first is the belief that the articles of faith are true. Faith in this sense is the acknowledgement of the 'great deeds' in God's creation, incarnation, passion, resurrection and glorification. This faith requires us to defer to the authority of Scripture or the Church. In Latin, this dimension of acknowledgment is designated by the term *fides quae creditur:* that is, the articles of faith that are believed and accepted. It is in this sense that faith can be defined as 'orthodox' or 'heretical'.

The second dimension is termed in Latin *fides qua creditur* (faith by which one believes): faith as a position or attitude vis-à-vis God, a relationship with God. The intensity of one's involvement with God determines whether one's faith is 'dead' or 'alive', 'cold' or 'passionate'.

'Mystical faith' is always closely associated with *fides qua creditur,* one's living association with God, yet can never be separated from *fides quae creditur,* the articles of faith. A living association with God can be imagined only within a complementary or even a tense relationship to faith in revealed truth as the necessary foundation of *fides qua creditur.* In turn, this living association with God can consciously attempt to transcend divine revelation when it seeks new revelations in mystical experience. Western mysticism attaches *fides qua* firmly to *fides quae.* It seeks to avoid the free-floating cosmic mysticism and speculation about the ages that is based on eastern Gnosticism. The experience of faith cannot circumvent the Confession of Faith. In the article of faith concerning the Trinity, at least in the West, the Spirit and therefore the spiritual person is bound to God's revelation in Jesus Christ by the *filioque* – the Spirit proceeds from the Father *and* the Son.

2. Mysticism and Mystical Theology

The other distinction required here is equally important, yet unlike the traditional pair of *fides quae* and *fides qua,* it is often overlooked. It is the distinction between mysticism and mystical theology. 'Mysticism' means the experience of faith tending toward union with God. However, the majority of our sources fall into the field of mystical theology, which abstracts in a didactic way from our experience and attempts to distinguish between true and false mysticism. This difference is not taken seriously enough even in our reference works, technical encyclopedias and source editions. Generally, mystical theology is cited without informing the reader that it does not provide any access to mysticism. The genre of mystical theology maintains a didactic distance in order to discuss 'mysticism'; its concern is to distinguish between true and false mysticism. Mystical theology attempts to develop general rules or 'spiritual laws' to interpret, regulate and allow people to reproduce the experiences of mystics. We have not yet begun in scholarly research to investigate to what extent these 'regulations' in their turn affected the experimental world of the mystics, who had been taught in advance which experiences and what order of experiences had been approved by mystical theologians as 'normal' or even as 'orthodox'.

Here are two examples. Around 1400, mystical theologians were issuing ever stricter warnings against tears as a concomitant 'symptom' and especially as 'proof' or evidence of mystical experience. Those mystics who imagined they could prove the authenticity of their feelings with tears were said to be entirely deceived and still enslaved to the 'outer man'. After 1410–20, mystical diaries and descriptions of mystical experiences contain hardly a word about the shedding of tears. We know that in some epochs of human history, tears came more easily than in others. Nevertheless, this behavioral change in mystical experience is a warning light: mystical theology did not communicate the experience of God in a merely ancillary and journalistic fashion, but actually exercised a corrective or regulatory influence on the reports filed by those who preceded us on the paths of mysticism.

The second example is doubtless better known: in 1545, one year before his death, Luther described how he arrived at his reforming discovery. He had already attempted to grasp the doctrine of justification using theological means; he had already, with the help of the Psalms, got a firm grip on how we are justified by God of his own free gift, without necessity or merit, but Luther was not yet able to find exegetical grounding for his discoveries in Paul. When he had finally understood Romans 1.17, he described his experience as 'Paradise opening itself up' to him. This is reminiscent of a medieval tradition, the tradition of the 'tower experience' (*Turmerlebnistradition*) concerning the joy of discovery and turning points in faith that break through earthly bounds. It is entirely believable that Luther experienced this *'Turmerlebnis'* precisely as he described it, but it is also probable that he communicated this breakthrough to his readers in a 'liturgical' language already molded by tradition. Luther's creative use of language is constantly surprising, but it occurs within the framework of established linguistic conventions. We must, therefore, listen carefully if we are to hear what is new in what he says.

We must turn to the historical record to discover whether descriptions of mystical experiences report new or 'original' mystical experiences that later led to new formulations, or whether mystics accommodated their reports to the expectations of mystical theologians. Mystics were always aware that they trod a fine line between genuine and false mysticism, between imagining things while beside oneself in ecstasy and the true experience of carefully attentive association with God.

The mystical theologians of the Middle Ages were conscious of the distance between their own experience and mysticism, and therefore insisted all the more often on their own lack of mystical experience. They pointed out that it is impossible to show colors to a blind man. This example shows why all talking about mystical experience is mere stuttering. We can 'really' communicate only with those who have had similar experiences. We are therefore faced with the fundamental difficulty of formulating a mystical theology for non-experts, for the inexperienced. Even the expression 'expert' comes from the field of mystical theology. One is *expertus* if one has had *experientia,* experience. Theologians, during the period of post-Reformation orthodoxy, clearly lost their knowledge of the unbridgeable gap between experience and the analysis of experience. Precise definitions of true mystical experience and the rules governing it were drawn up. This orthodoxy is dying, but as far as mysticism is concerned, it still holds sway in our reference works and encyclopedias – and thus it blocks access to mysticism.

3. Interpretation and Misinterpretation of Mysticism

Protestant reference books and manuals of the late seventeenth and eighteenth century rarely lead to genuine mysticism. Fearful concern for orthodoxy and denominational boundaries harrowed and dried out the field of experienced mysticism. As a result, our understanding of mysticism has also been prejudiced. There is little in Protestant orthodoxy that would be useful in exploring mysticism, because it sees mysticism as a phenomenon of a Catholicism far from Scripture, a Catholicism which, along with its sacramental and Marian mysticism, was refuted and superseded by the Reformation.

Roman Catholic manuals refer again and again to Philippus a SS. Trinitate, an established interpreter of Thomas Aquinas, who became famous for his *Summa Theologiae Mysticae,* first published at Lyon in 1656. His definition of mysticism is: 'Heavenly mysticism is that knowledge of God which is made possible through the union of the will with God and through the illumination of the intellect'. Everything else is false mysticism. Even first-rate students of St. Augustine have been forced under the pressure of this definition, which contemporary scholarship still uses, to conclude that St. Augustine had no mystical experiences. This assertion can only be maintained by sticking to this rigidly Thomistic definition of mysticism, a definition governed by the rules of Aristotelian logic.

The other possible definition of mysticism is based on a philological approach: mysticism is derived from the Greek verb *mýein,* which means 'to close one's lips and eyes'. Mysticism therefore is withdrawal from the distractions and dissipations of the world and concentration on one's spiritual powers and potential; detachment from everything that binds the self to time and place.

The original Greek meaning has at times provided support for the position that connects mysticism with a fundamentally negative theology. Genuine mysticism, in this view, is necessarily negative theology because it stems from the basic paradox that the experience of God's infinity has to be expressed in finite images, and therefore cannot be expressed. Consequently, all that is left is 'stuttering', a poor imitation of clear speech, since in every sentence, experiences are abridged. Negation becomes necessary because God cannot be grasped; he shatters the fetters imposed by our experiential language. Negative theology is the opposite of so-called positive theology, which today is termed systematic theology. Systematic theology concerns the interpretation and extrapolation of Holy Scripture and church doctrine. Negative theology is based on the premise that we can speak about God only in a state of amazement and with our tongues tied, stammering.

Negative theology has had its supporters in the West; it even inspired a wave of enthusiasm on the eve of the Reformation. The new, rising intelligentsia of the period, tired and disappointed by scholastic theology and the battles between various schools, saw negative theology as a new hope, a possible way to transcend the spiritually deadening disputes of the theologians.

A third way to analyze the content of mysticism is the observation of religious phenomena. Mysticism is a phenomenon found in all the 'great' religions. Given our present knowledge concerning world religions we can say that the goal of mysticism is the liberation of humankind, specifically of our soul's innermost core, which is overwhelmingly earth-bound and therefore in mortal danger. Mysticism projects us into absolute, pure original being, with our essence, thought, feelings and will safe and sound. This formulation, on which historians of differing religions can agree, is not specifically Christian. On the contrary; it neglects certain basic Christian truths. The soul's 'overwhelmingly earth-bound' condition is not what we mean when we speak of the Fall from grace. Even this quintessence furnished by religious phenomenology is therefore of no help in determining the essence of specifically Christian mysticism.

4. Christian Mysticism

What is the particular path of Christian mysticism? Starting with the mysticism of the Apostle Paul, we find in his Epistle to the Galatians the text that was cited again and again in medieval reports and books about mystical theology: 'I am crucified with Christ: nevertheless I live; yet not I, but Christ lives in me' (Galatians 2.19ff.). But if Christ is in us, then the opposite is also true: we are always in Christ (cf. Galatians 3.28ff.). These are fundamental texts of western mystical theology. The context makes it clear that Paul is speaking of liberation from the burden of the Torah. In its place the spirit of Christ has come to fulfill all believers, thus making them children of Abraham and showing them the one true way. The interpretation of Christian existence as 'being-in-Christ' has constantly been read in the western world in conjunction with Solomon's Song of Songs, particularly with the verse: 'My beloved is mine, and I am his' (Song of Songs, 2.16). This intimate friendship and the loving joy of the bride when the bridegroom is close serve as an image and model for the unification, the melding of the soul with Christ. 'Being-in-Christ' is transformed into a love relationship in which kisses lead gradually through a spiritual 'foreplay' to an emotional and psychological climax in the *exstasis*, 'being-outside-oneself', the *raptus*.

When Protestant church historians write about this mystical tradition, it is often dismissed as 'erotic mysticism'. I am happy to live in a time when the word 'erotic' has been rehabilitated, a time that allows the use of this term without a harsh moral judgement. Some may be of the opinion that monks and nuns 'merely' sublimated their sensuality; we can add that we are gradually gaining respect for the art of sublimation.

St. Augustine (+430) constitutes a second important stage on the road to occidental mysticism. He is a theologian of love. Not only is his great survey of history in *De civitate Dei* (*The City of God*) shot through with the theme of love, but his *Confessiones* (*Confessions*) take from the love of God and from God's love a new definition of the person. Reason and intellect do not place us in the cosmic hierarchy, contrary to what Augustine had learned while studying philosophy, but love. Love is *pondus*, and *pondus* is not a burden but rather gravity, and therefore determines the orbit into which a human being gravitates. Augustine assumes that there are only two sorts of people, who move in two different orbits. One sort rotates around themselves, the other sort, around God. Both orbits are determined by the love that seeks the center, either by *amor sui*, self-love, or by *amor Dei*, the love of God. In order to make the jump from the 'self-centered' orbit to the other one, human beings need the help of a sovereign act of God. God alone makes this jump from the old to the new orbit happen – by his grace alone, *sola gratia.*

As medieval scholars bit by bit discovered, translated and worked through the works of Aristotle, and as academic theology began its triumphal march, starting in the recently-founded universities, reason once again came to determine the center of man's world. Man is once again the *animal rationale,* a rational creature. He is distinguished from beasts by his reason, and this is therefore the characteristic that defines him. Not the direction of one's love, but the solid foundation of reason determines the place of man between God and the world, between heaven and earth. The mysticism that associates itself with scholasticism of an Aristotelian bent defines mysticism as *cognitio experimentalis,* an experience of thought and understanding. This applies to the high and the late Middle Ages, to Thomas Aquinas (+1279), Meister Eckhart (+1328) and Nicholas of Cusa (+1464).

5. High Mysticism and Its Alternatives

The Dominican monk Meister Eckhart expanded on Thomas' *cognitio experimentalis* and broke through the dividing line Thomas had drawn between the 'World of Man' and the 'World of God'. In the last phase of his life, when he was a professor at Cologne, he was accused of heresy by the archbishop Heinrich von Wernerburg. Meister Eckhart appealed a short time before his death to the pope. Nevertheless, twenty-six propositions of Meister Eckhart were condemned as erroneous on 27 March 1329, in the bull 'In agro dominico'. Three of these condemned propositions will be accorded a brief interpretation in the following pages: the first, because it illuminates – intensely, but only for a moment – Eckhart's highly complicated and speculative teaching; the other two because their condemnation determined the subsequent development of mysticism.

The first of the condemned theses answered the question why God had not made the world earlier: 'It was not possible for God to do so; as soon as there was God, he made the world. Therefore he could not make the world any earlier'. God is therefore not a free all-powerful Creator, but a necessary Being from whom the veil of mystery can be lifted through mysticism – God is brought down to the level of the 'secret principle' behind the world. A single Being embraces God and the world. The structure of unitary existence makes it possible for *human* beings to ascend to God. Eckhart can therefore say: that which is essential to man, is divine; indeed it is God himself in man.

The second thesis selected from the twenty-six condemned theses is the nineteenth, which reads as follows: 'God loves the souls, not the works of humanity'. This statement is typical not merely of Eckhart. The words of Heinrich Suso (+1366), John Tauler (+1361) and mysticism generally are characterized by insistence on the idea that the soul, at the moment of union with God, must be 'apathic', that is tranquil, absolutely calm. Here we find the starting point for the medieval concept of 'faith alone'. Eckhart's challenging formulation was, nonetheless, condemned by the Church because it might have amoral, dangerous effects. Mystical piety has never shown much respect for the moral boundaries set by solid burghers.

The tenth thesis made history on account of the opposition it elicited. Its condemnation decisively influenced the further history of mysticism. The tenth thesis reads: 'In mystical union we are entirely transformed and changed in God.' In a mystical experience, according to Eckhart, man is so enraptured in God that he loses his identity and therefore can no longer return to the world. The medieval Church thought this idea enormously dangerous. The contemplative life (*vita contemplativa*) would no longer need to be completed by the active life (*vita activa*), to which one was supposed to return strengthened after a mystical encounter with God. The condemnation of the idea that man loses his identity in the encounter with God exercised a profound influence on Eckhart's pupils. Tauler and Suso tried anxiously to escape this conclusion.

Nonetheless, a particular school of mysticism grew up around Meister Eckhart. From Tauler to Nicholas of Cusa, mystics tried to follow Eckhart and develop his intellectually oriented mysticism without straying into the dangerous territory on the other side of the border established by the condemnations of 1329.

Jean Gerson (+1429), the 'Church Father' of the fifteenth century, was responsible for the development of a parallel mysticism. He brought forth a new piety and a new mysticism, which Thomas à Kempis (+1471) adopted. Through his book *De imitatione Christi* (*On the Imitation of Christ*), Thomas has affected thinking on this topic right up to our own time. This 'alternative mysticism' does not draw primarily on intellectual vision. Rather, it is based on the *via amorosa,* the path of love. Thus, Augustine and Bernard of Clairvaux become relevant once again. The goal is no longer to penetrate into God's Being, but to encounter God as a person. God does not appear to the mystic as a substance, as the anonymous Being of the world, but rather as the Lord of history. This is the God who revealed himself as a person in Jesus Christ. The goal of mysticism is to unite oneself with the will, that is with the personal core of God. *Cognitio experimentalis* in this context does not mean transcendent reason, but the enjoyment of God in analogy to the experience of Adam when he 'knew' Eve his wife (Genesis 4.1) – the word in the Vulgate is *cognitio.* These two mystical traditions have their own different paths in history, and were furthered by factors specific to particular social groups and that can be described in sociological terms. Meister Eckhart's *cognitio experimentalis,* typical of Dominican mysticism, had a strong influence on contemplative religious communities. This form of mysticism is suited to 'intellectual aristocrats' who have enough leisure to prepare themselves through meditation for contemplation, and gradually to work toward the experience of absolute tranquility without being disturbed by mundane concerns, by the need for work and food, by screaming children. The alternative form – which can be described as urban mysticism – spread quietly from the smaller towns of the Low Countries as far as southern Germany and France. Urban mysticism appealed to urban artisans of modest means who wanted that 'mystical' experience which would make them a living member of the urban church community – without having to give up their livelihood. This form of piety led to the reading of Holy Scripture and to common prayer after work or during breaks at work. Mysticism was in this way 'democratized', made accessible to all believers. Contrary to high mysticism, urban mysticism aimed at an experience of faith common to all true believers.

6. Late Medieval Mysticism as a Sign of the Times

The late Middle Ages (1300–1500) saw a laicization of the *via amorosa,* the path of love. Augustine and Bernard of Clairvaux (+1153) became the best-loved spiritual guides. An important, non-monastic alternative to the *via rationis* (the path of reason) was thus created. Modern scholarship has not yet accorded this alternative mysticism the attention it deserves. When we think in a general way about medieval mysticism, we usually associate it with a spiritual movement that had turned away from the world, that was far from all social and political crises of the time. No matter how often this is repeated, it is still wrong.

Medieval mysticism must in fact be seen in conjunction with two late medieval movements. The first is the drive for continuous reform of the Church, the soul and the world. Life is a pilgrim's journey determined in its various stages from birth to death by the encounter with God. Before all encounters was the *first* arrival of God: God become flesh in Jesus Christ, a truth never forgotten because it transcends time in the embodiment given it in the Church. The Christian pilgrim is engrafted into the Church only by the second advent, that is the coming of Christ in his mercy to humanity. At the end of history, God in his glory encounters man, which is the third coming. On the way toward this third coming, humanity in the world needs constant reform, constant 'reformation' to a life in Christ.

Another great spiritual movement coincides with this drive for reform. It is called apocalypticism, the attempt to eavesdrop on history for signs of the End Time. Martin Luther and Thomas Müntzer (+1525) were not only opponents, but bitter adversaries in the battle over the reformation of the Church and society. Yet they agreed on one thing – namely that the way the world was going pointed to the speedy return of Christ, that the time had come to preach the Gospel on the spot and in its entirety. But contrary to Luther, Müntzer mobilized the true believers as the vanguard and executors of the Last Judgement: a clear path to the kingdom of God must be cut right now with the 'sword of Gideon'.

Late medieval mysticism cannot, therefore, be seen in isolation from the general contours of the time. Reforms set things in motion, starting with individuals. These reforms attempted to renew the Church and even forced a series of mystics out of their quiet corners into the apocalyptic final battle.

7. Varieties of Mystical Theology

We have already noted that mystical belief is not to be confused with mystical theology. Carefully chosen categories may help us to classify in a more appropriate way these various forms of piety. However, yet another stage of differentiation is needed within the two above-mentioned basic varieties of mysticism (the path of reason and the path of love). Despite the danger of distorting one's subject through excessive subdivisions and lists, I will risk a further examination of the multiple forms in which this theme appears. We can distinguish varieties of mysticism that are each oriented toward one of the sacraments – they are not mutually exclusive, but rather must be differentiated according to emphasis. If one imagines God to be a person, as a holy person with a holy will, then the mystical path demands union with his will, not merely courteous or even humble bowing and scraping before him. If we act 'in accordance with the law' it is not because God commands it, but because we transpose our will into God's will, we become one with him to such an extent that we no longer want anything other than what God wills. Even if God has decided in his holy providence that someone is damned to Hell, that union of wills remains so strong that the condemned sinner loves his judge. These mystics are interested in genuine penance. They would like to make certain that even the last drop of egotistical love is forced out of them: this unmasks whatever there is in one's love of God that is merely egocentric concern for one's own salvation. The basis for this is the discovery of the mystics themselves: outward piety hides self-love. We can describe this form of mysticism as 'penitential mysticism.'

Another form, 'marital mysticism', attracted a lively following throughout the Middle Ages. The highest point of union is depicted as an exchange of goods, as prescribed in Roman law for contracting a marriage. When a man and a woman marry, they have rights in regard to each other. Marriage creates a complete legal right to whatever is brought into the marriage by either party. This metaphorical transfer of marriage and marital rights to the Christian community is impressively described in Luther's treatise *Von der Freiheit eines Christenmenschen* (*On Christian Freedom*). Luther uses this metaphor entirely in the service of Reformation theology: 'Is it not a joyful household where the rich, noble, pious bridegroom Jesus Christ marries the poor, despised, impious little whore, frees her of all evil, adorns her with all goods?'.[1]

---

[1] *WA* 7, 26.4–7: 'Ist das nicht eine fröhliche Wirtschaft, da der reiche, edle, fromme Bräutigam Christus das arme, verachtete, böse Hürlein zur Ehe nimmt und sie entledigt von allem Übel, zieret mit allen Gütern?'

A third form is the mysticism of the Lord's Supper, which is based on the idea that men and women lose their identity in union with God, just as drops of water fall into the chalice of Christ's blood and disappear. In this form of mysticism, the image of the Lord's Supper signifies that men and women leave the world, are absorbed entirely into God, lose their consciousness of identity and with the loss of their sense of self also loses the last remnant of sin. It seems to me, however, that this search for the dissolution of the human person crosses the extreme boundary of Christian mysticism.

It is impossible to avoid the question of how mysticism and Reformation theology are related. Reformation scholarship has reached no consensus concerning whether or not Luther ought to be called a mystic. At least it is certain that without mystical theology, there would have been no 'young Luther'; without the experience of the mystical path from Augustine to Bernard of Clairvaux, Luther would not have developed his particular faith in Christ, vital and hungry for experience. He read those whom we today call mystics rather as genuine and substantial Christian writers. He also learned from them that he, the professor of theology, could not be satisfied with the technical instruments of theology that the humanists had provided. To fathom the Word of God, one must allow the living God, who speaks through and in his Word, to operate on oneself, one must suffer him, fight with him, but also allow oneself to be comforted and edified by him. Living experience always prevents Holy Scripture from being treated as mere words that can be twisted and bent: Scripture is indeed the object of biblical scholarship, but its goal is to make room for Scripture as the subject of faith. Luther treated Holy Scripture as Moses treated the stone: he struck the rock until 'living water' sprang forth. Like Moses, Luther had to beat the texts of Holy Scripture exegetically until they opened themselves up to him.

Luther, in the battle with the Church, still had no need to deviate from the basis of living faith he discovered in the monastery. Contrary to the monastic mysticism of the Middle Ages, which was dedicated to tranquility, the experiential dimension of the Joyful Change (conversion) meant for Luther not 'sweetness' but 'suffering' on account of Christ who lives in us and in our lives. The term 'theology of the Cross' refers to union with Christ crucified, not with the heavenly conqueror.[2]

8. The Significance of Mystical Faith: Between Detachment from the World and Secularization

During the era of Protestant orthodoxy and the Enlightenment, in the seventeenth and eighteenth centuries, and during the battle over the infallibility of Scripture, the Pope or Reason, discursive, reflective theology led to the intellectualization of faith. This process brought forth both the strengths and the weaknesses of what is now called academic theology. Its strength lies in the offer of faith to let itself be examined by scholarly and scientific means and to participate in penetrating the ideologically-charged fog surrounding the spirit of the age. Its weakness lies precisely where Bernard of Clairvaux had located it when he criticized the new university theological faculties of his time: in its lack of experience and therefore in the neglect of its *main task,* namely perceiving and clearing away obstacles on the 'path of love'. In the modern era, theological schools of thought and tendencies and ideas about faith and moral doctrines are subject to rapid change. This instability endangers the Church and leads to tired resignation unless these academic varieties of theology make good on their lofty claim to be experiments designed to help define and blaze for one's own time the 'path of love' between detachment from the world and secularization.

The dangers of mysticism are today no different than in the late Middle Ages, which display in overall terms surprising parallels to our own time. Mysticism entices one toward that elevated detachment or deep immersion through which it is possible to avoid the suffering imposed by an alienated, human – or all-too-human – society. Mysticism entices us toward that 'inner emigration' which makes the pilgrim between the second and the third meeting with God unable to live in the world, and unable to defend himself. It suggests seductively that we can grasp God's Being, God's wisdom or God's plan for history in countless new sects and religious communities – whether more theosophical or more anthroposophical – without worrying about God's revelation. This leap is sometimes successful

[2] For relevant examples and proof-texts, see my article 'Simul Gemitus et Raptus: Luther and Mysticism', in: *The Dawn of the Reformation,* Edinburgh 1986, 126–54.

due to an 'impatient heart', and sometimes because the established churches preach God's word in élitist and intellectual terms that confine it to an elevated, educated group; it is therefore not nourished and renewed by the experience of faith.

In addition to the historical-critical method, a tool which helps make Holy Scripture an object of analysis, we need the meditative, self-critical method that makes the reader a listener and the student a pupil. In addition to didactic preaching we need instruction and guidance on the path that leads to the inner discovery of faith. This instruction and guidance must take seriously our schizophrenia, the division of the self – not as an exception, but as the 'sickness unto death' of all people who live in a conscious manner. The pilgrim who is led through this sickness is, admittedly, not detached from the world, but mystically 'deranged'. He has been granted a sort of 'carnival license' that allows him to see and to see through the world *sub specie aeternitatis,* from God's perspective – because he is close to God. This makes for joyful Christians who can live their faith; for real professors and pastors who can build and sustain both church and community, who can direct their fellows in a time when Christians cannot count much longer on public tolerance, and must start to prepare themselves to establish small congregations of true believers.

In the absence of thoughtful and active faith there can be no Christian mysticism that is answerable to worldly concerns – but without Christian mysticism, there is no faithful and living Church to withstand the Hell of the Last Days. Without mystical faith, the Church that is called 'the salt of the earth' does not and cannot exist.

Chapter 5

WIR SEIN PETTLER. HOC EST VERUM.*
COVENANT AND GRACE IN THE
THEOLOGY OF THE MIDDLE AGES AND
REFORMATION**

* We are beggars. That is the truth.
** Inaugural lecture delivered on 1 June 1967, at the University of
Tübingen. To preserve the tenor of the address, the rather more
personal afterword has been retained.

1. The Problem

The first part of the above title is borrowed from Luther's last written
notes.[1] It seems more suitable as a topic for meditation than for clever
scholarly analysis, which, in this view, is itself an impoverished and
sterile exercise. Yet our title not only neatly summarizes Luther's
legacy to power-hungry Christianity, but also delineates a problem
fundamental to the interpretation of Luther's development. This
problem can only be hinted at here under the rather ambiguous
heading 'The Theology of Humility'.

In its original context, this phrase refers to the incapacity and
poverty of exegesis in relation to the inexhaustible riches of Holy
Scripture, and to the inability of all interpreters of Scripture to
identify, given the limits of their short life on earth, with the authors
of the Bible and to understand their message correctly: 'Let no-one
imagine he has tasted sufficiently of Holy Writ who has not led the
congregations for a hundred years with the prophets.'[2] Luther did
not, however, come to this realization suddenly, on his death-bed. As
early as three years before his death, he attacked the academic

[1] *WAT* 5, 318.2f., no. 5677.
[2] 'Die Heilige Schrift glaube niemand hinreichend verschmeckt zu haben, der nicht
hundert Jahre mit den Propheten die Gemeinden geleitet hat' (*WAT* 5, 317.16f.).
Concerning the translation and interpretation of this passage, see H. Bornkamm, *Luthers
geistige Welt*, Gütersloh 1960[4], 311–14.

theologians and ecclesiastical dignitaries: 'the *scioli* and big shots do not understand it [Holy Scripture], but the little folk and the simple do understand it'.[3] This is in turn merely the application of a principle enunciated again and again in the Bible and which we can trace in Luther's work from his first lectures on the Psalms (1513–15) as the basic tenor of his doctrine of justification: 'God resists the proud, but gives grace to the humble' (James 4.6; 1 Peter 5.5).[4]

Luther's interpretation of this particular biblical passage has loomed very large in Reformation historiography ever since Ernst Bizer's *Fides ex auditu* appeared in 1958.[5] In fact, it has been subjected to such intensive discussion that the broad range of pressing research tasks in the triangle formed by the late Middle Ages, Reformation and Counter-Reformation is in danger of being reduced to a constantly shrinking circle consisting of the Reformation, Luther, the young Luther, and the 'tower experience'. Nonetheless, our inquiry will start from this same point because Bizer's thesis, which dismisses all Luther's early works up to the lectures on the Epistle to the Hebrews[6] as belonging to the pre-Reformation era, represents so far-reaching a challenge that we cannot overlook it – we must examine at least a few of his conclusions concerning the first lectures on the Psalms.

According to Bizer, Luther in these lectures still understands 'God's righteousness as an accusing and punitive righteousness, as an accusing activity of God, which does in turn, of course, effect humility in us as the new righteousness'.[7] 'Luther speaks' – in his interpretation of the 71st (72nd) Psalm – 'of a *fides formata* ['formed faith'], which might possibly be described as "formed by humility".'[8] Indeed – as Bizer summarizes his interpretation – 'faith is merely another way of saying humility'.[9] The about-face happened only in the winter of 1517–18, when Luther arrived at a new concept of the

---

[3] '[D]ie scioli und grossen Hanse vorstehen sie [die Heilige Schrift] nicht, aber die geringen und einfeltigen vorstehen sie' (*WAT* 5, 168.20f., no. 5468).

[4] 'Deus superbis resistit, humilibus autem dat gratiam.' Cf. *WA* 3, 514.26–8; 515.16; 517.1–4 and 4, 254.37f.

[5] E. Bizer, *Fides ex auditu,* Neukirchen 1958 (1966[3]).

[6] See Bizer, 75 (3rd ed.: 93).

[7] '[D]ie Gerechtigkeit Gottes als anklagende und strafende Gerechtigkeit, als anklagendes Wirken Gottes, das dann allerdings in uns die Demut als neue Gerechtigkeit wirkt' (ibid., 22).

[8] ibid., 21.

[9] '[F]ides ist nur ein anderer Ausdruck für humilitas' (ibid., 20).

sacraments and of faith: 'Faith no longer means belief in the fate of Jesus, as told of in Scripture, but belief in the testament that Christ established.'[10] While for the pre-Reformation Luther – as one might summarize Bizer's thesis – it was the *humble* person, after 1518 it was the *believer*[11] to whom God gives his word of covenant, and through this word, righteousness. The interpretation of 'faith' as 'humility' seems to Bizer to belong to the pre-Reformation era; characteristic of the Reformation, on the other hand, is the understanding of grace as a testament or covenant.

Just as the monks of Wittenberg, according to Degering's well-known saying, swarmed like bees over the new editions of Gabriel Biel's *Collectorium* and *Commentary on the Mass* (bought by Luther in 1515) to adorn them with marginalia,[12] a swarm of scholars has surrounded Bizer. Their reviews, articles and monographs would fill a small library.[13] Because Bizer has shown himself to be – as he puts it – impenitent,[14] and also because he is by no means alone in this view, there is a danger that the lines between Bizer and his opponents will become firm, or that the coming generation of scholars will give up entirely if we are not able to get closer to a solution – or, even better, to break out of the entirely too narrow framework of this question poorly posed.

In my view, the debate about Bizer's thesis has not sufficiently considered two themes that are especially closely connected, nor thought them through in the broader context of medieval and Reformation-era theology. The first is the popular but still vague

[10] 'Glaube bedeutet nun nicht mehr Glaube an das Schicksal Jesu, wie es in der Schrift erzählt wird, sondern Glaube an das Testament, das Christus aufgerichtet hat' (ibid., 147 (3rd ed., 165)).

[11] ibid., 147, (3rd ed., 165).

[12] Cf. Luther's marginal notes on Gabriel Biel's *Collectorium in quattuor libros sententiarum* and on his *Sacri canonis missae expositio*, Lyon 1514, ed. H. Degering, Weimar 1933 (Festgabe der Kommission zur Herausgabe der Werke Martin Luthers zur Feier des 450. Geburtstages Luthers. 10 November, 1933), VIII.

[13] See O. H. Pesch OP, 'Zur Frage nach Luthers reformatorischer Wende: Ergebnisse und Probleme der Diskussion in Ernst Bizer, *Fides ex auditu*', in: *Catholica* 20 (1966), 216–43 and 264–80. The opinion of Pesch is 'dass die in der Vorrede berichtete neue Erkenntnis zu Röm. 1,17 insofern sie psychologischen und theologischen Durchbruchscharakter hat, erst 1518 gewonnen wird' (276, n. 101).

[14] See the preface to his book *Theologie der Verheissung. Studien zur theologischen Entwicklung des jungen Melanchthon (1519–1524)*, Neukirchen 1964, as well as the afterword to the third edition of *Fides ex auditu*, Neukirchen 1966, 179–204.

concept *humilitas* (humility) or rather *humilitas*-theology. Since all scholars involved emphasize that in Luther's first lecture on the Psalms humility can no longer be meant as the medieval monastic virtue, Bizer forces us to distinguish *three* varieties of humility: (1) the so-called monastic virtue, (2) humility as understood by the early Luther of the first lectures on the Psalms and the commentary on Romans and (3) humility as understood by Luther in his later works, up to and including his spiritual testament, 'We are beggars. That is the truth.'

The second question concerns the relationship between faith and testament. This relationship, as it is presented in the lectures on Hebrews is, according to Bizer, the germ of Luther's Reformation breakthrough.[15] The concepts 'testamentum' and 'pactum' (covenant) play an important role not only in medieval theology, but also – in a way that has not yet been examined – in the works of the young Luther. If we keep in mind that the 'covenant' that God made with humanity is often understood in Scholastic circles to mean that God promised not to withold his grace from the 'humiles' (humble or meek), then we can discern at least the rough outlines of the issue under consideration: covenant and grace.

2. Humilitas and the Cloaca

There is one crucial point of the discussion that we have not yet mentioned, namely the dating of the Reformation breakthrough described by Luther in 1545, which is commonly referred to as the 'tower experience'. We will need to handle this experience delicately and make careful distinctions, because Luther's description is a *topos* that must be understood against the background of a tradition of tower experiences that existed well before Luther's time. Similar tower experiences, in which the secret meaning of a particular Bible passage is revealed to the searching exegete, are to be found not only in the eighth book of Augustine's *Confessions,* which served as Luther's model,[16] but also in Thomas Bradwardine, Richard FitzRalph, Jean Gerson, Andreas Karlstadt, Gasparo Contarini and John Calvin.[17]

---

[15] See especially *Fides ex auditu,* 73–5 (3rd ed., 91–3).

[16] See *WA* 3, 549.26–32; see also E. Wolf, *Staupitz und Luther,* Leipzig 1927, Quellen und Forschungen zur Reformationsgeschichte 9, 145ff.

[17] Cf. my article '"Iustitia Christi" and "Iustitia Dei"', in: *Harvard Theological Review* 59 (1966), 1–26, 9f.

Of even more importance is the fact that Luther evidently had this experience on many occasions. As early as 1516 he proposed as a general rule 'that anyone who meditates on God's law quickly and suddenly [*breviter et subito*] learns many things'.[18] This sudden insight is characteristic of a theological breakthrough seen in its entirety and cannot, therefore, be related exclusively to a supposed single moment in which Luther discovered the 'real meaning' of Romans 1.17. For this reason we will no longer be able to draw a clear, temporally-defined dividing line between Luther's development before and after 'the breakthrough'. Instead, we must trace by means of painstaking individual studies the various overlapping layers that comprise the process of his development.[19]

We will not, therefore, consider here the much-discussed question of when the 'tower experience' took place. We will instead examine the tradition, much less common in Luther scholarship, that seems to concern the *place* of the experience. In a 'table talk' of the year 1532, according to the testimony of the generally very reliable Rörer, Luther said: 'This art' – namely the correct interpretation of Romans 1.17 – 'was given to me by the Spirit of God on this *cloaca*.'[20] While Protestant Luther scholarship has always insisted that *where* Luther's discovery took place is absolutely irrelevant,[21] and the Catholic

---

[18] *WA* 55II, 16.2f.; cf. the excursus in *WA* 55II, 55.39–57.10. On dating this passage, cf. H. Boehmer, *Luthers erste Vorlesung*, Verhandlungen der Sächisischen Akademie der Wissenschaften zu Leipzig, Phil-hist. Klasse 75, 1923, H.1, Leipzig 1924, esp. 38, and E. Vogelsang in: *Luthers Werke in Auswahl* 5, ed. Vogelsang, Berlin 1933, 40f.

[19] We can start with G. Ebeling's results ('Die Anfänge von Luthers Hermeneutik', in: *ZThK* 48 (1951), 172–230), namely that Luther's first and fundamental hermeneutical awakening was based on his first discussion of the Psalms, as a solid and proper basis for further research. Indeed, even the Luther whom we encounter three years earlier, in 1509–10, as commentator on Peter Lombard cannot, without doing him great violence, be classified as belonging to any of the schools known to us, including the Augustinian; cf. my article 'Facientibus quod in se est deus non denegat gratiam. Robert Holcot, OP and the beginnings of Luther's Theology', *Harvard Theological Review* 55 (1962), 317–42, esp. 330–42.

[20] 'Diese kunst hat mir der Geist Gottes auf dieser cloaca eingegeben' (*WAT* 2, 177 n. 1 (to no. 1681); cf. also 177.8f. and *WAT* 3, 228.22f; no. 3232b). Concerning the value of Rörer's transcriptions, see E. Kroker, *Luther-Jahrbuch* 1 (1919), 81–131; 112–16. In more recent studies, cf. G. Pfeiffer, 'Das Ringen des jungen Luther un die Gerechtigkeit Gottes', in: *Luther-Jahrbuch* 26 (1959), 25–55; 42; Pfeiffer is however – evidently without knowledge of Kroker's study – rather reticent concerning the transmission of '*cloaca*'.

[21] See for example G. Kawerau, *Luther in katholischer Beleuchtung. Glossen zu H. Grisars Luther*, SVRG 105, Leipzig 1911, 6f., and A. Harnack, *Theologische Literaturzeitung* 36 (1911), 302.

scholar Hartmann Grisar[22] ascribes nothing like the importance to
the statement transmitted by Rörer that Protestant replies might lead
one to believe,[23] this testimony has attracted in recent times the
particular attention of two psychoanalysts.

The first of these, the Dane Paul Reiter, contents himself with a
passing shot at Luther's 'earthiness'.[24] Erik Erikson criticizes Reiter's
work as superficial, and in his congenial psychoanalytic-historical
study *Young Man Luther*,[25] he interprets the report handed down by
Rörer as a description of a psychosomatic process: 'A revelation . . . is
always associated with a repudiation, a cleansing, a kicking away; and
it would be entirely in accord with Luther's great freedom in such
matters if he were to experience and to report this repudiation in
frankly physical terms.' Indeed, Erikson continues: 'The cloaca, at the
"other end" of the bodily self, remained for him sometimes wittily,
sometimes painfully, sometimes delusionally alive, as if it were a "dirt
ground" where one meets with the devil, just as one meets with God
in the *Seelengrund,* where pure being is created.'[26]

Since this interpretation still enjoys a broad dissemination,
particularly in the English-speaking countries – e.g. John Osborne's
play *Luther*[27] – it would be irresponsible if we were, as 'serious'
professional historians, to ignore the interpretation of a psychoanalyst.
Rather, we must investigate carefully to what extent Erikson's
interpretation explains and does justice to the historical record.

[22] *Luther I,* Freiburg 1911 (1924³), 323f.

[23] See the justified defense of Grisar, in the third volume of his work, Freiburg 1912
(1925³), 978–980, as well as his book *Martin Luthers Leben und sein Werk,* Freiburg 1926
(1927²), 98.

[24] 'Derbheit'; P. J. Reiter, *Martin Luthers Unwelt, Charakter und Psychose* II,
Copenhagen 1941, 321f.

[25] New York 1958 (1962²); cf. H. Faber and W. J. Kooiman 'Een psychoanalyticus over
Luther', in: *Nederlands Theologisch Tijdischrift* 20 (1965), 17–48; most devastating is the
evaluation of David Stannard in his *Shrinking History: On Freud and the Failure of
Psychohistory,* Oxford 1980.

[26] *Young Man Luther,* 199f. (2nd ed., 205–6).

[27] New York/London 1961, 24: 'There's a bare fist clenched to my bowels and they
can't move, and I have to sit sweating in my little monk's house to open them.' Cf. *Young
Man Luther,* 198 (2nd ed., 204): 'Luther refers to a *secretus locus monachorum* [= my little
monk's house!], *hypocaustum* [= sit sweating] or *cloaca.'* Cf. also Osborne, 62f.: 'It came to
me while I was in my tower, what they call the monk's sweathouse, the jakes, the john or
whatever you're pleased to call it . . . My pain vanished, my bowels flushed and I could get
up. I could see the life I'd lost. No man is just because he does good works.'

As early as 1919, the editor of the table talk in question, Ernst Kroker, insisted that 'Sch(m)eißhaus' – the expression probably used by Luther – should be understood in a figurative sense.[28] And although he cites a passage in which Luther describes all earthly life in this way,[29] his interpretation so far has met with no scholarly agreement whatsoever.[30] Yet Kroker seems to have perceived something quite real; indeed, it can be demonstrated that behind Luther's statement there is a firm medieval tradition in which concepts like *cloaca, latrina, faeces* or *stercus* (filth) were used simultaneously in the physical and in the metaphysical sense.[31]

The starting point of this tradition is the widespread notion[32] that the *cloaca* is a preferred spot of the devil or other unclean spirits. Thietmar of Merseburg (+1018) tells of demons that arise from the *cloaca* to tempt a monk.[33] Other medieval authors address the question as to whether one should even pray in so unclean a place. While an Irish monastic rule answers in the negative,[34] the author of the *Summa Theologica* ascribed to Alexander of Hales says 'yes', since everything is clean to those who are clean.[35] Gabriel Biel, who copied this passage of the *Summa,* adds that one might pray to God even in Hell, if it were done with the right *affectus* (emotional

---

[28] 'Luthers Tischreden', in: *Luther-Jahrbuch* 1 (1919), 81–131; 116–20.

[29] *WAT* 4, 191.31f.; no. 4192.

[30] The only exception is Grisar, *Martin Luthers Leben und sein Werk,* 528, n. 34, but he does not discuss Kroker's view in any detail.

[31] Luther also seems to have had this tradition in mind when he says in a table talk (*WAT* 1, 136.14–17): 'When I was a monk, I was a craftsman of allegory . . . I even allegorized 'cloaca' and everything.' ('In allegoriis, cum essem monachus, fui artifex . . . allegorisabam etiam cloacam et omnia.')

[32] See also beside the following evidence, R. Otto, *Gottheit und Gottheit der Arier,* Giessen 1932, 62.

[33] *Chronicon* IV 72 (ed. Holtzmann, *MGH.* SS, NS IX, Berlin 1935, 215, 11–14).

[34] W. Reeves, 'On the Céli-dé, commonly called Culdees', in: *Transactions of the Royal Irish Academy,* 24, Antiquities II, Dublin 1864, 209, gives the following translation of the Irish text: 'Now the privy-houses and the urine homes they are the abodes of demons. Let these houses be blessed by anyone going thither, and let him bless himself when he enters them, and it is not lawful to say any prayers in them, except "Deus in adjutorium" to "festina".' This exception refers to Ps. 69.2(70.2): 'Deus, in adiutorium meum intende; Domine, ad adiurandum me festina' ('God, turn to my aid; Lord make haste to help me').

[35] *Summa Theologica,* Norimbergae (A. Koburger) 1515–16, p. IV, Q. 94, M.2. (f. 347ʳ): 'Legitur . . . de beato Gregorio quod cum purgaret ventrum et psalmum diceret, apparuit ei diabolus querens quid faceret: et respondit ventrum meum purgo, et deum meum laudo. opera enim nature perfectis turpia non videntur.'

state).[36] Luther also expresses his approval of this position in a table talk.[37]

The context in which Augustine discusses this problem is particularly characteristic. A pupil of the Church Father Licentius had sung a verse from a psalm on the toilet and had therefore been censured by Augustine's mother, Monica. Augustine defends him, however, arguing prayer to be entirely appropriate to the place, where, after all, people free themselves from the filth of carnal life.[38]

In Augustine we see the foundations of a symbolic interpretation of the concept 'cloaca' that was widespread in the later Middle Ages. According to Biel, a bad conscience is a stinking latrine.[39] Gerson interprets a dream in which a man falls into a latrine and tries in vain to climb out of the filth with the help of a stick, as follows: the man in the latrine is a symbol for the hopeless position of the sinner, and the stick is a symbol of our own efforts, which cannot ever suffice without God's help.[40] Geiler von Kayserberg also offers the same explanation in a sermon on Sebastian Brant's *Narrenschiff*.[41] 'To fall into the *cloaca*' meant in the late Middle Ages 'to fall into sin', particularly to be pulled down by fleshly lusts, away from the *Seelengrund*, where God lives in mankind.

This is the background necessary to understand Luther's declaration:

[36] *Canonis Misse expositio,* lect. 62 F (ed. Oberman, Courtenay, Wiesbaden 1963–6, III 27).

[37] *WAT* 2, 143.1–9; no. 2307. On the topic of the general notion, cf. also *WA* 54, 174.6–12, where Beelzebub is described as a big fly that likes to dig 'in the secret room' ('auf dem heimlichen gemach') in human excrement.

[38] Augustine, *De ord.* I 8, 22 f.; *PL* 32, 987f. The word *cloaca* does not, however, occur in this Augustine text.

[39] *Canonis Misse expositio,* lect. 87 E (ed. Oberman, Courtenay, IV 145).

[40] Gerson, *De praeparatione ad Missam, post pollutionem nocturam* (ed. DuPin, Antwerp 1706, III 332A): 'Fuit cuidam per somnium ostensa visio talis: Praecipitatus in cloacam erat, et a quodam baculo stercoribus infixo sustentari, ne profunderetur, sategebat. At vero baculus ille fundotenus demittebatur assidue cum foetore intolerabile. Sentiens ille periculum, tota mente ad Dominus conversus, relicto baculo, confestim ereptus est. Sane conscientia nostra quantumlibet munda, est cloaca quaedam, plena stercoribus foedis defectuum quotidianorum. Baculus ille, nostra est industria, per quam emergere quaerimus; sed proculdubio quousque levemus oculos in coelum, unde veniat auxilium nobis; quousque fiduciam nostram totam in Deum jactemus, quanto plus innitimur solo nostrae industriae baculo, tanto in profundiorem abyssum nostrae pravitatis demergimur, et non nisi foetorem tetrum et horridum reportamus.' Cf. E.J. Dempsey Douglass, *Justification in Late Medieval Preaching,* Leiden 1966, 112, n. 4.

[41] See Douglass, 112, n. 3.

What then is a pure heart? Or what does it consist in? Answer: it is quickly said – you may not try to climb up to heaven nor run after it in a monastery and try to create it with your own thoughts. But rather be wary of everything that you know to be your own thoughts in yourself, as of useless mud and filth, and know that a monk in a cloister, when he sits in his most sublime state of meditation and thinks of his Lord God, as he himself paints and dreams him, and wants to throw the world right out of his heart, he is sitting (begging your pardon) in shit, not just up to his knees, but right up over his ears, because he is dealing only with his own thoughts, without God's Word.[42]

The authentically 'Lutheran' part of this passage is not the reference to *cloaca* and *stercus,* but the idea that the historically revealed, incarnate Christ is absolutely necessary for salvation.

The use of the words *cloaca* and *stercus* is suggested by certain formulations in the Vulgate. Philippians 3.8: 'Omnia . . . arbitror ut stercora' ('I count all things . . . but dung'). Even more effective is Psalm 113.7 (112.7): 'Suscitans a terra inopem et de stercore erigens pauperem' ('He raiseth up the poor out of the dust/And lifteth the needy out of the dunghill'). In interpreting this verse Peter Lombard glosses *stercus* as 'carnal desire', from which man is freed 'by grace alone'.[43] In an extensive study of this verse,[44] Jacob Perez ponders various interpretations[45] and likewise understands *stercus* primarily as sin, from which man is cleansed by the sacrament of penance.[46] God's

---

[42] 'Was jst denn nu ein rein hertz? odder worinn stehets? Antwort: Es jst bald gesagt, und darffst nicht gen himel klettern noch jnn ein Closter darnach lauffen und mit eigen gedancken ausrichten, Sondern hute dich fur allen, was du fur eigen gedancken bey dir weissest, als fur eitel schlam und unflat, und wisse, das ein mönch jm Closter, wenn er jnn seiner hohesten beschauligkeit sitzet und an seinen Herrgott dencket, wie er jn selbs malet und treumet, und wil die wellt gar aus dem hertzen werffen, der sitzet (mit urlaub) jm dreck, nicht bis an die knye, sondern uber die oren, Denn er gehet mit eigen gedancken umb on Gottes wort' (Weekly sermon on Matthew 5–7 (1530–32), here Matthew 5.8; *WA* 32, 325.23–31). It should be noted that Luther or at least the contemporary editor of the sermons apologizes for the use of the word 'dreck'. Therefore, it is not permissible to take the sting out of such statements with the argument that sixteenth-century Europeans were less shy than us about 'natural functions' and used spicier language.

[43] 'Per solam gratiam', *Comm. in ps.; PL,* 191, 1017B; cf. Augustine, *En. in ps.* CXII 7 and Cassiodorus, *Exp. in ps.* CXII 7.

[44] Ed. Venetiis 1581, p. 827 A–F.

[45] ibid., 827 D: 'exaltauit . . . discipulos de stercore, [et] fimo artis piscatorie'; 827 E: 'suscitauit apostolos . . . de stercore cerimonialium'.

[46] ibid. 827 E: 'per pauperem erectum de stercore intelligit quemlibet peccatorem a sordibus peccatorum per poenitentiam mundatum, [et] eleuatum. Nam ille erat mortuus in terra: [et] iste iacebat inuolutus in stercore peccatorum.'

omnipotence[47] and the efficacy of predestination[48] are manifested in this cleansing, which takes place 'by grace alone' according to Perez as well.

In his first lecture on the Psalms, Luther started out in agreement with his predecessors, and interpreted *stercus* as 'vices and sins'.[49] But he then breaks new ground, independent of tradition: in the verse 'Suscitans a terra inopem et de stercore erigens pauperem' there appears a 'new rule of Christ', not known under the old covenant.[50] This 'new rule' means the same thing as the verse cited at the beginning, 'God resists the proud, but gives grace to the humble'.[51] Everyone is humbled, *de facto,* by God; however, his promise applies only to those who actually acknowledge this fact, that is, to those who know that they are *pauperes* (beggars) and *in stercore, in cloaca* (in filth, in the latrine).[52]

In the third and last part of our inquiry we must also ask to what extent these 'rules of Christ', as formulated by Luther, go beyond the limits of the medieval doctrine of justification. We can summarize the results of our study up to this point as follows:

1. Even though Erikson is justified in referring to Luther's life-long digestion problems and his attitude toward the natural bodily functions as more open than that of recent times,[53] the attempt to interpret the 'tower experience' as a dramatic psychosomatic event seems doomed to fail in the light of the medieval *stercus/cloaca* tradition, which lives on in Luther's work. Psychoanalysis of a historical figure is at best possible in collaboration with a historian. This objection is especially apposite in the case of Erikson's Luther biography, which is both a brilliant analysis and a garbled distortion – because it is unhistorical.

---

[47] ibid. 827B: 'ostendit etiam Deus magis suam omnipotentiam, cum ex hominibus . . . suscitavit, [et] eleuauit quosdam per gratiam'; 827 D/E: 'ecclesia Christi ex pauperibus, [et] simplicibus congregata est, [et] eleuata, [et] suscitata. [et] in hoc magis ostensa est Christi potentia.'

[48] ibid., 827 B: 'tunc erexit de terra inopem, [et] pauperem, quando hominem sauciatum, [et] expoliatum redemit, [et] per gratiam elegit. Et tunc inter principes populi sui collocauit, quando inter hierarchias angelorum collocauit.'

[49] *WA* 4, 254.19.

[50] *WA* 4, 256.26f.

[51] Cf. *WA* 4, 256.10f.

[52] *WA* 4, 256.21–6. Cf. also the scholion to Psalm 82(83).11; *WA* 3, 635.22–4.

[53] *Young Man Luther,* 199.

2. Luther's use of the terms *stercus* and *cloaca* is rooted in a medieval tradition, but it is not stuck in the past. When Luther says in his lecture on Galatians: 'Works meriting partial grace are filth',[54] he seems to be following late medieval theologians who called human works, in their insufficiency and uncleanliness – after Isaiah 64.6 – 'the cloth of a menstruating woman'.[55] In reality, however, Luther is not concerned with works (the fruit), but with the sinful person (the tree).[56] His theology of humility does not refer to the humbleness of works, but to the humility of the person who does the works. This humility requires belief in the promise that not just anyone, but precisely the beggars (*pauperes*) and 'those who lie in excrement' (*in stercore iacentes*) are blessed.[57] While medieval man was urged to flee the *cloaca,* the place of temptation, Luther insists that it is where the spirit of Christ acts and operates. Whereas in scholastic anthropology the *cloaca* is the opposite of the *Seelengrund,* that is, the stronghold of sin and the devil, the *cloaca* for Luther is the location of Christ's advent.

3. Luther's statements must be understood in relation to this idea of *duplex peccatum* ('double sinfulness'). Anyone who wishes to justify himself, and claims to be without sin, thereby doubles his sinfulness because – as in 1 John 1.10 – he 'makes God a liar'.[58] God's salvific

---

[54] '[O]pera congrui ist ein dreck' (*WA* 40I, 235.12). Cf. also ibid., 137.24f.: 'Erat . . . iustitia illa mea nihil aliud quam latrina et suavissimum regnum diaboli.'

[55] '[P]annus menstruatae'. See Adolar Zumkeller, 'Das Ungenügen der menschlichen Werke bei den deutschen Predigern des späten Mittelalters', *Zeitschrift für katholische Theologie* 81 (1959), 265–305; 271 and nn. 19, 30, 31, 37, 44, 47, 81, 98, 115 and 117. However, this is only a partial uncleanliness; cf. for example the words of Pelbartus of Temesvár cited in n. 98: 'iustitia nostra est impura et vitiis mixta', which goes no farther than the position of Bernard of Clairvaux cited in n. 5 (*PL* 183, 358 A), 'Nostra . . . (si qua est) humilis est iustitia, recta forsitan, sed non pura'. Zumkeller maintains on page 305 that his study confirmed the results of J. Lortz and showed 'daß . . . auch für das Deutschland des 14. und 15. Jahrhunderts die Fabel von der katholischen Werkheiligkeit wirklich nur Fabel ist'. However, there is evidence to the contrary. For Luther, at least, human righteousness is not merely 'mixed with sin' (*vitiis mixta*), but 'nothing but sin' (*nihil nisi peccatum*); scholion on Psalm 118(119).163; *WA* 4, 383.9.

[56] Luther says in characteristic fashion: 'humana natura . . . est menstruata'; Gloss on Psalm 71(72).2; *WA* 3, 458.20.

[57] Cf. also the scholion on Psalm 118(119).163; *WA* 4, 383.7–11.

[58] *WA* 56, 230.23f, scholion on Rom. 3.5. Cf. also *WA* 55II, 2.11–3.5: '[peccator] facit primum peccatum duplex . . . Hoc est autem duplex peccatum: stare, defendere, resistere corrigenti et revocanti . . . seipsum Iustificare, postquam peccavit' and 55II, 30.12f.: 'suum sensum statuere, sua opera et facta Iustificare et defendere . . . est duplex peccatum'.

action therefore begins with the sinner being led back *in stercus,* into filth, that is, the sinner is unmasked as 'humble in the face of God' (*humiliatus coram Deo*). In the extreme terms Luther once used, 'the just must become sinners'.[59] The humility which this implies, and which is discussed in the earliest version of the first lecture on the Psalms,[60] is not, however, simply a psychologically refined form of 'medieval monastic virtue'. The term *humilitas* always had for Luther the same sense as the expression *extra nos* (outside ourselves): it means the realization that all we find in ourselves is excrement.

Faith and humility are, therefore, without a doubt so closely connected that it is tempting to understand them as interchangeable terms. But they are not entirely interchangeable, particularly not in a medieval sense. First, humility in this context is not a prerequisite of faith, but presupposes faith;[61] second, as we will demonstrate in what follows, humility is conceived of in such radical terms that it is not a virtue for Luther, but the attitude appropriate to a person conscious of standing before God with empty hands.

4. In January or February of 1519 – that is, even if we accept Bizer's dating, *after* the Reformation breakthrough – Luther defined the principle which we have met in the garb of the 'new rule of Christ' as 'the wonderfully beautiful difference between law and faith'. He does not allow himself to be held back by the actual wording of the text he is interpreting (Psalm 5.2), but explains in accordance with Phil. 3.8 that the *people of the law* do not seek God's mercy (*misericordia Dei*), but trust in their own works, whereas the *people of faith* only hope for God's mercy and regard their own righteousness as excrement. As we might expect he bases this idea on the principle that 'God gives grace to the humble and resists the proud'.[62]

It might be difficult to see here a third variety of *humilitas–* theology distinct from the second understanding just discussed. Indeed, we can go one step further and refer to a *Tischrede* from the winter of 1542–43,

---

[59] *WA* 56, 230.6–8, scholion on Rom. 3–5: 'docet nos fieri peccatores . . . Quomodo fit peccator, qui prius Iustus erat.' Cf. *WA* 40I, 224.4–7, on Gal. 2.16.

[60] *WA* 55II, 30.12f. (see n. 58).

[61] See my article 'Simul Gemitus et Raptus: Luther and Mysticism', in: *The Dawn of the Reformation,* Edinburgh 1986, 126–54; 147ff.

[62] *AWA* 2, 223.14f.; *WA* 5, 127.17–27.

which says: 'Previously [that is, before the discovery of Romans 1.17] I had no reason to distinguish between the law and the gospel; I thought it was all one and the same and said Christ did not differ from Moses except in time and degree of perfection. But when I found the distinction – that the law is one thing and the gospel another – I broke through it all.'[63] Now if this distinction is identical with the 'new rule of Christ', according to which God's promise applies particularly to beggars (*pauperes*) and the 'humbled' (*humiliati*), and if this means the same thing as the formula *extra nos* (outside ourselves), then Luther's Reformation discovery consists in an insight, a realization, that he held onto until the end of his life, but which he spelled out in his earliest lecture: We are beggars. That is the truth.

3. Covenant and Grace

We are not accustomed – and quite properly so – to think of Luther as a 'covenant theologian'. The idea of covenant does not dominate or overshadow other elements in his theology. In this regard, Luther is very different from Reformed theologians, especially Cocceius,[64] but also Bullinger, who considers the common topic and goal of all the books of the Bible – of the Old *and* New Testaments – to be the historical covenant of God, understood in the infralapsarian context. God commits himself to his people on the basis of this covenant;[65] in it is manifested the promise sealed by Christ.[66] Yet the idea of the covenant, in a certain form, was both problematic and helpful to the young Luther, in a way that is directly connected to the development of his *humilitas*–theology. This development was not entirely novel. The theologians of the Middle Ages, particularly of the later Middle Ages, were also concerned with God's covenant, which obliges us to turn our attention to this tradition.

The objective and subjective concepts of the covenant correspond to the two points of view from which Augustine considered the

[63] *WAT* 5, 210.12–16; no. 5518.

[64] See K. Müller, RE³ IV 189.45–191.40, and P. Jacobs, RGG³ I 1519f.

[65] See J. Staedtke, *Die Theologie des jungen Bullinger*, Zurich 1962, 65. It is of particular importance with regard to baptism and the Lord's Supper that there is only one covenant; cf. 232 and 248.

[66] See *Confessio et expositio simplex orthodoxae fidei* (1566) XVI, in: *Bekenntnisschriften und Kirchenordnungen der nach Gottes Wort reformierten Kirche*, ed. W. Niesel, Zurich 1938 [1985], 246.12f.

question of Christian sanctification in his disputes with the Donatists and Pelagians. The first is rooted in Augustine's belief that God does not allow his salvific work to be compromised by sinful instruments.[67] This emphasis on the concept *ex opere operato* (spiritual effects are achieved by ritual or spiritual actions – not by the merit of the person who performs the action) led, in the wake of the radical changes that followed the rediscovery of Aristotle, to an explicit idea of covenant. This idea addressed primarily the question whether, and if so, how, the sacraments impart grace. In opposition to Thomism,[68] representatives of the Franciscan school from Bonaventure[69] through Duns Scotus[70] and Ockham[71] up to Gabriel Biel[72], argued ever more insistently that the sacraments owed their efficacy to 'God's covenant with the Church' (the *pactio* or *pactum dei cum ecclesia*). Biel, for instance, says that in the Eucharist, Christ himself, because of the pact he has made with the Church, his bride, effectuates the transubstantiation.[73] Everything that happens *ex opere operato* is based on a covenanted divine obligation. Even circumcision, the only Old Testament sacrament through which sins were forgiven, was efficacious *ex opere operato,* merely because it was rooted in God's covenant with his people.[74]

The subjective idea of the covenant developed out of the views Augustine represented in his fight against the Pelagians. Yet there were abridgements and changes, because although the second Synod of Arausio (529) largely confirmed Augustine's radical teachings on grace, it became necessary to bring this doctrine into harmony with the practical exigencies of the cure of souls in the Church. This process produced the axiomatic principle 'facientibus quod in se est deus non denegat gratiam' (God does not deny grace to those who do what it is in their power to do). This position, prepared by early Scholasticism,[75]

---

[67] See for example Augustine, *De bapt.* IV 4.5.

[68] Cf. Thomas Aquinas IV *Sent.* d.1 q.1 a.4 quaestiunc. 1–4.

[69] IV *Sent.* d.1 p.1 a.1 q.4 (ed. Quaracchi 1949, IV 17ᵇ).

[70] *Oxon.* IV d.1 q.5; *Rep.* IV d.1 q.4.

[71] IV *Sent.* q.1 C–M.

[72] *Canonis Misse expositio,* lect. 47 R–X (ed. Oberman, Courtenay, II 224–8).

[73] ibid., 47 T (226).

[74] Cf. Bonaventure, IV *Sent.* d.1 p.1 a.1 q.5 (ed. Quaracchi 1949, IV 20ᵇ) and Biel, lect. 47 X (228).

[75] See A. M. Landgraf, *Dogmengeschichte der Frühscholastik* I 1, Regensburg 1952, 249–64.

was unanimously accepted by the theologians of the Franciscan
school – Alexander of Hales, Duns Scotus, Ockham, Holcot, Gerson,
d'Ailly and Biel – as well as by the young Thomas.[76] God covenanted
before all time – entirely of his own free will and from pure merciful
grace – to give his grace to everyone who makes all possible efforts
according to his or her capacity, and to reward justly the works that
are accomplished in relation to this grace. The granting of grace
follows *merita de congruo* ('corresponding merits': merits resulting
from works that help to earn partial grace); while the 'final reward'
depends on *merita de condigno* ('absolute worthiness'). Strictly
speaking, *merita de congruo* are rewarded on account of God's own
generosity, and only *merita de condigno* are rewarded in accordance
with a historical covenant. However, these varieties of merit are so
closely connected to each other that God's covenant is manifested
even in rewards *de congruo*. In both cases God's grace or glory is given
by necessity – though not by absolute necessity, but rather by
necessitas immutabilitatis (the principle of unchangeability) in
accordance with which God remains true to himself and therefore
also to his covenant.

This brief overview should be rounded out by a few remarks
concerning the principle *facere quod in se est* (do what you are able to
do). Dionysius the Carthusian explains in his interpretation of
Proverbs 16.1 – 'hominis est animum praeparare' ('men must make
ready their soul') – that this verse concerns not only the unbelievers,
who must use their free will and natural reason, but also Christians in
a state of sinfulness, who can rely on their *fides informis* (inborn
faith), the remnants of lost virtues and their knowledge of the
commandments. It even applies to Christians in a state of grace, who
have prepared themselves for the increase of grace through prayer,
meditation and listening to sermons.[77]

[76] See Leif Grane, *Contra Gabrielem,* Gyldendal/Copenhagen 1962, 214ff., and my
article 'Facientibus quod in se est deus non denegat gratiam', *Harvard Theological Review*
55 (1962), 317–42 and more recently in Heiko A. Oberman, *The Dawn of the Reformation,*
Edinburgh 1986, 84–103.

[77] *Opera omnia* VII, Monstrolii 1898, 105 D–106 B: 'Hominis est animum praeparare,
id est se ad gratiam Dei disponere, faciendo quod in se est, hoc est, quod per naturam et per
dona sibi data facere potest: quod dum toto conatu peregerit, Deus certissime gratiam ei
infundet. Verumtamen Deus diversimode praevenit homines, et quosdam tam pie, ut
etiam dum vitiosis actibus sunt intenti, trahat eos valenter et prorsus piissime ad se, sicut et

Talking about *facere quod in se est* does not necessarily betray a crass Pelagianism; the element of human cooperation which it presupposes can be reduced to a minimum. Thomas Marsilius von Inghen (+1396) demonstrates the process of salvation, for instance, in a parable about a man who falls into a pit and is pulled out by a powerful rescuer. Of course, the man also does what he can, but in reality he hinders his rescue by his weight more than he helps by his efforts. It is not on account of his actual help, but exclusively on account of his serious efforts that the sinner receives grace *de congruo*.[78]

According to Alexander of Hales, the natural potential of fallen man consists chiefly in his knowledge of a merciful God, and in knowing that he can call on God for help. This position illustrates the transition from the principle *facientibus quod in se est deus non denegat gratiam* to the statement *humilibus deus dat gratiam* (God gives grace to the humble). Kaspar Schatzgeyer (+1527), Luther's opponent of later years, clearly expresses this connection of ideas. According to Schatzgeyer, man is capable as an *animale rational* (a being endowed with reason) to live according to the dictates of reason. If he actually does so, he is doing his best (*facit quod in se est*) and therefore is

---

Paulum pergentem Damascum ad persequendum Christifideles. Semper tamen in adultis requiritur consensus, et cooperatio quaedam liberi arbitrii: quia, ut asserit Augustinus, qui creavit te sine te, non justificabit te sine te. Itaque per liberum arbitrium naturalemque rationem, aptat se homo ad gratiam, recedendo a malis, bonisque actibus cohaerendo, secundum naturalis rationis dictamen, et quantum possibile est per vires naturae: et ita se possunt aptare infideles. Credentes vero, sed in mortali vitio exsistentes, etiam per fidelem informem, reliquiasque virtutum quas amiserunt peccando, et per notitiam mandatorum, possunt et debent se praeparare ad divinorum infusionem charismatum; similiter acquiescendo angelicis et divinis occultis instinctibus, quibus homines etiam vitiosi ac perfidi multipliciter retrahuntur a malis, atque ad bona misericorditer instigantur. Denique non solum est hominis, animum suum praeparare modis jam tactis ad gratiae infusionem; sed et hi qui gratiam habent, virtutibusque ornantur, se debent [praeparare] ad caritatis profectum, ad gratiae incrementum, ad devotionem ardentem, Dominum invocando, scripturas pensando, sermones attente audiendo, et bonis sibi concessis rite utendo. Imo et ad ipsam orationem debet se homo praeparae recolligendo cor suum.'

[78] Marsilius, *Quaestiones super quattuor libros sententiarum,* 1. II q. 18 a. 3 concl. 4 sol. (ed. Straßburg 1501, fol. 300ᵗᵇ): 'sicut qui in fossam cecidit, sua gravitate plus resistit extrahenti, quam ad sui extractionem suis viribus faciat. Tamen congruum est, cum efficaciter libenter coageret, ut esset extra, fortis liberator existens extra eum de fossa trahat. Ita etiam benignissimus ille deus preveniens tractu spirituali peccatorum plus peccati pondere deorsum tendentem quam sua opera ad gratie consecutionem facere potest. Quia tamen attritus est et tractus ad gratiam anhelat, congruum est ut ipsum de servitute peccati eripiens ad gratiam reaccipiat.'

preparing himself *de congruo* for grace. However, the Fall generated a tendency to evil that constantly threatens this life based on reason. Since the Fall it has therefore been necessary, in order to receive grace, to recognize one's own failings and to know oneself to be as wretched as anyone can be; for the meek will be exalted by God.[79]

With Schatzgeyer we have arrived at the eve of the Reformation. In summarizing once again the medieval tradition sketched above, we must keep in mind that the objective and subjective idea of the covenant not only come from the same source, but also remain, in the course of their development, closely connected to one another.[80] In the same way that the sacraments convey objective grace, meritorious works procure subjective grace – on account of a covenant in which God bound himself to his Church and his faithful followers.

Luther's position toward both medieval versions of the covenant idea is unequivocal. When he was working through the Lyon edition of Gabriel Biel's *Collectorium* and *Commentary on the Mass* shortly before or shortly after the first lecture on the Psalms, he came across the assertion that biblical passages such as Luke 11.9 – 'seek and you shall find' – actually mean *facere quod in se est*. Luther remarked: 'As if those words meant that it is in our power to seek and to convert ourselves, when it says in Psalm 13 [14.2] that no-one understands or seeks God!'[81]

---

[79] Schatzgeyer, *De perfecta atque contemplativa vita*, Conventus Monachiensis 1501, Dir. 17; *Opera omnia*, Ingolstadt 1543, fol. 324: 'Cum enim omnes creaturae possint (posita Dei generali influentia) exire in actus suae naturae competentes, et illi actus conveniant homini inquantum animal rationale, ut videlicet secundum rationem vivat, colligitur quod potest talia facere cum Dei generali influentia. Patet etiam hoc in paganis et infidelibus, quorum multi habuerunt virtutes morales, et vixerunt secundum rationem, propter quod inexcusabilis est homo si non vivat ut homo. Hoc enim modo secundum rationem vivendo disponit se de congruo ad gratiam gratum facientem, et facit quod in se est. Verumtamen, quia sensus et cogitatio hominis prona sunt ad malum . . . necessaria est gratia sibi, prout est specialis dei influentia, retrahens a malo et disponens ad bonum . . . Ex quo fiet, ut quanto amplius nos humili aestimatione evacuamus, tanto ad gratiam suscipiendam capatiores erimus. Requiescit enim Spiritus Dei super humilem; quanto ergo maior es, humilia te in omnibus, ut Deus te exaltet, qui humiles respicit [Luke 1.48–52].'

[80] Cf. Eck, *Chrysopassus*, cent. III 75: 'sufficit nobis illa gratia dei, quod ex mera liberalitate illas regulas nobis praescripsit, sacramenta instituit: quibus si conformaremur, vitam aeternam adipisceremur' and Biel, *Canonis Misse expositio*, lect. 47 X (ed. Oberman, Courtenay, II 227).

[81] Luther's marginalia to Gabriel Biel's *Collectorium in quattuor libros sententiarum* and to his *Sacri canonis missae expositio*, Lyon 1514; *WA* 59, 45.25f.; 46.4–6.

Luther answered Biel's extenuating explanation that grace is at least required to make the *facere,* the doing, easier: 'Pelagius said the same thing.'[82]

Luther's judgement concerning the objective covenant idea is no more positive. He accuses Biel and the other Scholastics of failing to see what distinguishes a sacrament from the rest of creation:[83] 'They disregard the fact that the spoken word in the sacraments is God's word.'[84] Luther's real concern is revealed even more fully in the following marginal note: 'When will anyone ever speak of faith?'[85] The last comment on Biel's doctrine of the sacraments is also fundamentally in opposition to the medieval covenant idea, and summarizes both points of view emphasized by Luther: 'It is clear that they know neither of the promise, nor what faith is.'[86]

These comments have – to the extent that they have ever been noticed – in many cases led to the assumption that the covenant idea had only a negative significance for Luther's Reformation discovery.[87] This assumption implies not only a failure to recognize a decisive phase in Luther's development, but also a failure to recognize one of the most important foundations of his early *humilitas*–theology.

A detailed comparison with the exegetical tradition will show that the covenant idea is a constant in Luther's first lectures on the Psalms. Preliminary results can be summarized in five points:

1. The concept of *pactum* (covenant) is known to Luther not only via the systematic tradition, but also via the exegetical tradition. It is characteristic of this latter tradition for *pactum* to be identified with *testamentum.*[88] Following this tradition, Luther also equates the two terms (with a demonstrable debt to Jerome's *Psalterium*

[82] *WA* 59, 46.21–3 and 29.

[83] *WA* 59, 49.8–10.

[84] *WA* 59, 49.12f.

[85] *WA* 59, 49.24f.

[86] *WA* 59, 51.26f.

[87] Even Leif Grane, who has made an important contribution to research in this field, emphasizes in regard to the passages in which Luther speaks of the *pactum dei* 'daß diese Terminologie erst ziemlich spät [in the first lecture on the Psalms] auftaucht und . . . bald wieder verschwindet'; *Contra Gabrielem,* 299, n. 43.

[88] See for instance Peter Lombard, *Comm. in Ps.* 82.5; *PL* 191, 782 B.

Hebraicum[89]) and thus arrives at a covenant theology that corresponds only partially – or perhaps forms a counterpoint to – that of the Franciscan school.

2. It has been noted frequently in the scholarly literature that Luther, in the first lecture on the Psalms, still uses *Gesetz* (law) and *Evangelium* (Gospel) as interchangeable terms. It seems fair to assume that he had not yet formulated the difference between them. If we keep in mind that *lex* (law) can also serve as a periphrasis for *pactum* or *testamentum*,[90] we can analyze the concept 'covenant' in such a way as to arrive at a more detailed and judicious appreciation of the problem.

As far as I can see, Luther deviates from the existing exegetical tradition – as well as from later reformed theology – in that he distinguishes strictly between the old and new covenant, that is, between the old and new law. The old covenant is for him a two-sided bond of works, which can be cancelled if the covenanted obligations are not met. The new covenant, however, is a one-sided bond that is based solely on God's merciful compassion and therefore cannot be revoked. When believers of the new covenant sin, they are punished, but the covenant itself remains.[91]

It should be recognized that Luther in this context starts from the objective covenant idea of medieval theology. Much more important

---

[89] *WA* 3, 282.4–6: 'Qui ordinant testamentum eius super sacrificia [Ps. 49(50)]. Primo (id est pactum Christi feriunt pro sacrificio: sic enim Hebr.) qui legem eius suscipiunt, ut eum colant sacrificio.' See S. Raeder, *Das Hebräische bei Luther,* Tübingen 1961, 322. See also *WA* 57II, 24.21f., gloss on Gal. 3.15: 'Dicit B. Ieronimus "testamentum" hoc loco pocius sonare "pactum", ut est in Hebreo.'

[90] See *WA* 3, 306.25 on Ps. 54(55).21; and 552.5f., on Ps. 77(78).10; as well as *WA* 4, 42.4 on Ps. 88(89).40.

[91] See *WA* 4, 41.15–29 on Ps. 88(89).35: 'lex nova sicut non ex operibus et meritis nostris incipit, ita nec demeritis nostris ruit. Sed ex mera promissione et misericordia et veritate Dei incipit, stat et perstabit. Vetus autem lex non. Quia data fuit sub conditione tali, scilicet si implerent ipsam, staret, si autem non implerent, rueret. Quia erat fundatum (sic!) in operibus eorum et non in misericordia et promissione pura Dei, sed cum inclusione operum illorum. Unde Jer. 31.[32] "pactum quod irritum fecerunt". Ipsos dicit irritum fecisse, quod tamen suum erat, scilicet quia non servaverunt. Sed non sic Christi, quod nullus homo potest irritare quantumvis omnes peccent, quia stat in gratia Dei, non in operibus nostris. Et hec sunt misericordie, quas cantat iste psalmus [v. 34], magnifice certe et cantande. Unde ps 131[.12] non dicit, ut hic, sed hic: "Si custodierint filii tui testamentum meum etc." Hic [Ps. 85.32–4] autem: "Si non custodierint, etiam adhuc misericordiam meam etc." Unde et quando peccant fideles, tota Ecclesia flagellatur, mali cum bonis, sed non irritum fit pactum. Olim autem etiam si pauci pecassent, solvebatur pactum, quia fundatum erat in operibus eorum.'

to our task, however, is that the covenant concept just sketched also exercised a decisive influence on Luther's teachings on the law. When the *testamentum dei* (God's covenant) is referred to in the first lectures on the Psalms as 'law', 'through which God has attested to future grace',[92] Luther does not mean a law for the faithful, but rather a law which God in his one-sided covenant has decreed for himself, as it were.

3. But are there no new covenanted obligations that must be fulfilled? The new covenant is eternal because it leads to eternal salvation.[93] Mark 16.16 describes its content and the way in which it leads to salvation: 'He who believes ... shall be saved.'[94] God therefore committed himself in his covenant not to those who perform good works, but to those who *believe*. Luther binds the objective and subjective covenant ideas together, forming a new unity, yet he also modifies the idea of covenant in a decisive manner: the covenant 'produces' justification and salvation and it furthers belief in Christ.

Let us consider this matter from another angle. Samuel Preus, in the course of a debate with Gerhard Ebeling, wrote an important study on the hermeneutic function of the concept *promissio* in the Middle Ages and the works of the young Luther. In this work, Preus demonstrates convincingly that Luther could not accept without reservations a tropological correspondence between Christ and the believer because he agreed with the unanimous view of the Middle Ages that one cannot really speak of Christ having *fides*.[95] However, the other objections raised by Preus can be overcome at least in part if

[92] *WA* 3, 552.5f. on Ps. 77(78).10. See also *WA* 4, 193.34–7 on Ps. 104(105).10f.

[93] *WA* 4, 246.18f. on Ps. 111(112).9.

[94] *WA* 4, 193.10–21, gloss on Ps. 104(105).8–10: 'Memor fuit exhibendo sicut promisit in saeculum testamenti sui, in quo promisit gratiam Christi futuram: verbi fidei future, quod mandavit suscipiendum pro mandato posuit, ut qui crediderit, salvus erit. Benedictio fidei enim promissa est ei in omnes gentes . . . Quod verbum fidei disposuit . . . Et statuit illud verbum fidei promissum Iacob filiis Iacob in praeceptum, quia credere in Christum tenentur: et Israel populo ex Israel in testamentum aeternum, i.e. quod ex verbo fidei promisso et tandem impleto et exhibito, si ipsum servarent pro precepto, haberent vitam eternam. Fides enim est eternum testamentum.'

[95] J. S. Preus, *From Shadow to Promise. Old Testament Interpretation from Augustine to the young Luther,* Cambridge, MA, 1969, 226–33. Cf. also his article 'Old Testament promissio and Luther's new Hermeneutic', *Harvard Theological Review* 60 (1967), 145–61.

we consider the idea of the covenant, particularly as it is formulated in the interpretation of Psalm 100(99).4f.: 'bless [the name of the Lord], for . . . his truth endureth to all generations'.

To ancient and medieval exegetes, 'truth' (*veritas*) in this context meant the 'faithfulness' (*fides*) with which God fulfilled the promise he made in his covenant.[96] Luther also substitutes 'faithfulness' (*fides*) for 'truth' (*veritas*), and glosses *fides* as *fides Christi* (the faithfulness of Christ[97].) This expression, however, must be understood as both a 'subjective genitive' (*genitivus subjectivus*) and an 'objective genitive' (*genitivus objectivus*): the *fides Christi* (faithfulness of Christ) is, according to Luther's interpretation, both God's faithfulness to his covenant, 'through which everything that once was promised is given to us', and the believers' faithfulness to the covenant, 'through which we are justified and saved.'[98]

We can now return to our point of departure: in his earliest lectures – and therefore not only in the lectures on Hebrews of 1517–18[99] – Luther transforms the medieval notion of the covenant into something completely new by joining objective and subjective conceptions of the covenant, thus emphasizing the necessity of faith.

4. Inquiry into the relationship between the covenant and humility, between *pactum* and *humilitas,* leads us directly to the 'worst bone of contention for interpreters of Luther' – as Axel Gyllenkrok put it in his book on justification and sanctification in Luther's early evangelical theology.[100] He means not only an isolated statement, but a whole series of passages, especially in the later part of the first lecture on the Psalms, where Luther appears to have advocated the doctrine

---

[96] Cf. Jerome, *Psalterium Hebraicum* and Peter Lombard, *Comm. in ps.,* ad loc. (*PL* 191, 900 B).

[97] Following Jerome's *Psalterium Hebraicum;* cf. S. Raeder, *Das Hebräische bei Luther,* 337.

[98] Cf. to the preceding *WA* 4, 127.17–20: 'veritas eius exhibitio misericordie promisse, seu hebr. "fides eius". Fides enim est ipsa gratia et misericordia olim promissa, quia per illam iustificamur et salvamur. In fide enim Christi omnia nobis donantur, que promissa sunt olim.' The transition from the 'subjective genitive' to the 'objective genitive' takes place explicitly for the first time in the gloss on Rom. 3.20 (*WA* 56, 36.13f.): '"fides Christi" . . . non qua credit Christus, sed "qua creditur in Christum".'

[99] See n. 91.

[100] 'Der schlimmste Stein des Anstoßes für alle Lutherinterpreten'; *Rechtfertigung und Heiligung in der frühen evangelischen Theologie Luthers,* Uppsala 1952, 40, n. 2.

of *facere quod in se est,* or rather, of *meritum de congruo.*[101] Thus, following Matthew 7.7 – 'Ask, and it shall be given you' – he can say: 'On the basis of this passage, scholars correctly say that God unfailingly gives grace to those who do their best [*facienti quod in se est*]; and although man cannot prepare himself for grace *de condigno* . . ., he can at least prepare himself *de congruo,* because God has made this promise and sealed his covenant of mercy [*pactum misericordie*].'[102]

A statement like this cannot be dismissed as a mere remnant of pre-Reformation theology.[103] The argument that Luther always presupposed *gratia praeveniens* (pre-existing grace) where the *facere* was concerned cannot by the same token be used to support the thesis that the Reformation breakthrough occurred even before the first lectures on the Psalms:[104] other theologians such as Marsilius von Inghen or Johannes von Staupitz[105] also presuppose *gratia praeveniens.* Nevertheless, Luther broke with the medieval tradition as early as 1515, at least on one decisive point: concerning the particulars in which the *facere* (the actions of the faithful in the context of the covenant) consists.

In Luther's view, the *facere* of the human party to the covenant consists in our hope (*exspectatio*)[106] and in our prayers (*petitio*).[107] Man is a beggar (*pauper, mendicans*)[108] who can do no more than yell

---

[101] The most important passages are cited by Steven E. Ozment in his book *Homo Spiritualis. A comparative study of the anthropology of Johannes Tauler, Jean Gerson and Martin Luther (1509–16) in the context of their theological thought,* Leiden 1969, 159–66.

[102] *WA* 4, 262.4–7, scholion on Ps. 113B(115).1.

[103] This might well be raised in objection to the solutions proposed by K. Holl, *Gesammelte Aufsätze zur Kirchengeschichte* I, 31, n. 2 and p. 156, and E. Vogelsang, *Die Anfänge von Luther Christologie,* Leipzig 1929, 70. On the other hand, S. Ozment has taken the problem far more seriously in his *Homo Spiritualis,* 159–83, see esp. 159: 'the issue of a highly refined Pelagian facere quod in se est and meritum de congruo is something more than a strawman.'

[104] Cf. *WA* 4, 446.31–4, gloss on Ps. 143(144).2, as well as 520.30f., gloss on Ps. 118(119).50.

[105] For Staupitz see D. C. Steinmetz, *Misericordia Dei. The theology of Johannes von Staupitz in its late medieval setting,* Leiden 1968, 93–7.

[106] See *WA* 4, 262.8–17 and R. Hermann, *Luthers These 'Gerecht und Sünder zugleich',* Gütersloh 1930, 240 and n. 4.

[107] See *WA* 4, 262.2f.; see also the following notes.

[108] *WA* 4, 350.13f.: 'pepigit nobiscum fedus, ut daret nobis petentibus gratis ac mendicantibus'; cf. 256.16–25

(*clamare*).[109] In other words, the actions of the believer are his sighs (*gemitus*), that is, the sighs of one who knows he can find salvation only outside himself (*extra se*), in Christ.[110] The humility encouraged by the covenant, therefore, is not some variety of virtue, but rather a recognition of our indigence and our fundamental instability.

5. The great shift from *sola gratia* (by grace alone) to *sola fide* (by faith alone) occurred largely in the form of a debate with the medieval idea of the covenant; it was part of the development of Luther's own covenant theology. Luther accepted as a consequence of this change the possibility that his work might be misunderstood as Pelagian. God can be the God of the covenant in Christ only for the meek and for beggars. This is not merely the view of the so-called pre-Reformation Luther. Even at the end of the second lectures on the Psalms (1520–21), he was able to say – rather boldly – that 'Christ did not become a bridegroom merely on account of his incarnation, but rather because his Church approved of the covenant [*pactum*] in faith ... For agreement is the foundation of marriage; before that, man is more a suitor [*procus*] than a bridegroom.'[111] Written in 1530, Luther's interpretation of the Psalm 111 shows that the preceding statement was not meant in a Pelagian manner at all. Clearly analogous to the medieval doctrine of the efficacy of the sacraments *ex opere operato*, Luther writes:

> Praise God ..., who founded his merciful covenant of forgiveness of sins not on our merits but on his Word, and who commanded and still commands that it stand firm forever; not topple when we sin; and not rise up again when we are pious, but it stands there on its own by God's command, so that we may approach it at any time and always find forgiveness of sins.[112]

Who are those who can approach the covenant so full of hope and 'find forgiveness of sins'? The beggars! According to Luther's actual words at

---

[109] Cf. Ozment, *Homo Spiritualis*, 176–8.

[110] Cf. my article 'Simul Gemitus et Raptus' (see n. 61), 150ff.

[111] *WA* 5, 550.11–15.

[112] 'Gott [ist] zu loben ..., Der seinen gnadenreichen bund der vergebunge der sunden nicht auff unser verdienst sondern auff sein wort gegründet hat und geboten und noch gebeut, das er sol stehen fest und ewiglich, nicht umbfallen, wenn wir sundigen, auch nicht auffstehen, wenn wir frum sind, Sondern da stehet er fur sich selbs auff Gottes befelh, das wir alle augenblick mügen zu jhm gehen vnd jmer vergebung der sunden finden' (*WA* 31I, 423.34–424.4).

the end of the first lectures on the Psalms, the beggars can see themselves even in faith as 'shithouses, cloaca, which . . . is true'.[113] Some will merely be shocked by this; some will seek to clear away myths by resorting to psychoanalysis; others see in such statements merely the remnants of medieval theology, or even try to understand them as evidence for a 'pre-Reformation Luther'. All overlook a fascinating connection which we have only just begun to discover and research:[114] the connection between covenant and grace, between freedom within the covenant and poverty in Luther's testament: We are beggars. That is the truth.

Permit me to end this inaugural lecture in accordance with an academic tradition from the Netherlands with a few personal words first to my predecessor and then to the Tübingen students, the audience and faculty. I am conscious that I am heir to a legacy that has been cultivated and developed by you, Mr. Rückert, for three and a half decades. That is not always the case when an academic chair is newly occupied, either because there is nothing left as a legacy, or because the successor wants to demonstrate his independence by

---

[113] '[L]atrina et cloaca, quod . . . verum est' (*WA* 4,448.33).

[114] Any approach to the tasks that remain to be done in this field ought to address the following points:

1. Even though the concept of *pactum* tended after the lectures on Romans to be absorbed into the terms *promissio* and *evangelium*, it still designates the objective and dependable context of faith, and therefore also the boundary of Luther's thesis 'If you believe, then you have it' ('Glaubst du, so hast du').

2. Whereas the *pactum dei* is the basis for *merita de condigno* in Scholasticism, for the Luther of the *Dictata super Psalterium* it refers to the coming of Christ in the flesh, in the spirit and in glory. This understanding not only eliminates the *merita de condigno*, it also dispenses with the medieval distinction between *merita de congruo* and *merita de condigno*, between *gratia* (salvific grace) and *gloria* (overpowering glory), justification, sanctification and salvation. One who is *iustus* (justified) is also *salvus* (saved) already – which in principle provides the believer with certainty of salvation.

3. The covenant based on the coming of Christ as an event that embraces the entire process of salvation therefore is not a pact concluded between God and the elect before the beginning of history, as Gregory of Rimini implicitly and Johannes von Staupitz explicitly interpreted Augustine. However, this does not mean that there is a multiplicity of temporary pacts or *foedera*, as in later reformed federal theology, which follow one another over the course of Christian history. Rather, the covenant is unique and eternal (*WA* 3, 491.10f.) and it consists in the advent of Christ who brings human beggars both justification and salvation – whereby the gospel is precisely in this way the 'power of God unto salvation' (Rom. 1.16) that brings together the past (his coming in the flesh) and the future (his coming in glory) in the present tense (and tension) of faith.

rejecting the legacy. I hope that in the coming years, you will be pleased as an observer, advisor and friend that there is a certain continuity – despite all our apparent differences – of goals and of commitment to the same ends: Incipientes vos publice salutamus!

Ladies and gentlemen, my dear doctor–father, Professor Maarten van Rhijn, expressed the desire at the end of his inaugural lecture at Utrecht, some forty years ago, that his contact with students should not be comparable to administering eye drops from the twentieth floor of a skyscraper. It is clear to me that my peculiar relationship to the German language may create yet another kind of distance, since it involves more than just differences in accentuation. On the other hand, this shows all the more clearly that you will find in me a teacher who is himself *in statu discendi,* who is still learning and wishes to carry out his duties in such a way as to allow you to participate in his own search for truth.

Since we owe to the Reformation the new understanding of divine justice that we have achieved, I would like to hand on to you the old prayer:

Sol iustitiae, illustra nos.

Chapter 6

WITTENBERG'S WAR ON TWO FRONTS: WHAT HAPPENED IN 1518 AND WHY

1. Martin Luther's Manifesto: From Provincial University to the Church Universal

Luther's theses concerning indulgences had already been condemned, but there had not yet been any substantial response to them. True, two series of theses published in 1518 were intended to 'unmask the heretic', but they did not answer Luther: Wimpina's theses appeared in January, and those of Tetzel – the Dominican preacher who had stirred so many hearts and pens with his sermons on indulgences – in late April/May. The debate soon left the original topic behind, and finally concentrated so exclusively on the central issues of ecclesiology and the doctrine of salvation that the question of indulgences played a secondary role in Eck's 404 articles, presented at the Diet of Augsburg in 1530.[1]

The Council of Trent did in fact deplore the abuses and defects in the system of indulgences – but this issue was accorded star billing neither at Trent nor in the relevant sessions at the Second Vatican Council. In any case, the functionaries in charge of indulgences had been warned against abuses in the instructions given them in 1515 and in the regulations concerning indulgences of 1516. Accordingly, the Tridentine position cannot be understood merely as a Counter-Reformation response in the spirit of the renovation of the Catholic Church.

On the one hand, Luther's 95 Theses are in danger of being eclipsed by the continuing debate over when and whether the theses were posted.[2] On the other hand, the theses are often seen merely as

[1] On the main theological themes of Eck's writings associated with the Imperial Diet of Augsburg, see Klaus Rischar, *Johann Eck auf dem Reichstag zu Augsburg 1530*, Münster 1968.

[2] Erwin Iserloh has collected his arguments against the posting of the 95 Theses in a book entitled *Luther zwischen Reform und Reformation. Der Thesenanschlag fand nicht statt*, Münster 1966, 65–80; likewise see Klemens Honselmann, *Urfassung und Drucke der*

the initial impetus, in terms of ecclesiastical politics, that got Luther's program under way – that is, brought it to the attention of the authorities in Rome. Seen from the perspective of theological history, however, the Reformation theology of the theses was cloaked in so medieval a mantle that it took on clear and recognizable features only in response to the challenges posed by later critics. Luther's Reformation teachings on the Church and salvation were indeed contained in the 95 Theses, no matter how careful and seemingly respectful their formulation. In a short article that nonetheless contains a wealth of information, Ernst Kähler has conducted a precise inquiry into the goals of Luther's theses, probably because the goals have received inadequate attention in contemporary scholarship. Some scholars refer to Luther's own comment that the theses were intended to pose only a few questions for debate in a small circle of learned colleagues,[3] while others

---

Ablaßthesen Martin Luthers und ihre Veröffentlichung, Paderborn 1966. Heinrich Bornkamm provides a balanced overview of the various positions in 'Thesen und Thesenanschlag Luthers', in: *Geist und Geschichte der Reformation, Festgabe Hans Rückert*, ed. Heinz Liebig and Klaus Scholder, Berlin 1966, 179–218. Hans Volz refutes Honselmann's arguments and, indirectly, the premises of Iserloh's work: 'Die Urfassung von Luthers 95 Thesen', *ZKG* 78 (1967), 67–93. See Honselmann's response in *ZKG* 79 (1968), 68–76; also Volz's rebuttal, ibid., 206f, and Volz, 'Um Martin Luthers Thesenanschlag', in *Luther* 38 (1967), 125–38. For subsequent developments in scholarship see Oberman, *Werden und Wertung der Reformation*, Tübingen 1979², 190–2, n. 89.

[3] Cf. Erwin Iserloh, *Luthers Thesenanschlag, Tatsache oder Legende* Wiesbaden 1962, 28, 51. Although the relevant texts have for the most part been collected and used in the course of the debate set off by Iserloh's book, I would like to direct the reader's attention to a passage in Eck's 'Obeliscus' XXVI that has received scant attention. Iserloh refers only to Luther's answer to this passage. Eck charges that Luther made the theses known to more than just the competent authorities (bishops and theologians): 'Quod si Lutherus pio afficiebatur amore, non coram pusillis, qui alioqui facilius scandalisantur, sed coram his quorum interest, talia proponere debuerat, Et forte quis scit, si Deus incrementum dedisset et profectum?' (*WA* 1, 311.3–6). On 24 March 1518, Luther mentions Eck's attack for the first time; Otto Clemen feels that it might have been known to him even before this date. *WAB* 1, 153 n. 9. However, so much had occurred before that time – from the invitation to Eck extended by Bishop von Eyb to when Luther received the 'Annotationes' – that Luther must have published his theses much earlier. There might not have been enough time for Eck to have used the Latin-German edition of Nuremberg (January 1518? See *WA* 1, 230). Moreover, concerning the posting of Luther's theses, it is important to keep in mind that it seems to have been quite common at Wittenberg to post theses publicly. For instance, when Karlstadt sent his 151 theses to Spalatin (18 April 1517), he explicitly states, in the accompanying letter, that he had posted these *conclusiones* publicly two days earlier: 'Quas nuper Dominica Misericordia Domini [= 26 April] dieque sancta ostensionis venerabilium reliquiarum conclusiones centum quinquaginta duas [sic] publice affici . . .' (Hermann Barge, *Andreas Bodenstein von Karlstadt*, I: *Karlstadt und die Anfänge der Reformation*, Leipzig 1905 [Nieuwkoop 1968], excursus I, 463).

doubt that the fateful encounter with Cardinal Cajetan at Augsburg (October 12–14, or rather 13–15, 1518) really concerned indulgences,[4] since they were discussed only as an appendix to the Leipzig Disputation with Eck (27 June to 15 July, 1519).[5] Kähler, however, after a recapitulation of the final theses (92–95), comes to this conclusion: 'These are neither theses for a formal disputation, nor guidelines for preaching, but the powerful climax and conclusion of a general proclamation.'[6] He refers above all to theses 42 through 51, in which Luther repeated nine times the programmatic call: 'Christians are to be taught . . .' (*Docendi sunt christiani . . .*).

It is an out-and-out manifesto. From the perspective of rhetoric alone, Luther's performance is pitched for a new and much larger stage than that of the Wittenberg lecture hall. Now he is conscious of an educational responsibility that extends out and over the walls of the university into the Church as the 'congregation of the faithful' (*congregatio fidelium*). There existed at Wittenberg, according to the regulations of the (Wittenberg) faculty of arts (25 November 1508), a corps of so-called 'reformers' of the university[7] – a tradition that in

---

[4] According to Gerhard Hennig, *Cajetan und Luther. Ein historischer Beitrag zur Begegnung von Thomismus und Reformation,* Stuttgart 1966, 71, n. 103, in opposition to Heinrich Bornkamm's position in the article 'Luther, Leben und Schriften' in *RGG³* IV, 484.

[5] Otto Seitz, *Der authentische Text der Leipziger Disputation (1519),* Berlin 1903, 171–82. Although the text reconstructed by Seitz is a considerable improvement on the Weimar edition text (*WA* 2, 254–383) and in addition includes Eck's debate with Karlstadt, a modern edition of Karlstadt's portion with an apparatus containing the history of the text is still needed urgently. Unfortunately, *WA* 59 has not taken up the disputation with Karlstadt.

[6] 'Das sind keine Disputationsthesen, es sind auch kein Predigtsätze, sondern das ist der kraftvolle Höhepunkt und Abschluß eines Aufrufs.' ('Die 95 Thesen. Inhalt und Bedeutung', in: *Luther* 38 (1967), 114–24; 123).

[7] W. Friedensburg, *Urkundenbuch der Universität Wittenberg* I, Magdeburg 1926, 56: 'Quilibet legat a principio foras usque in finem, voce clara et intellegibili legat imprimis textum plane . . . dein textum continuet et dividat. magistri deputentur ad lecciones ordinarias per reformatores.' On the reformation of the *series lectionum,* see Luther's letter of 11 March, 1518 to Spalatin. Here Luther describes his discussion with Karlstadt 'de lectionibus studii nostri initiandis vel instituendis' (*WAB* 1, 153.5) and says that the enclosed plan offers a 'vera occasio omnium universitatum reformandarum' (*WAB* 1, 153.11f). The detailed proposal of 23 February, 1519, directed to the Prince-Elector was signed by Luther and Karlstadt, among others (*WAB* 1, 350.43f.).

The 'reformers of the University' were responsible not only for implementing university reform, but also for administrative duties. For example, Valentin Polich, brother of the influential Martin Polich von Mellerstadt (+1513), noted in February of 1517 'vor den Reformatoren der Universität 186 Gulden und 13 Groschen für verkaufte Tartarete [a

1517 produced the great series of theses against scholastic theology published by Andreas Karlstadt (26 April) and Martin Luther (4 September) who together pursued the reformation of theology in both form and content. Luther, however, appears in his theses of 31 October (or 1 November) for the first time as a reformer of the *Church*, who is no longer addressing just his colleagues and students, but a much broader circle of educated laymen. Right from the very beginning at Wittenberg – and not only at Augsburg or Leipzig – Luther's challenge, which initially concerned indulgences, had two polemical 'spear-heads'. These were intended to distinguish between false 'certainty of salvation' (*securitas*) and true atonement (*satisfactio*) as well as their ecclesiastical – that is to say papal – legitimation.

In the following pages, I would like first to examine briefly the prelude to the *Acta Augustana* – Luther's dispute with Cajetan's older fellow-Dominican, Sylvester Prierias. This episode is important mainly because Luther prepared himself theologically and psychologically in the course of this dispute for the discussion at Augsburg.[8] The debate with Prierias furnishes the required historical context, without which their subsequent meeting cannot be understood.[9] Questions of

Scotistic textbook] . . .' (Gustav Bauch, 'Wittenberg und die Scholastik', in: *Neues Archiv für sächsische Geschichte und Altertumskunde* 18 (1897), 285–339; 308). Bauch sees the role of the reformers in the battle between scholasticism and humanism and in general in the life of the University of Wittenberg from 1508 on as a prelude to the attack on scholastic theology mounted in 1517 (ibid., esp. 326, 328f.).

Although the Wittenberg theses, especially the series of theses of 1517, ought to be seen as a part of the history of the university itself, the theses in question were not necessarily meant for Wittenberg alone. Just as Karlstadt requests help from the Prince-Elector in his letter to Spalatin (see n. 3) to 'certos ex sua provincia Saxonia ad futurum certamen Theologicum destinare', so Luther sought contact with colleagues at Erfurt and Nuremberg concerning his September theses (against scholasticism); he declared himself to be 'paratissimum venire et publice seu in collegio seu in monasterio de iis disputare, ut non putent me in angulum ista velle susurrare, si tamen nostra universitas tam vilis est, ut angulus esse possit videri' (Letter of 4 September, 1517, to Johann Lang, *WAB* 1, 103.13–15. Concerning only the *praecepta* (the sermons on the Ten Commandments; cf. *WAB* 1, 104, n. 7), not the 'theses', Luther writes: 'Praecepta ideo tibi utraque lingua misis, ut, si quando volueris ad populum de iis praedicare (sic enim ego illa docui, ut mihi videor, ad evangelicum morum), haberes' (ibid., 103.15–104.18).

[8] Luther received Prierias' 'Dialogus' along with the summons to Rome on or before 7 August; his answer was printed by 31 August (*WA* 1, 645f.). On 8 August, Luther wrote to Spalatin : 'Dialogo Silvestrino vere sylvestro et penitus inculto iam respondeo, quod totum mox habebis, ut paratum fuerit' (*WAB* 1, 188.21f.; cf. 192.31f.).

[9] Hennig (see n. 4) does not deal with Prierias, nor does he accord a detailed treatment to what I think is the highly important dispute between Cajetan and Jacques Almain

ecclesiastical obedience were first discussed at this meeting, and consequently, so were principles of ecclesiology. As a second step, I would like to liberate not only Luther's theses, but his entire performance from an artificial isolation that is constantly being recreated, and place the man and his theses squarely within the circle that was starting to appear at Wittenberg. Whereas Luther himself often speaks of his friends who 'exhort' him at critical moments, 'admonish' and 'counsel' him, and 'convince' him,[10] these figures have too frequently been reduced in Luther scholarship to the role of a silent backdrop, useful only to define and provide contrast for the artificially sharp outline of 'Luther, the pioneer'. From the end of 1516, at the very latest, until after the Leipzig Disputation, there was at Wittenberg an intimate circle of theologians – including Luther as well as Andreas Bodenstein von Karlstadt. Not only in his attack on scholastic theology (1517), but also in the debate with John Eck – during Luther's absence and without his agreement – Karlstadt beat Luther to the punch and delivered the first blows.

I will, therefore, examine the dispute between Eck and Karlstadt more closely. In the course of this chapter, I will pay close attention to the fact that this dispute is far more concerned with the issue of the true Christian existence than that of ecclesiastical obedience or discipline. The reason for this is not simply that Eck – even according to his own judgement – had proven himself, by the publication of his *Chrysopassus Praedestinationis* in 1514, to be an outstanding expert in the scholastic discussion of predestination. The decisive reason is rather that Eck, in his private annotations for the Bishop of Eichstätt,

---

(+1515). The triangular relationship between Prierias, Cajetan and the Parisian conciliarist, that is, the splits within the Roman curia and the tension between Rome and Paris (as they were expressed in the *conciliabulum* of Pisa), must have made it easier for Luther to appeal from Cajetan to the Pope, and even to hope for quite some time after the Leipzig Disputation for a positive or at least a neutral *Gutachten* from Paris. See also Francis Oakley, 'Almain and Major. Conciliar theory on the eve of the Reformation', in: *American Historical Review* 70 (1965), 673–90; 689. Cf. Almain's writings: *Quaestio resumptiva de dominio naturali, civili et ecclesiastico* (1512) and esp. *Tractatus de auctoritate ecclesiae et conciliorum generalium adversus Thomam de Vio* (1512), both in *Johannis Gersonii Opera omnia*, ed. du Pin, II, Antwerp 1706, col. 961–76 and 976–1012.

[10] On 24 March 1518, Luther writes, for instance, to Sylvius Egranus in Zwickau that he would be ready 'absorbere patientia' Eck's 'Obelisci', but, he adds, 'amici coegerunt, illi ut responderem, sed privata manu' (*WAB* 1,158.24f.). Any attempt to 'identify' these *amici* can be nothing more than conjecture. However, the addition *sed privata manu* seems to suit Spalatin rather better than Karlstadt.

Gabriel von Eyb (which Eck referred to as 'Obelisci'[11]), does not insist as strongly as Prierias and Cajetan on the question of ecclesiastical primacy.[12] Eck starts from a completely different position than that of the Thomistic theologians of the papal curia. These deliberations now lead us back to Eck's *Chrysopassus,* which must be read with a completely new set of 'lenses': those in use up to now have made the *Chrysopassus* appear to be nothing more than a prerequisite for the exchange of theses with Karlstadt.[13]

2. Sylvester Prierias: Roman Papalism

One of Luther's earliest opponents, Sylvester Prierias OP (1456–1523)[14] perceived quite clearly the ecclesiological significance of the 95 Theses. He does not deserve the bad reputation that he has today in both Catholic and Protestant camps. His arguments are the most sincere of contemporary attempts to answer Luther. He attempted to refute Luther not merely by condemning him, but with well thought-out arguments, many of which are not made hopelessly outdated – important for today's denominational situation – by the subsequent development of Catholic dogma, as are the arguments advanced by Wimpina, Tetzel and Eck. Prierias at times selects with great sensitivity the most decisive points: those which have lost none of their power to divide the Church, even after Vatican II.

---

[11] '[P]auca adnotabimus et (ut dici solet) Obelisco signabimus' (*WA* 1, 282.24). The introduction to the *Asterisci Lutheri adversus Obeliscos Eckii* in *WA* 1, 278 does not take seriously enough the private character of Eck's annotations.

[12] He is hesitant in *WA* 1, 296.36f.; 301.1 and 302.11–16 (where he makes the charge that wounds Luther so deeply: '[Q]uod nihil aliud est quam Bohemicum virus effundere'; cf. also 305.6f.); more characteristic of Eck is *WA* 1, 305.18: 'At irreverentia in eis ponderanda est summi Pontificus sanctitati'; continuing in 307.35f.; cf. also 312.6–8. However, at 311.5f. (see n. 3) he does not assume that Luther had made a deliberate attack on the Pope, but rather a viable suggestion for reform: had Luther not published (posted?) his theses, but directed them only to the competent authorities, 'Et forte quis scit, si Deus incrementum dedisset et profectum?' But he is cautious toward the end when he says at 312.14: 'Propositio sonat [!] falsa et capitis Ecclesiastici derogativa.'

[13] See Joseph Greving, *Johann Eck als junger Gelehrter. Eine literatur- und dogmengeschichtliche Untersuchung über seinen Chrysopassus praedestinationis aus dem Jahre 1514,* Münster 1906. Walter L. Moore's *Between Mani and Pelagius. Predestination and Justification in the early writings of John Eck,* Diss. Harvard University, Cambridge MA, 1967 is of much more use.

[14] The following characterization of Prierias' *Dialogus* is a revised version of my short note 'Roms erste Antwort auf Luthers 95 These', in: *Orientierungen* 31 (1967), 231–3.

Prierias' many-layered *De potestate papae dialogus* (not: de indulgentiarum virtute!) was composed at the beginning of January, 1518, probably on the basis of a copy of the 95 Theses that the Archbishop of Mainz had prepared and sent to Rome. Although he was less suited, as a Dominican, to render judgement against his fellow-Dominican Tetzel in the Luther affair, Prierias was, on account of his office as papal chief inquisitor and his thorough preparation – he discussed the question of indulgences exhaustively in the so-called *Summa Sylvestrina* of 1514 – the expert appointed by the curia.

Unlike Luther's other opponents, Prierias wrote not just negative theses, but prefaced his presentation of the discussion with 'Martinus' – who delivers his own theses, and is answered by 'Sylvester' – with prolegomena and four axioms (*fundamenta*). These axioms represent a parallel to the first four of Luther's 95 Theses, insofar as the translation and interpretation of Christ's call, 'Do penance', lays the foundation for the subsequent conclusions.[15] However, Prierias replaces Luther's exegetical foundation with an ecclesiological one as a means of distinguishing truth from heresy in the course of the dispute.

In the first *fundamentum,* Prierias represents the structure of the Church as two concentric circles. The center of the world is the Church of Rome; the center of the Church is the Pope.[16] Sure of his goal and consistent in his argument, he adds a second *'fundamentum',*[17]

---

[15] However, closer inspection reveals that in both cases, only the first statement can be called 'axiomatic' in the true sense of the word. It seems to me that Erasmus alludes to Prierias; see *Opus Epistolarum,* ed. P. S. Allen and H. M. Allen, III, Oxford 1913, 531.104–6 (Antwerp, 14 April 1519, to Prince-Elector Frederick): 'Nunc quidam noua comminiscuntur fundamenta, sic enim vocant, hoc est nouas leges condunt, per quas doceant haereticum esse quicquid non placet.'

[16] 'Fundamentum primum est: Ecclesia universalis essentialiter est convocatio in divinum cultum omnium credentium in Christum. Ecclesia vero universalis virtualiter est ecclesia Romana, ecclesiarum omnium caput, et Pontifex maximus. Ecclesia Romana repraesentative est collegium Cardinalium, virtualiter autem est Pontifex summus, qui est Ecclesia caput, aliter tamen, quam Christus' (*D. Martini Lutheri opera Latina varii argumenti* I (= *EA* var. arg. I), Frankfurt and Erlangen 1865, 346). Translation: 'First fundament: The universal church is in essence the assembly of all believers in Christ for divine worship. This church however is according to its power and might the Roman Church, the head of all churches, and the Pope. The Roman Church is represented by the College of Cardinals, but according to its power and might, by the Pope, who is the head of the Church, although in a different way than Christ.'

[17] 'Fundamentum secundum: Sicut ecclesia universalis non potest errare determinando de fide aut moribus, ita et verum concilium, faciens quod in se est (ut intellegat veritatem) errare non potest, quod intellego incluso capite, aut tandem ac finaliter, licet forte prima

claiming that the universal Church, and consequently a true Council, can never err; he expressly includes the Pope as the head of councils. But since the Pope is the center of the universal Church, it is not surprising that infallibility is ascribed to him not only as the leader of councils, but also in his office as the head of the Church.[18] Finally, the last two *fundamenta* state that in the Church of Rome – and therefore in the Pope – the believer experiences the truth of Scripture, of doctrine and of tradition as authoritative.[19] Without repeating the details of Prierias' further discussion, I would like to note four main points:

---

facie fallatur, quousque durat motus inquirendae veritatis, imo etiam aliquando erravit, licet tandem per spiritum Sanctum intellexerit veritatem, et similiter nec ecclesia Romana, nec pontifex summus determinans ea ratione, qua Pontifex, id est, ex officio suo pronuncians, et faciens quod in se est, ut intellegat veritatem' (ibid. 347). Translation: 'Second fundament: Just as the universal church cannot err when it decides concerning faith or morals, so a true Council, when it does its best to perceive the truth cannot err, at least not in the final result – and this I understand to include the head of the church. For even a Council can be deceived at the beginning, so long as it is still searching for the truth; indeed a Council has sometimes erred, although it finally recognizes the truth with the aid of the Holy Spirit. Correspondingly, the Roman Church cannot err, nor can the Pope when he makes decisions in his capacity as Pope, that is, when he makes them officially and does his best to perceive the truth.'

[18] There is a significant parallel not only in the words, but also in the intentions of a large minority of the conciliar fathers to the church constitution 'Lumen Gentium' of the Second Vatican Council. Given the concept *nota praevia*, Prierias could have agreed entirely with this constitution. This risky jump from the sixteenth to the twentieth century is justified because it shows that compared to later developments in Catholic ecclesiology, Luther found in Germany and Italy not only – as is constantly claimed – interlocutors who were seriously contaminated by 'late medieval symptoms of decay' and who therefore distorted 'true' Catholicism. On this see Hennig (see n. 4), 10f., who has hit the nail on the head.

[19] 'Fundamentum tertium: Quicunque non innititur doctrinae Romanae ecclesiae, ac Romani Pontificis, tanquam regulae fidei infallibili, a qua etiam sacra Scriptura robur trahit et autoritatem, haereticus est.

'Fundamentum quartum: Ecclesia Romana sicut verbo ita et facto potest circa fidem et mores aliquid decernere. Nec in hoc differentia ulla est, praeter id quod verba sunt accomodatiora quam facta. Unde hac ratione consuetudo vim legis obtinet, quia voluntas principis factis permissive aut effective exprimitur.

'Et consequenter, quemadmodum haereticus est male sentiens circa scripturarum veritatem, ita et male sentiens circa doctrinam et facta ecclesiae in spectantibus ad fidem et mores haereticus est.

'Corollarium [and transition to the real topic]: Qui circa indulgentias dicit, ecclesiam Romanam non posse facere id quod de facto facit, haereticus est' (*EA* var. arg. I, 347).

'Third fundament: Whoever does not hold fast to the teachings of the Roman Church and of the Pope as the infallible rule of faith, from which even Holy Scripture draws its strength and authority, is a heretic.

1. It is not easy to determine exactly where Prierias' assertions are to be placed on the various levels of authoritative ecclesiastical doctrinal statements. But since the *Dialogus* was included in the first summons to Luther, it is not unreasonable to describe it as a sort of court record of the first part of proceedings against Luther – as they would have gone, if Luther had been forced to defend himself at Rome in person.

2. Prierias took a certain amount of care to find support for his counter-theses. He argued with a will, and often well; he chose to support his arguments more often from the works of Saint Thomas than from Scripture, but he certainly was not content with mere denials. However, he did not enter into a disputation with Luther as a 'fellow doctor of Holy Scripture', which was what Luther had expressly asked for in the 95 Theses.[20] In his prolegomena, Prierias addressed Luther from the very beginning as a heretic. He treats Luther accordingly in the response that follows.

3. Even the most recent Luther scholars – and not only the Catholics – accuse Luther of gross vulgarity. But it should be remembered that it was precisely here, on the path toward the final schism, that Prierias' innumerable patronizing remarks rise (or sink) again and again to the level of deliberate and crass insults. Prierias' comments reflect in part an Italian's feeling of superiority toward a German, in part the cocksure arrogance of an old Roman university professor in the face of a greenhorn from provincial Wittenberg. We cannot understand this style of argument without noting that according to

---

'Fourth fundament: The Roman Church can decide matters of faith and morals both by word and by deed. And there is no difference between the two, except that words are better suited than deeds. In this sense, custom also receives the force of law, because the will of a prince expresses itself in deeds that he allows or does. And just as he is a heretic who thinks wrongly about the truth of the Scriptures, so he is a heretic who thinks wrongly about the teachings and the deeds of the Church, so far as these pertain to faith and morals.

'Conclusion: Whoever says in relation to indulgences that the Roman Church cannot do what it in fact does, is a heretic.'

[20] Outwardly, Prierias is willing to enter into a real dialogue with Luther: 'non aliter imprimis tecum congredi velim, quam tuarum falsarum positionum opposita sustinendo et defensando, ut quibus innitaris fundamentis edoceas' (*EA* var. arg. I, 346). However, the dedicatory epistle to Pope Leo X shows that Prierias is not very sympathetic: 'Martino nescio cui Luther, qui in veritatem ipsam et sanctam hanc sedem cervicem elevatam ostentat, me scutum opponerem pro Sedis huius proque veritatis honore ac maiestate . . .' (ibid. 345).

canon law, a much greater reparation (*restitutio*) was prescribed for
the theft of someone's good reputation (*fama*, or rather *honor*) than
for the theft of 'temporal goods'. Since Luther, according to Prierias,
has infringed upon the *honor* of the Pope and the Church, he is paid
back in the *Dialogus* in the same coin. The irritability and the harsh
tone on the one hand, and – as a polar opposite – the flattering mode
of address and strings of reverent epithets on the other, both of which
were characteristic of sixteenth century reformers, humanists and
counter-reformers, make little sense to us unless we see them against
this legal background.[21]

4. In the prolegomena, Prierias does not begin with a point-by-point
refutation of Luther's theses. Instead of attacking Luther's critique of
indulgences and penance and the doctrine of justification behind this
critique, Prierias first restates the principles of ecclesiology by
reaffirming the authority and infallibility of the Church and the Pope
– without, however, referring to any sort of standard content, which
is the decisive characteristic of such so-called *fundamenta*. It is not the
Eck of the Leipzig Disputation who first forces Luther to reconsider
the ecclesiological components of his call for a reformation of the
Church, but Prierias. But Luther was not unprepared, because he had
already begun, in his first lectures on the Psalms (1513–15), to
understand the relationship between the Church and justification in
a new way.[22] On the basis of this new understanding, Luther would
immediately have seen that what Prierias had to say on the topic was

---

[21] Cf. Johannes Altenstaig, *Vocabularius Theologiae* (with a dedication to Johann von
Staupitz), Hagenau 1517, fol. 85[r-v]. Gabriel Biel, *Collectorium* in IV Sent. dist. 15 q.16 art.
1 nota 2B; Gabrielis Biel *Collectorium circa quattuor libros Sentantiarum*, ed. W. Werbeck,
U. Hofmann, Tübingen 1973–84; *Collectorium* IV, 2,334.B1–335.B2. In the *Canonis
Misse expositio*, lectio 74 O, ed. H. A. Oberman and W. J. Courtenay, Wiesbaden 1966,
231, Biel ranks *fama* after *bonae animae* and *bonae corporis*, in third place; however:
'praeferenda est [fama] temporalibus divitiis . . .' As in the *Collectorium*, he refers to the
variant opinion, according to which *fama* is ranked above the *bonae corporis*, right below
the *bonae animae*: 'Verum Richardus et Nicholas de lyra videntur famam preferre corpori'
(ibid.; Richardus de Mediavilla, IV Sent. dist. 19 art. 3 q. 1; Lyra on Matthew 18.15).
Concerning *honor* see also Altenstaig, fol. 103[ra]: 'Et honor est maximum bonorum
exteriorum . . .' Luther writes Eck on 19 May, 1518: 'ecce misi ad te asteriscos contra tous
obeliscos . . . in quibus sane ita parco honori tuo, quod nolui illos edere, sed privatim ad te
dirigere, ne redderem tibi malum, quod mihi fecist' (*WAB* 1, 178.18–21).

[22] Joseph Vercruysse, *Fidelis Populus*, Wiesbaden 1968, has gathered and clearly
organized the necessary material. Comparisons with the medieval tradition are now needed
to uncover specific continuities and discontinuities.

not the true catholic doctrine of the Church, because it was not based on Scripture.

To Prierias, the Church or rather the Pope was infallible because it or he was inspired by the Holy Spirit – as long as a council or a pope did its/his best (*faciens quod in se est*). Since early scholasticism, however, this principle was more at home in the doctrine of justification than in ecclesiology. It occupied the central place in teachings on justification in the formulation 'God does not deny grace to those who do their best' (*Facientibus quod in se est Deus non denegat gratiam*).[23] On the one hand, the theologian can argue – in accordance with Augustine – that the sinner is hopelessly lost without grace; on the other, that our duty to do our best is not cancelled by the doctrine of grace. By the summer of 1516 at the latest, Luther attacked this position, which makes the reception of grace dependent on a condition, as neopelagianism.

Luther's understanding of the Church as the hidden people of God led by the Holy Spirit and fed (*pascere!*) by the priests and heads of the Church with God's Word is so far from Prierias' position that it is practically antithetical. As such, Prierias' position served to confirm Luther's view that justification by faith alone is closely linked to the Church that stands beneath the Cross. Luther became more and more certain that the Pope, in his constant efforts to 'do his best' in order to defend the Gospel, relied less on the power of the Gospel than on his own claim to infallibility – thereby silencing the voice of Christ in the Church, rather than allowing it to ring out and be heard.

This confrontation with so papal, indeed so papalistic an ecclesiology – together with the subliminal German suspicion of Italian financial and power politics – can only have confirmed Luther's feeling, during the sixty days that were left before his perilous journey to Augsburg, that Cajetan would be more interested in a formal retraction than an explanation of the issues at stake. Thus, Augsburg was much less a dramatic climax than some colorful descriptions would lead us to believe. Luther's meeting with the

[23] Concerning *facere quod in se est* in Prierias' doctrine of justification, see my article 'Das tridentinische Rechtfertigungsdekret im Lichte der spätmittelalterlichen Theologie', in: *ZThK* 61 (1964), 251–82; 260f.; expanded in *Concilium Tridentinum,* ed. R. Bäumer, Darmstadt 1979, 301–40; 311f.

cardinal cannot have been a sudden disappointment of real hopes for a settlement. Rather, this meeting confirmed what Luther must already have known about Prierias' position.[24]

For Prierias, the reliability of papal doctrinal decisions was based on a theologoumenon (a non-dogmatic doctrinal position) that Luther had long ago unmasked as the central hereditary defect afflicting the scholastic doctrine of justification (the principle of 'doing one's best'). Prierias and Cajetan think along the same lines, both politically and ecclesiastically, in terms of Boniface VIII's bull *Unam Sanctam* (1302) with its triumphalist ecclesiology and its reference to 1 Corinthians 2.15: 'The spiritual man makes judgments about all things, but he himself is not subject to any man's judgment.'[25] Before turning to Eck and the second front on which the

[24] Cf. Luther's letter written on the eve of his departure for Augsburg: 'Cras versus Augustam ibo . . . concurrunt praedicatores [Tetzel, Cajetan and, in my opinion, Prierias], Velut Lupi ad agnum deuorandum. Viuat Christus, Moriatur Martinus et omnis peccator, sicut Scriptum est [Ps. 103.35f.], pereant peccatores et iniqui de terra ita, vt non sint. Exaltetur autem deus salutis meae [Ps. 17.47f.]. Valete bene et perseuerate Scientes, quoniam necesse est vel ab hominibus vel a deo reprobari, Sed est deus "mendax" verax, homo autem mendax [Rom. 3.4]' (Nuremberg, 4 October, 1518, *WAB* 12, 14.13–19).

[25] Denzinger, *Enchiridion symbolorum,* 873 (469). Prierias' relationship to the bull *Unam sanctam* in his *Opera omnia* deserves further research. I understand the clause 'prout iura decernunt' toward the end of the *Dialogus* in which Prierias answers Luther's 90th thesis not as a qualification, but as a specific reference to the political authority of the Pope: 'Ecclesia Romana, quae in Romano pontifice virtualiter inclusa est, temporalis et spiritualis potestatis summa in papa apicem tenet, et saeculari brachio (prout iura decernunt) potest eos, qui fide primo suscepta, deinde male sentiunt, compescere, nec tenetur rationibus certare ad vincendos protervientes . . .; hostes autem se irridentes et corporales et spirituales solet ecclesia ad nihilum (deo iuvante) deducere' (*EA* var. arg. I, 376f.). Luther's answer starts with this point: 'Ultimo tribuis Pontifici iterum, ut sit virtualis Ecclesia et Imperator et Pontifex, potens et brachio seculari compescere etc. Ista opinione tua stante vellem doceri, an etiam sitis homicidae? Cur ego iura non permittunt Ecclesiae ad corporalis vitae periculum poenitentiam imponere?' (*Ad dialogum Silvestri Prieratis de potestate papae responsio* (1518); *WA* 1, 686.20–3). For Prierias, see also his *Replica,* which Luther received at Leipzig on 7 January 1519, esp. *WA* 2, 53.31–6, where he sets Gerson ('de potestate Pontificis pessime sensit et scripsit') against other – curialist – *doctores* from Luther's own order. On the topic of the bull *Unam sanctam* see Luther, *Resolutio Lutheriana super propositio sua decima tertia de potestate papae* (printed 27 July 1519), *WA* 2, 219.11–225.28. At the end, Luther directs his barbs against papal authority in matters of doctrine: 'cum contra verba hominum iudicanda sint secundum verba dei, quod iudicat omnia.' Regarding Cajetan, see Hennig (see n. 4), 24–9. 'Papa . . . in nullo eventu nulloque casu nisi haeresis proprie sumptae iudicari aut deponi possit, nisi ab ipso Domino Jesu Christo' (ibid., 29).

Wittenberg theologians had to defend themselves, we ought to note that parallel to his work on the *facere quod in se est* and closely related to this work in content, Luther had for some time accorded central importance to the 'spiritual man'. In his marginal commentaries (1516) on Tauler's sermons, in debate with both Gerson's and Tauler's anthropology, Luther construes this spiritual man in such a way as to exclude all varieties of 'doing one's best': 'The spiritual man [is he] who strives [not by the height of his mental powers, not by synteresis, but] by faith; the Apostle calls this man spiritual [1 Cor. 2.14f.], and true Christians are not unlike him.'[26] Here Luther laid the anthropological foundations for the de-anthropologization of medieval soteriology. The believer is called away from himself, like Abraham from his kin; indeed, in the language of mysticism, 'torn out of himself' (*rapi*). Here we find an outline of Luther's principle 'outside ourselves' (*extra nos*), according to which the true Christian does not rely on his spiritual foundation or on his conscience in whatever sublimated form it may take. Here is the indispensable root of the Reformation principle 'Christ alone' (*solus Christus*). But Luther is originally and fundamentally a medieval Doctor of Scripture. Anyone who is willing to acknowledge this first, and not precipitously to declare him a 'modern man', will see immediately that it is impossible to follow Luther's reinterpretation of the spiritual man without linking it simultaneously to a fundamental ecclesiological statement.

---

[26] 'Homo spiritualis [is he] qui nititur [not *apice mentis*, not *syntheresi*, but] fide, Hunc Apostolus [1 Cor. 2.14f.] videtur vocare spiritualem, Et hunc attingunt Christiani veri' (*WA* 9, 103.41–104.3). The fundamental significance of Luther's new understanding of the *homo spiritualis* has been demonstrated in a convincing fashion by Steven E. Ozment, *Homo Spiritualis. A comparative study of the anthropology of Johannes Tauler, Jean Gerson and Martin Luther (1509–16) in the context of their theological thought*, Leiden 1969, esp. 197. This is connected in a systematic way to the basic view that 'Christus enim non nisi in peccatoribus habitat' (*WAB* 1, 35.29; Ozment 184). What Ozment has demonstrated concerning Luther's anthropology and doctrine of justification has a direct influence – not merely against the background of the bull *Unam sanctam* – on Luther's ecclesiology. For an early medieval equation of *homo spiritualis* with *monachus* – in contrast to *saecularis* (*PL* 174, 876) – in the area of monastic theology, see Ulrich Faust, 'Gottfried von Admont. Ein monastischer Autor des 12. Jahrhunderts', in: *Studien und Mitteilungen zur Geschichte des Benediktiner-Ordens und seiner Zweige* 75 (1964), 272–359; esp. 303ff. A study of the idea *homo spiritualis* in the Middle Ages and Reformation is a much-needed project that would bear considerable fruit.

What Innocent III said about the Pope is applied by Luther to the true Christian. What Innocent III understood as the definition of the Pope is for Luther the determining characteristic of a true Christian.

3. John Eck: Papal Conciliarism

When Luther returned to Wittenberg from his victory at Heidelberg (26 April, 1518), he found a thorny problem awaiting him. During his absence, Karlstadt had – without his knowledge and against his wishes[27] – taken on Luther's defense against Eck. By 9 May, six days before Luther's return, Karlstadt had prepared 380 theses against the Ingolstadt theologian. Karlstadt was in such a rush that twenty-six more were added during printing. On 19 May, Luther did write Eck a reproachful letter, but did not break with him altogether.[28] On 15 June, he enclosed in a letter to their mutual friend Christoph Scheurl[29] an offer of friendship to Eck – a letter which has, unfortunately, been lost. However, the gulf between Karlstadt and

[27] *WAB* 1, 183.11. Karlstadt naturally was under no obligation, as a *Doctor theologiae* in his own right, to obtain Luther's permission.

[28] 'Optionem habes, dilectionem servabo, si voles, impetum tuum laetus excipiam; neque enim (ut video) in theologia aliquid nosti praeter siliquas opinionum scholasticorum' (*WAB* 1, 178.31–3). Cf. n. 84.

[29] On 19 May 1518, Luther wrote a letter to Eck as 'inter amicos singulari' (*WAB* 1, 178.3), doubtless in the ambivalent sense of *singularitas*. Christoph Scheurl, who had criticized Eck very sharply in connection with the question of interest on 15 November 1514 (see n. 31) assured the by now well-established protector of the University of Ingolstadt on 13 September 1516, that he was not stirring things up against him ('nihil tibi adversum moliar. . .'), and would rather consider him as a friend ('me ama, id quod muto facies'); see *Christoph Scheurl's Briefbuch, ein Beitrag zur Geschichte der Reformation und ihrer Zeit*, ed. Franz Freiherr von Soden and J. K. F. Knaake, Potsdam 1867–72 [Aalen 1962]; and behaves in a manner ever more friendly toward Eck ('Eckium meum', to Eck in October of 1516; I 163; 'celebris Eckii fama . . .' to Trutfetter on 10 December 1516; I 167). On 14 January 1517, he recommends the Wittenberg theologians to Eck, promises to send Eck the German and Latin editions he had done of Staupitz' treatise on predestination and confirms 'scedas tuas . . . Wittenburgensibus communicavi' (II 13f.). In the accompanying letter to Karlstadt, Scheurl betrays his great knowledge of human nature and of his friends: '[Eck] disputator acerrimus, amicus meus, quem in plerisque animi dotibus tibi iudicavi similem . . .' (II 131; 31 October 1517!). We ought to bear in mind that Karlstadt and the Wittenberg circle have been shown to have had access to Eck's Vienna theses. After two attempts, we now have a full bibliography of Scheurl's works, which could be the basis of a much-needed monograph on this key figure perched between Nuremberg, Erfurt and Wittenberg (just to name a few places): Maria Grossmann, 'Bibliographie der Werke Christoph Scheurls', in: *Archiv für die Geschichte des Buchwesens* 70 (1969), 658–70 (Lit.). See also the valuable study by Wilhelm Graf, *Doktor Christoph Scheurl von Nürnberg*, Leipzig 1930 [Hildesheim 1972].

Eck could not be papered over. Luther could attempt only to move Eck not to answer Karlstadt more harshly.[30] When a person's *fama* or reputation is held to be as important as it was at that time, one insult necessarily evokes another. Luther cannot have welcomed this exchange because Karlstadt, who never thought in terms of tactics, only in terms of his principles, was thus forcing the Wittenberg theologians into a war on two fronts, a war that might have disastrous consequences. Although Eck could not have shown the Wittenberg group any sympathy, they might have expected at least a neutral position of non-intervention from the professor at Ingolstadt, for two reasons. First there is evidence that Eck, as a Swabian theologian, shared the German national sentiments that had been growing very fast since the middle of the fifteenth century.[31] In his *Chrysopassus,* Eck adds up in two long lists the names of ninety-three authors

[30] *WAB* 1, 183.20.

[31] Cf. Lewis W. Spitz, *The religious Renaissance of the German humanists,* Cambridge MA, 1963, 53, 85f., 99, 164, 261. Eck's position on the question 'de licitis usuris' should not be seen as pro-Italian. (For the postlude to his Augsburg disputation (1514), in which he defended the so-called 'contractus trinus' as well as the novel 'contractus quinque de centum', see Joseph Schlecht, 'Dr. Johann Ecks Anfänge', in: *Historisches Jahrbuch* 36 (1915), 1–36; 20–30 as well as the literature cited here.) Although in Germany Adelmann and Fabri at Augsburg, Cochleus and Pirckheimer at Nuremberg and Ulrich von Hutten called Eck a 'Fuggerknecht' (a lackey of the Fuggers), in Italy Prierias, for example, stuck more closely to tradition and rejected the taking of interest. In 1514 he stated that anyone who denied that interest-taking was a sin, was a heretic: 'Quarto quaeritur utrum sit haereticus, qui asserit usuram non esse peccatum? Et dico quid sic . . .' (*Summa Sylvestrina,* (1514), Lyon 1594, under *haeresis* I, para. 4(7); cf. also under *usura,* one of the most exhaustive of all the articles in this alphabetically-ordered *summa* of moral theology). Cajetan's opinion on interest was also unfavorable; but compare John T. Noonan, Jr., *The scholastic analysis of usury,* Cambridge, MA, 1957, 211f., and J. Schneid, 'Dr. Johann Eck und das kirchliche Zinsverbot', in: *Historisch-politische Blätter für das katholische Deutschland* 108 (1891), 241ff. There is no dividing line between the Franciscans and the more conservative Dominicans and Augustinians; rather, it runs right through their ranks – at least through the OP and the OFM – as Julius Kirshner has demonstrated in 'A document on the meeting of the Chapter General in Florence (1365)', in: *Archivum Franciscanum historicum* 62 (1969), 392–9 – directed against the positions of Noonan (122) and R. de Roover, *The rise and fall of the Medici Bank 1397–1494,* Cambridge, MA, 1963, 22. Even though Eck sought a papal decision, no binding doctrinal statement was issued. On the relationship of Eck to the Fuggers, see Götz Freiherr von Pölnitz, *Jakob Fugger: Kaiser, Kirche und Kapital in der oberdeutschen Renaissance,* Tübingen n.d. [1949–52] I 313–18; II 327–93. Concerning Eck's journey to Bologna he writes: 'Auf seiner gesamten Reise, die zum Triumphzug des oberdeutschen Kapitals werden sollte, blieb Eck von Fuggers Schutz überschattet' (I 317). For further details, see von Pölnitz, 'Die Beziehungen des Johannes Eck zum Augsburger Kapital', in: *Historisches Jahrbuch* 60 (1940), 685–706, esp. 689ff.

'whose positions have been cited from the original works'[32] and another series of authors whose works he has cited indirectly.[33] These lists are not simply testimony to his own pride in his work, because he also notes carefully each of the authors who can be called German (*Germanus*). In the first list alone, there are twenty-six. In order to sweep away all doubt, Eck gives Albert the Great double billing as 'the glory of the Swabians and of the Germans – a German!'[34] The Italians Prierias and Cajetan, however, are mentioned in neither list, although Eck dealt with them as well, as his discussion shows.[35]

More important even than the national feelings that link Eck to the Wittenberg group[36] is his originally non-curialist ecclesiology. Three statements – noteworthy in a book that stays so close to its theme[37] – bear directly on this position. The first is in his 'Primum Evidentiale', where Eck argues that God is the first and last standard of righteousness. A thing is righteous because God wills it; God does not will a thing *because* it is righteous. So Eck propounds the same teaching that appears in Ockham and Biel and which has again and again provoked in scholarship charges of arbitrary voluntarism and ethical relativism.[38] But Eck goes one step farther in his deliberations.

[32] '[Q]uorum sententiis ex originali desumptis'; *Chrysopassus*, Augsburg 1514, fol. b ii'.

[33] Formulated as follows : 'Tabella theologorum quos vel non vidimus aut visos non legimus' (fol. b ii'). Concerning the individual authors and works named by Eck, see Greving (see n. 13), 19–65.

[34] See also his nicely-written dedication 'Iohannis maioris Eckii suevi [!] theologi epistola' (fol. a ii').

[35] For Prierias, see *Chrysopassus* C III 30, fol. Giiii' (C = Centuria; Eck's main division into six parts), where Eck quotes from Prierias' *Compendium seu abbreviatura in Capreolum* (1497). For Cajetan, see n. 41 below.

[36] Christoph Scheurl, the former rector of the fledgling University of Wittenberg and admirer of Staupitz, provided a connecting link between the Wittenberg theologians and Eck. On the other hand, there was a certain inner-German rivalry between universities: 'tam florens et famigeratum ... factum est gymnasium nostrum', Eck says, 'ut cum omnibus totius Germaniae Achademiis celebriate contendat, cedat nulli' (fol. a iiii'). I am inclined to believe Eck's statement in his letter of 28 May, 1518, that he is a friend of the Wittenberg theologians (V.E. Löscher, *Vollständige Reformations-Acta und Documenta*, I–III, Leipzig 1720–9, II 64f).

[37] The title *Chrysopassus* was chosen from Rev. 21.20, where the chrysopras is named as the tenth gemstone signifying the 'communi doctorum interpretamento decimum articulum fidei, qui est sanctorum communio' (fol. b'; cf. Greving (see n. 13), 2–4). The Augustinian link between the *Sanctorum communio* and predestination is mentioned here, but not dealt with at any length.

[38] Cf. Oberman, *The Harvest of Medieval Theology. Gabriel Biel and Late Medieval Nominalism*, Durham, NC, 1983³ (1963), 96 and 97, n. 24.

He notes that there is an interpretation in the tradition of canon law according to which the principle of 'Absolute God' (*Deus absolutus*) can be extended to the pope, such that any of his actions, simply by virtue of being done by him, *ipso facto* are unimpeachable and righteous. Eck also challenges a parallel gloss, according to which the pope is a being situated between God and humans. His answer is unequivocal: 'we must reject this as extraneous to the question'.[39] With this, Eck announces his direct opposition to Prierias' *fundamentum quartum* in the *Dialogus* against Luther, which states that the will of the Church – i.e. of the pope – becomes law not only through its verbal decisions, but also in what it actually does.

In another passage of the *Chrysopassus* that has received just as little attention as the preceding one, Eck turns away from Cajetan over the question of whether or not confirmation communicates an added grace that increases the grace of baptism. Eck endorses Gerson's view (against Johannes Maior, +1550) that confirmation should not be delayed until a baptized child has grown up. A child must be confirmed as soon as possible, because a sacrament enjoined in the New Testament 'does what it represents'[40] and thus provides new grace. Most importantly here, Eck attributes particular authority to Gerson's position because the Chancellor stated it not just anywhere, but at the Council of Constance, 'where errors and schisms were destroyed, not sown – contrary to what Cajetan says.'[41]

---

[39] C I 92, fol. C iiii^r: 'Et glossema ibidem super verbo "ratione" extendit evidentiale nostrum etiam ad papam, quod ubi papa aliquid faciat quod videtur iniustum ubi nos rationem assignare non possumus, quod nichilominus iustum sit. Similem glossam reperies alibi, quod papa nec sit deus, nec homo. Sed haec extraria reiiciamus.' Cf. Innocent III, *Sermo II in consecr. pont.*, *PL* 217, 658 A: 'Inter Deum et hominem medius constitutus, citra Deum, sed ultra hominem: minor Deo, sed maior homine: qui de omnibus iudicat, et a nemine iudicatur'; cf. Johannes Andreae (+1348), *Glossa ord. ad Clementinas*, proem., under *papa:* 'Nec Deus es nec homo, quasi neuter es inter utrumque.' See M. J. Wilks, *The problem of sovereignty in the later Middle Ages. The papal monarchy with Augustinus Triumphus and the Publicists*, Cambridge 1963, 164, n. 5. On the notion that the pope is *supra ius* and *legibus solutus* see Wilks, 173, n. 3. On the principle 'papa a nemine iudicatur' see Wilks, 471, nn. 2–5.

[40] C III 13, fol. G^r.

[41] C III 15, fol. G^r: 'Sed quia argumenta sua [Johannis Maioris] non sunt nervosa (nisi quid urgentius afferat) assentimur domino cancellario [Gerson] in illa doctrina [the grace of confirmation ought to be achieved as soon as possible] quam procamavit in eo loco (puta in concilio Constantiae), ubi errores et schismata fuerunt extirpata, non seminata: contra Caietanum.'

Before we examine in detail the controversy between Karlstadt and Eck, and its background in the *Chrysopassus,* we must be certain of two things. First, Prierias and Eck, the two most important opponents of the Wittenberg theologians, disagree sharply on matters of ecclesiology. This split meant that Eck (in the wake of the 95 Theses) thought in terms of the 'Church of sinners' (*ecclesia peccatorum*) and not of the bull *Unam sanctam* – with its triumphalist ecclesiology of the 'Church without blemish or wrinkle' (*ecclesia sine macula et ruga*) – which portrays the pope in analogous fashion to 'God who is above the law' (*deus exlex*).[42] This approach alone made dialogue possible, since the latter position (based on *Unam sanctam*) would have been unthinkable for a disciple of Staupitz – to whom Christ is the only lord or 'apex' of the Church.[43]

Second, we now see that Eck suspected Luther of Hussitism not primarily for tactical reasons; if he led Luther on at Leipzig to compromising statements about the infallibility of the Council of Constance, it was not out of mere enjoyment of tactical maneuvering. Eck's position grew organically out of the theology of his early years. Over the five years between 1514 and 1519, his ecclesiology shows signs of an increasingly papal tendency. Eck nevertheless did not – even in his far-ranging book *De primatu Petri* (1521) – convert to the extreme variety of papalism represented, for instance, by Prierias. Even at Leipzig, Eck's ecclesiology was characterized by his high regard for the Council of Constance (not that of Basel) such that he can be described even in 1519 *mutatis mutandis* as a 'Gersonist'.[44]

---

[42] Augustinus Triumphus, 'De potestate collegii mortuo papa', in: Richard Scholz, *Die Publizistik zur Zeit Philipps des Schönen und Bonifaz' VIII,* Stuttgart 1903, 503: '[E]cclesia ipsa, cuius papa sponsus existit . . .' Cf. Innocent III, *Sermo III in consecr. pont., PL* 217, 662 C; Wilks (see n. 39), 39, n. 2.

[43] Cf. the *Libellus de exsecutione aeternae praedestinationis,* Nuremberg 1517; *Johann von Staupitz. Sämtliche Schriften,* 2II, ed. L. Graf zu Dohna and R. Wetzel, Berlin 1979, esp. ch. IX, XI and XV.

[44] These remarks presuppose the convincing analysis of Gerson's ecclesiology offered by G. H. M. Posthumus Meyjes, *Jean Gerson, Zijn Kerkpolitiek en Ecclesiologie,* 's-Gravenhage 1963. 'Mutatis mutandis' because 100 years after the Council of Constance (1414–18), given the sobering effects of the bull *Execrabilis* (1461) and in particular the Mainz *Stiftsfehde* (1459–63), 'Gersonism' could be only a middle way between the old conciliarism and a new resurgence of curialism. See the introduction to the *Defensorium Oboedientiae Apostolicae et alia documenta,* ed. H. A. Oberman, D. E. Zerfoss and W. J. Courtenay, Cambridge MA, 1968, esp. 52ff.

4. Gregory of Rimini: The Secret Master of Wittenberg Theology

Eck's theses,[45] which he finished on 1 August 1518 and which were directed against his prospective opponent at Leipzig, were based on shared ecclesiological foundations but were developed in a very different way. Unlike Prierias, Eck was willing to accept the 'Church of sinners and at least of the weak' (ecclesia peccatorum saltem infirmorum) as a starting point. He rejected Karlstadt's accusation[46] that he taught 'the militant church has no need of penance'.[47] Both noblemen and others who heard his preaching could certify that he had always thought the Church needed penance, although only penance understood as a sacrament. For this reason, Eck felt Karlstadt[48] should not attempt to cast the lex orandi, the liturgical prayers of the Church, in the role of a lex credendi – 'a law of belief' – in arguing against him. The demand for penance at all times, throughout life (per omnem vitam) raised by Luther and supported by Karlstadt could not, therefore – if penance is understood in sacramental terms – be sustained. Penance as 'baptism' happens only now and then, hic et nunc.

Eck then turns to Luther and Karlstadt's linking of 'penance we do' (poenitentia activa) with 'penance visited on us' (poenitentia passiva).[49] Eck skillfully boxes Karlstadt in by remarking on the contradiction between the claim that penance is necessary 'at all times' and the liturgical prayer – used to support this claim –

---

[45] CC I 46.2–47.12 (CC I = Corpus Catholicorum, I: Johannes Eck, Defensio contra amarulentas D. Andreae Bodenstein Carolstatini invectiones [1518], ed. J. Greving, Münster 1919).

[46] According to Karlstadt in his letter of 11 June 1518; Löscher (see n. 36), II 649; cf. CC I 35, n. 3.

[47] CC I 46.1–3: 'Miror, unde D. Bodenstein venerit in mentem, ut dicat, primam conclusionem Eckii velle in fundamento, ecclesiam militantem non indigere poenitentia, cum hoc nullibi in adnotatione mea reperiatur.'

[48] CC I 39.4–11: '5.<106> . . . Dicit [ecclesia] item: "Deus, qui culpa offenderis et poenitentia placaris" etc., et: "flagella, quae meremur, averte." Non dicit: "meriti sumus", sed "meremur". Item adverte: "poenitentia placaris". 6.<107> Et in alia collecta: "Parce, Domine, parce populo tuo, ut dignis flagellis castigatus in tua miseratione respiret." 7.<108> Nonne ecclesia seu populus Dei petit, se castigari? Quod si non est poenitere, Eckius iudicabit.'

[49] CC I 47.13–17: 'Quamvis autem mirum sit, quomodo pro fundamento D. Bodenstein imponat Eckio, quod nunquam cogitavit, id tamen non minus mirum est, quod a poenitentia, quam agere debemus ex praecepto D. Iesu, ipse se transfert ad poenitentiam, qua flagella et poenas a Deo inflictas patimur.'

'turn away the scourges that we merit':[50] if this prayer really applied to 'penance visited on us' (*poenitentia passiva*), it would mean that the Church actually begs God to free it from true penance.[51] While Eck maintains vis-à-vis Luther that the command of Christ to 'Repent'[52] is to be understood as applying to the 'penance we do' (*poenitentia activa*),[53] he thinks he has proven, in opposition to Karlstadt, that the 'law of prayer' (*lex orandi*) of the Church not only has nothing to do with Eck's concept of sacramental penance, but that Karlstadt uses it in a loose and irrelevant way (*impertinenter*).[54]

One-and-a-half months later (on 14 September 1518), in his last written statement before the meeting at Leipzig, Karlstadt addresses Eck's objection explicitly, arguing that the word *flagella* (scourges) means the *flagella irae* (scourges of [God's] wrath) and that the prayer in question is therefore intended to avert God's wrath.[55] Although this distinguishes clearly between ecclesiastical penance and divine

---

[50] Karlstadt, thesis 106; *CC* I 39.4–7; Löscher II 68 (thesis 5), cited in n. 48.

[51] *CC* I 47.18–21: 'Et vere mirandum est, quod hanc vocarit poenitentiam, et tamen ecclesia petat, hanc averti a populo Dei, itaque petit, poenitentiam averti a populo Dei, quam tamen posterius affirmat in bonis per omnem vitam durare.'

[52] Matthew 4.17, cited in the first of the 95 Theses (*WA* 1, 233.10f.), interpreted esp. in the last three theses (*WA* 1, 238.16–21).

[53] *CC* I 48.3–6: 'Nam cum venerandus pater Martinus Luther meminerit poenitentiae, de qua dominus et magister noster Iesus Christus dixit: "Poenitentiam agite" etc., ego, ab eo dissentiens, de poenitentia, quae a nobis agitur, non qua patimur, manifeste sum locutus.'

[54] *CC* I 48.7–9: 'Quare liquet, collectas et orationes ecclesiae non solum mihi non adversari, sed multum impertinenter adduci; orat enim ecclesia, Deum nos protegere a periculis imminentibus etc.'

[55] Löscher II 129: 'Ut penetremus negotium, non dixi, D. Ecki, Ecclesiam deprecari, ut Deus poenitentiam avertat (oratio Ecclesiae satis plana est). Sed quod Deus flagella averti [sic], aliud poenitentiam, sicut res alia atque alia existit poenitentia et flagellum.

'Non te movet quod scripsi ex Ecclesiae oratione, populum fidelem et iustum deprecari, ut flagella irae avertat, prout in conclusione mea CXI. lucidissima habet linea. Ecclesia ita preces Sabb. Dom. I. in quadrag, fundit: Et ab eo flagella tuae iracundiae clementer averte. Quae tamen alibi orat, ut de pio verbere proficiat, pia verbera Ecclesia tolerat, sed ab iracundiae plagis petit liberari. Sed cum tu sanctos Ecclesiae precatus aspernis, rideas, contemnas, canonicam obiicia scripturam. Advertistine usquam David iustum, sanctumque in eodem contextu dicere se in flagella paratum, et dolorem suum esse in suo conspectu semper [Ps. 37.18]? Qui in exordio eiusdem Ps. [37.2] ita orat: Domine, ne in furore tuo arguas me, neque in ira tua corripias me. Petit, ait Chrysostomus, ne in ira, id est vehementer arguatur, et neque in furore, id est absque venia, corripiatur.' See also Löscher (n. 36 above), II 131f. (on Eck's twelfth thesis).

punishment,[56] in his more fundamental answer to Eck's eighth thesis Karlstadt demonstrates that both kinds of penance are closely linked. According to Karlstadt's 'theology of the cross,' 'following Christ' implies no mere human activity or effort, but the suffering of Christ's cross, as the event where penance and punishment meet.[57] This means that in penance, Christians must bear the 'scourge of God' (*flagella Dei*) – penance understood as the acceptance of God's just punishment.[58]

This answer could not satisfy Eck because it begs the question of why the Church can pray to be spared the divine punishment contained in this kind of penance. But to Karlstadt – and this is the decisive point – predestination and justification are so closely linked that he assumes the elect, the true believers, will accept God's righteous punishment in penance and, simultaneously, remain

[56] Cf. this line in the text just cited: 'res alia atque alia existit poenitentia et flagellum'. It is a mistake to try to explain Karlstadt's *tribulatio*– and *flagella*–theology unilaterally from the perpective of the *Theologia Deutsch*, as many Karlstadt scholars have done – from R. Stupperich, 'Karlstadts Sabbat–Traktat von 1524', in: *Neue Zeitschrift für systematische Theologie* 1 (1959), 349–75; 369 to H. Hillerbrand, 'Andreas Bodenstein von Karlstadt. The prodigal Reformer', in: *Church History* 35 (1966), 379–98. Noteworthy here is Staupitz' importance for Karlstadt's break with his scholastic past, particularly Staupitz' *Libellus de exsecutione aeternae praedestinationis*. Here themes are developed that cannot have been influenced by Luther because they are announced as early as 1498 in Staupitz' Tübingen sermons: 'Prorsus ad deum tuum refer flagellum tuum . . . "Flagellat autem omnem filium, quem recipit ad Hebr. XII [v.6]". Nec te sine flagello speres futurum, nisi cogites exhereditari . . . Haec ergo tribulacionis considerata utilitas rectum principium est, quo generatur in nobis ad voluntatem divinam nostrae voluntatis conformitas' (*Tübinger Predigten, Sermo III*, ed. G. Buchwald and E. Wolf, Leipzig 1927, 17.11–18). Luther adopts this idea without modifications, e.g. in his gloss on Hebr. 12.6 (*WA* 57 III, 77.12–24). It is precisely this type of mysticism 'per conformitatem voluntatis' that Karlstadt will continue to preach. Cf. n. 59.

[57] Löscher II 125: 'tollat crucem suam et sequatur me [Matt. 16.24], non faciat, sed post te et curremus [Songs 1.3]. Nemo enim venit ad Christum nisi pater eum traxerit [John 6.44]. Si venire debemus, trahat nos pater. Si crucem nos, Christe, accipere iubes, circumda nos tuo scuto veritatis! Circumdabit ergo scuto, hoc est cruce circumdabit te veritas eius, et non timebis a timore nocturno [Ps. 90.5]. Foeliciter crucem portas, si Christus suam crucem imposuerit, dicit scuto circumdabit (vide semper passivam vel susceptivam, non activam voluntatem) te veritas . . .'

[58] Löscher II 125: 'Timor nocturnus poenas noctis habet et damnationis; verum ut ab his non timeamus, datur nobis donum crucis, quod ingerit nobis peccata quae fecimus, propter quae cum propheta dicimus: Quoniam ego in flagella paratus sum, et dolor meus in conspectu meo semper. Quoniam iniquitatem meam annuntiabo et cogitabo pro peccato meo [Ps. 37.18f.]; propter peccata nostra excogitantes aeterna supplicia, universa quae patimur delicias reputamus, exclamantes cum Daniele [3.26–28]: Iustus es, Domine, et iuste induxisti haec mala super nos propter peccata nostra.'

hopeful through prayer that they may be spared God's wrath at the end of time.[59] It is therefore no surprise that Karlstadt addresses Eck concerning this problem and asks him why he separates predestination from justification, since the Pauline doctrine of justification rests on the doctrine of predestination.[60] Eck counters that Karlstadt has dragged the question of predestination in 'by the hair'[61] and that it has nothing to do with the issue they are debating. However, he stresses that he would be glad to undertake a separate disputation on this point,[62] especially since he has already dealt with it in detail in his *Chrysopassus*.[63] This prepared the ground for the Leipzig Disputation, where Karlstadt would once again try

[59] Later Karlstadt made it even clearer that he understood the prayer 'flagella quae meremur, averte' as a plea for certainty of salvation on the part of those who, as *praedestinati,* are most aware of their alienation from God. In the theses of March 1521 we find a more unequivocal response than in those of May and September 1518. Their main topic is once again *poenitentia passiva,* which precisely in its 'semi-sacramental' version lends itself to an 'anti-sacramental' interpretation in the traditional sense of the word; cf. for example thesis 4: 'Baptisati spiritu et aqua tribulacionis vere sunt baptisati' and thesis 6: 'Tribulatio spiritualis sacramentum est.' The word *averte* of 1518 must be understood as it is formulated in thesis 8, which expresses humanity's alienation from the true Church and from God ('Dolor et sensus alienati a sanctis dei aut abscisi spiritus a deo . . .') when we confront our own sins ('in conscientia infirmitatis et peccatorum recordatione'). The theses concerning predestination are no mere add-on, but refer in a rigorous fashion to the entire text: on the one hand, this sort of doubt is a reliable sign that one belongs to the predestined (theses 2f.); on the other, the Church is said to pray for the spiritual welfare only (*tantum*) of the predestined: 'Orationes justorum tantum praedestinatis sunt salubres ad vitam aeternam' (thesis 20) (T. Brieger, 'Thesen Karlstadts', in: *ZKG* 2 (1890), 479–83).

[60] Löscher II 128: 'Si profundum inspexeris et amussatius adverteris [averteris Löscher], fateberis ex praedestinatione omnia pullulare, de quibus concertamus, et te nimis impudenter affirmasse materiam praedestinationis operibus esse extraneam atque impertinentem. Nam apostolus [Eph. 2.10] ait: Ipsius sumus figmentum creati in bonis operibus, quae praeparavit Deus, ut in illis ambularemus. Praescivit, ait Augustinus, et praedestinavit bona opera se datura electis. Quam ob causam negas praedestinationem operibus esse pertinentem et intrinsecam? Hoc enim scilicet quod Deus iustificat, nimis occulte facit; ex hoc enim incipiunt bona opera ex quo iustificamur, non quia praecesserunt iustificamur. Si enim gratia esset ex operibus, iam non esset gratia [Rom. 11.6]. Latitudo perseverantiam habet.'

[61] *CC* I 65.13–66.1: 'Quamvis autem clare posuerim adnotationem meam, tamen D. Bodenstein quasi per capillos detorsit in materiam praedestinationis, adducendo omnia quae sequuntur, ad hunc finem quod nulla sit ratio praedestinationis . . .'

[62] *CC* I 66.11–67.2: 'Neutram tamen partem hic suscipio defendendam, quod praedestinationis negotium sit proposito impertinens et omnino extrarium. Unde nescio, quo spiritu D. Bodenstein tam impertinenter in hanc materiam excurrit. Si tamen placuerit sibi, ventilare hanc materiam in studio eligendo, placet mihi, positiones in ea dare et super his respondere aut respondenti opponere.'

[63] See *CC* I 66.8f.

systematically to use this point as a fulcrum for the lever of his argument. A thankful disciple of Staupitz, whose *Libellus de exsecutione aeternae praedestinationis* helped him to break with scholasticism,[64] Karlstadt sees the inner coherence of predestination

[64] See the dedicatory epistle addressed to Johann von Staupitz for his commentary on Augustine's *De spiritu et litera*, in: Ernst Kähler, *Karlstadt und Augustin. Der Kommentar des Andreas Bodenstein von Karlstadt zu Augustins Schrift De spiritu et litera*, Halle 1952, 5.15–21; cf. 4*ff. Kähler is justified in noting that in Karlstadt's description of Staupitz' treatise ('hortatorium tuum . . . epistolium, quo Christi dulcedinem, quam hii, quo puro corde in sacris literis Christum videntes, non qui eas velo obductas iudaice extrospicientes pregustant, egregie extulisti . . .', 5.17–19), there is no direct reference to the *Libellus de exsecutione aeternae praedestinationis* (7*). It is, therefore, tempting to identify the *epistolium* with the *De amore Dei libellus*, on account of the direct parallels. See I. F. K. Knaake, *Johann von Staupitzens sämtliche Werke* I: *Deutsche Schriften*, Potsdam 1867, 88–119, esp. 97: 'allein ist ein trost darbey, das vnter dem buchstaben der geyst vorborgen ligt, das allt gesetz schwanger ist vnd tregt Cristum, durch den die gnade got vber alle ding zelieben geben wirt. Die diesen geyst funden haben, vnd Christum ym gesetz verborgen erkenen, den ist die geschrifft zu nutzbarer lere vnd, alls Paulus sagt, zu troste kommen, vornehmlich in deme, das sy bey der kranckheit die sterckung, bey dem tod der natur die lebmachung der gnaden funden, durch Ihesum christum vnsern hern, in welcher sy auch got vber alle ding lieben vnd das gesetz volkommenlich verpringen mogen'; and 98: 'Dis vnd der gleichenn bringt der buechstab des newen testaments, vnnd todtet. Vnnd ob ehr schon Christum in die augenn bringt, und sein lere in die ornn, weil er doch den geist Christi nit vermag in das hertz zubringen, dient ehr allein zu schwererm todt. Die iuden hetten Christum inn augen, in den orn, und in henden, sy hetten aber den geist Christi nit ym hertzen, darumb waren sy verdamlicher den die heidenn.' But even if Knaake can show that this treatise 'iam 1517 adumbratum et conceptum sit' (90), this is still too late to explain Karlstadt's dedication to Staupitz, dated 18 November 1517. Yet Karlstadt is fully justified in claiming that he had based his position on a basic strand of Staupitz' theology, a strand to which Karlstadt gave concentrated and coherent form for the first time in 1518.

On the other hand, three factors can be adduced against the argument that Karlstadt is alluding to Staupitz' treatise on predestination:

(1) the headings of chapters 15 and 17 of Staupitz: 'De praegustu salutis' and 'De dulcedine sermonis Christi ad cor christiani';

(2) chapter 16, esp. the first sentence 'Christum acceptistis signis quibusdam amoris sui dulcedinem in intimis animae palam facere . . .' (§122) and the key phrase 'Lex quoque Christi ad litteram durissima est . . .' (§126);

(3) the main thesis: Staupitz understands the principle *gratia gratum faciens*, in deliberate opposition to its customary scholastic interpretation, not as a sacramentally infused habitus, which makes us 'acceptable' or 'pleasing' to God, but as the love of God, in which God becomes pleasing to us: 'Haec est gratia gratum faciens; non hominem Deo, sicut multi exponunt, quia hoc ipsa electio fecit, sed solum deum facit placere et gratum esse homini per caritatem, quae restituit, quam rapuit concupiscentiam, oboedientiam, qua Deo, non nobis, et recte et iuste sumus et vivimus' (Staupitz 2 II (see n. 43), cap. VI §36; cf. cap. VII §40; cap. VIII §47; cap. XVI §131 and cap. XVIII §152). To clarify this third point, we must undertake a more detailed comparison of the positions of Staupitz, Karlstadt and Luther against the background of Augustine.

Let us now compare the thesis set forth in (3) above with the following passages from Augustine's *De spiritu et litera*: 'Charitas quippe Dei dicta est diffundi in cordibus nostris,

and justification, and it is precisely on this point that he attacks his opponent.

Yet it seems that Eck does not want to decide about the 'reason for predestination' (*ratio praedestinationis*), about the basis – whatever it

---

non qua nos ipse diligit, sed qua nos facit dilectores suos; sicut iustitia dei, qua iusti eius munere efficimur; et Dominus salus, qua nos salvos facit; et fides Iesu Christi, qua nos fideles facit. Haec est iustitia dei, quam non solum docet per legis praeceptum, verum etiam dat per spiritus donum', (cap. XXXII 56; *PL* 44, 237) and the exegesis of Rom. 1.16f. and Hab. 2.4 offered in the same treatise: 'Haec est iustitia dei, quae in Testamento Veteri velata, in Novo revelatur: quae ideo iustitia Dei dicitur, quod impertiendo eam iustos facit; sicut "Domini est salus" [Ps. 3.9], qua salvos facit. Et haec est fides, ex qua et in quam revelatur, ex fide scilicet annuniantium, in fidem obedientium: qua fide Jesu Christi, id est, quam nobis contulit Christus, credimus ex Deo nobis esse, pleniusque futurum esse quod iuste vivimus' (cap. XI 18; *PL* 44, 211). Four conclusions are suggested:

(1) Staupitz' main thesis *contra multos* (the scholastics), i.e. his 'own' interpretation of the *gratia gratum faciens,* is rooted in Augustine.

(2) Just as in Karlstadt's commentary, Staupitz understands *fides caritate formata* on the basis of *sola gratia;* the question as to how *caritas* thus emphasized relates to the traditional concept of sacramental grace remains open. Cf. Karlstadt: 'Cui consequens est charitatem dei utiliter operari. per ista iam nolo ambagiosam questiunculam de vi sacramentorum dissolvisse, suo loco aptius explicandum' (Kähler 95.15–17); the phrase *suo loco* was to come home to roost in the sacramentarian controversy with Luther!

(3) Whereas for Augustine the righteousness of God is *velata* in the Old Testament, but *revelata* in the New, Staupitz and Karlstadt agree that the letter as such is veiled and veils the truth, in both the New and the Old Testaments. Both theologians thus shift the crux of the problem from the field of hermeneutics or rather from the historical process of salvation as set down in the Bible to the field of anthropological or even cosmological inquiry.

(4) Both Karlstadt and Staupitz make common cause against Luther when they reinterpret the word *sicut* in the first Augustine quote as meaning a consecutive *ut.* According to Luther, the genitive phrases *opus Dei, virtus Dei, sapientia Dei, fortitudo Dei, salus Dei, gloria Dei* are concepts analogous to the mysterious *iustitia Dei* – 'colligebam etiam in aliis vocabulis analogiam' (*WA* 54, 186.11); Augustine also compares *caritas Dei, iustitia Dei, salus Domini* and *fides Christi* using the term *sicut.* Karlstadt and Staupitz probably come closer, with their consecutive interpretation of *fides* and *caritas,* to Augustine's position than does Luther.

Kähler points to the emphasis 'auf der praktischen Abzweckung der Gnadenmitteilung, eben ihrer Verwirklichung in einem christus-förmigen Leben' as the common ground shared by Staupitz and Karlstadt (7*). For an accurate analysis of this relationship based on all the works of Staupitz, see David C. Steinmetz, *Misericordia Dei. The theology of Johannes von Staupitz in its late medieval setting,* Leiden 1968, 171–81. On the importance of Augustine's *De spiritu et litera* for Luther's development, see Bernhard Lohse, 'Die Bedeutung Augustins für den jungen luther', in: *Kerygma und Dogma* 11 (1965), 116–35, esp. 131. In his *De doctrina christiana* (III 33.46; *CChr* 32, 105), Augustine says explicitly that *de spiritu et litera* is another way of saying *de promissis et lege,* Tyconius' third rule for interpreting the Old Testament. On the importance of this rule to medieval hermeneutics and to Luther's early theology, see J. S. Preus, *From shadow to promise. Old Testament interpretation from Augustine to the young Luther,* Cambridge MA, 1969, esp. 11.

might be – for predestination in each member of the elect. On the one hand, he admits that it is a general notion (*communis sententia*) that everything we have is a gift of God. He refers this idea specifically to Gregory of Rimini (+1358) as a representative of the Augustinian tradition.[65] On the other hand, he notes that there is a whole series of theologians who disagree.[66] Eck's portrayal at first sight seems to be a purely descriptive exercise in the history of dogma.[67] However, the decision not to take sides 'here' since the doctrine of predestination has nothing to do with the Church's teaching on true penance, human responsibility, or with the will in the play of forces between God and the world – that is with a theological anthropology[68] – is a

[65] *CC* I 65.15–66.4 (cont'd from n. 57): 'quod nulla sit ratio praedestinationis, sed omnia bona nostra sint a Deo, quae est communis theologorum sententia, et latissime per Gregorium Ariminensem ad mentem Augustini distinctione 27. secundi [libri] tractata et distinctione xl. primi.' At a disputation on 7 July 1515 at Bologna organized by the Provincial of the German Dominicans, Eck attacked this thesis: 'nullam esse praedestinationis rationem'; see Johannes Eck, *Disputatio Viennae Pannoniae habita (1517)*, ed. Therese Virnich, Münster 1923 (= *CC* VI), 46, n. 3. Not opposed, however, is his third thesis, which he defended five days later at Bologna: 'Nullam fore praedestinationis causam, celebris est opinio; attamen meritorum praescientiam esse praedestinationis rationem, ut Bonaventura et Ales loquuntur, sit multum probabile' (*CC* VI, 46.12–14). In his *Chrysopassus*, Eck had already rejected unequivocally any *causa praedestinationis*, but accepted the notion of *ratio praedestinationis*. The most important shift in this issue between 1515 and 1518 is the replacement of *praedestinationis causa* (1515) by *praedestinationis ratio* (1518); Eck can share the *opinio celebris* (1515), but not the *opinio communis* (1518), as described by Gregory in his *Sentences* commentary. As can clearly be seen in the *Chrysopassus*, Eck's twelfth thesis is an attack on Gregory of Rimini: 'Non omnis infidelium actus est peccatum, licet omne, quod non ex fide fiat, sit peccatum.' *CC* VI 47.9–24: '6. Sicut opera satisfactoria etiam in pecato [sic] mortali utiliter satisfaciunt, ita et indulgentiae mortuis non tantum per modum suffragii, sed autoritative a papa dari possunt. Corollarium. [7.] Illa clausula "permodum suffragii" in bullis apostolicis non diminuit, sed ponitur declarative. 8. Existens in purgatorio est quodammodo viator et ita super terram, sicut et sanctus Paulus in raptu fuit viator simpliciter. 9. Eadem ratione non confesso et non contrito actu vel proposito indulgentiae dari possunt, licet non nisi super contritis et confessis. 10. Quare papa pro maiori parte de plenitudine potestatis purgatorium evacuare posset, non tamen totum, sicut Christus fecit in resurrectione, attamen residuis per modum suffragii prodesse potest. 11. Peccatum veniale nec de "per se" nec de "per accidens" punitur aeternaliter in inferno.'

[66] *CC* I 66.5–10: 'Plures tamen boni et sancti theologi rationem praedestinationis suo modo admisere, ut seraphicus doctor Bonaventura, s. Thomas in scripto, Alexander de Ales, Henricus de Gandavo, Thomas Argentinus, Gabriel Biel, Silvester de Prierio et alii, quorum in Chrysopasso memini. Hi solvere habent pro maiori parte hic per D. Bodenstein inducta.'

[67] According to Leif Grane in his study 'Gregor von Rimini und Luthers Leipziger Disputation', in: *Studia theologica* 22 (1968), 29–49; 33: 'Die nächste These fängt gerade mit folgenden Worten an: Neutram tamen partem his suscipio defendendam . . .'

[68] *CC* I 66.11f., see n. 62. Cf. as the context of this statement the entire exposition starting with *CC* I 63.2.

decision *against* Gregory of Rimini! When Eck, to support his concept of the will, invokes Sirach 15.14–17, which states that human beings are free to decide between 'water' and 'fire',[69] he knows very well that Gregory cites this passage in reference to the state of humanity before the Fall, and therefore rejects any appeal to this passage as against the teachings of Augustine.[70] He also knows that Gregory's discussion ends abruptly in the following *distinctio* with the statement that no-one in the world achieves penance unless God has illuminated him beforehand and converts him out of sheer mercy.[71] Since Eck challenges Karlstadt to orient himself better on the basis of the *Chrysopassus,* we ought also to have a glance at it to get a firm grip on Eck's own position, behind his 'analytic history of dogma'. Without attempting to answer the question concerning Gregory's importance for the genesis of reforming theology,[72] we can establish the following points:

1. In Wittenberg – as elsewhere – Gregory was added as required reading to Thomas Aquinas and John Duns Scotus when the new

[69] *CC* I 64.4–8.

[70] Gregory of Rimini, *In 2 Sent.* dist. 26–8 q. 1 art. 3 ad 12; *Gregorii Ariminiensis OESA Lectura super Primum et Secundum Sententiarum,* tom. VI, ed. D. Trapp and V. Marcolino, Berlin 1980, 77.7–78.27.

[71] *In 2 Sent.* dist. 29 q. 1 art. 2; 173.14f.; after Pseudo-Augustine (= Fulgentius of Ruspe), *De fide ad Petrum* 74; *CChr* 91A, 755.

[72] For this, see rather Manfred Schulze, *Von der Via Gregorii zur Via Reformationis: Der Kampf um Augustin im späten Mittelalter,* Diss. theol. Tübingen 1980. Leif Grane (see n. 67) has introduced to the discussion the important argument that Karlstadt did not make full use at Leipzig of Gregory's discovery: that the *Epistola ad virginem Demetriadem,* which Eck cited as a work of Jerome, was actually written by Pelagius (35–7) (cf. Gregory, *In 2 Sent.* dist. 26–8 q. 1; 23.1–5; 84.31–85.5). Grane concludes: 'Deshalb darf man wohl davon ausgehen, daß diese Feststellung alle weiteren Vermutungen einer genaueren Kenntnis Gregors durch die Wittenberger vor der Leipziger Disputation ausschließen muß, auf jeden Fall so lange, bis neue Argumente auftauchen' (37). However, there are three points that must be made in response to Grane:

(1) We know that Eck had studied Gregory carefully. Nonetheless, that did not prevent him from ascribing the *Epistola* to Jerome, both in his *Chrysopassus* (C II 13; fol. D ii^r and C III 79; fol. I ii^r) and in the Leipzig disputation (Seitz [see n. 5], 34f.).

(2) Karlstadt adduces Erasmus as an authority on the passage in question; Erasmus in turn refers to Augustine and the Venerable Bede (cf. Grane 36, n. 22). Since Erasmus enjoyed considerably more respect in 1519 than Gregory, it is natural that Karlstadt preferred to follow the honored, non-partisan humanist of Rotterdam, rather than the leader of the scholastic *via Gregorii.*

(3) Even a quick glance at Eck's *Chrysopassus* shows that appealing to Gregory in this disputation would not have persuaded Eck in the least.

statutes of the faculty of arts were introduced in 1508[73]; Eck was conscious that he was facing, if not disciples, at least readers of Gregory.[74]

2. Eck analyzed Gregory so carefully that he saw, 450 years before Louis Saint-Blancat, that Gregory was used a great deal by Pierre d'Ailly. Eck called Pierre's knowledge 'practically an epitome of Gregory's first book'.[75]

3. Whenever Gregory takes a stance on the doctrine of predestination, and particularly when he refers to the inseparable bond between justification and predestination, Eck disagrees. Finally Eck makes a general statement: 'Gregory of Rimini, that powerful doctor, has a singular character and way about him' ('Gregorius Ariminensis, valens ille doctor more suo sit singularis') – and being 'singular' (*singularitas*) does not mean being 'odd' or 'unique', but by definition represents a first step toward heresy.[76] Despite the

---

[73] Friedensberg (see n. 7), 53 (ch. 3: De eleccione decani): 'eligatur decanus . . . quicumque ille fuerit, seu religiosus seu secularis, Thome, Scotho sive Gregorio mancipatus.' ibid. 56 (ch. 10: De horis leccionum et modo legendi . . .) 'indifferenter profiteatur via Thome, Scoti, Gregorii. estate quinta, hieme octava libri phisicorum et de anima, quibus finitis parva naturalia, similiter per tres vias. hora duodecima minor logica, id est Petrus Hispanus, similiter per tres vias, secunda libri ethicorum et post illos metaphisica, item in mathematica, tercia grammatica.'

[74] C V 88, fol. Vʳ: 'Audite, domini, qui legitis Gregorium: nam ipse assumit Augustinum ac si imposuerit Manicheo dixisse se esse spiritum sanctum. Divus tamen Augustinus in eo loco hoc non fecit . . .'

[75] C I 69, fol. B viʳ: 'Sed quicquid sit de dicto Gregorii (quem tamen dictus cardinalis [Cameracensis] ut plurimum sequitur ut eius scientie videantur quasi Epitome primi libri Gregorii . . .)'; see Louis Saint-Blancat, 'La théologie de Luther et un nouveau plagiat de Pierre d'Ailly', in: *Positions Luthériennes* 4 (1956), 61–81.

[76] C III 79, fol. I iiʳ; cf. C II 31, fol. Eʳ: 'In caeteris vero auctoritatibus ad idem propositum scilicet quod nullum actum bonum agit homo vel coagit nisi ad coagendum moveatur et iuvetur a deo, remitti Gregorius adnotata per eum in dis. XXVI. secundi: quas hic brevitate studentes lubenter etiam dedita ope resecamus: In ea enim distinctione quam citat amplectitur opinionem quae nobis in alto et basso displicet. Sed regia via procedamus . . .' and C II 76, fol. Fiiᵛ: 'omitto quae Gregorius Ariminiensis ponit dis. XXVI. secundi . . . Nam omnino adversatur nobis Gregorius, sed occultus facile intelleget oppositum suarum conclusionum esse verum. Ostendatur ergo illud evidentiale primo in generali quoad primam partem per beatum Gregorium [Magnum] qui etiam dona naturalia per gratiam dari testatur . . .'

On *singularitas*, see Gerson, *Contra curiositatem studentium*, ed. Mgr. Glorieux, *Oeuvres complètes* III, Paris 1962, 230: 'Superbia scholasticos a poenitentia et fide viva praepediens, duas in eis filias infelices, nisi providerint, gignere solita est, curiositatem et singularitatem.' Cf. 'Signum curiositatis et singularitatis poenitentiam atque credulitatem impedientis apud

ornamental epithet 'that powerful doctor,' there is no other
theologian with whom Eck deals so thoroughly and so ruthlessly. The
reason for this is to be found in Eck's own statements, which show
him in all respects to be one of those who, according to Gregory, are
'more in error than Pelagius himself'.[77]

Eck's own position has already been accorded a thorough treatment
by Greving.[78] The following points must be considered in order to
understand the amazing symmetry between the battles the
Wittenberg group had to conduct on two different 'fronts':

1. Double predestination in the sense of an 'unmotivated' rejection by
God appears nowhere, which is not surprising: according to the
general trends in thought of the fifteenth and early sixteenth century,
the rejection of a human being without cause, that is, undeserved
damnation, would make God into a blood-thirsty tyrant.[79]

---

scholasticos est gaudere potius in impugnatione doctorum aut in defensione unius pertinaci
quam ad eorum dicta concordanda operam dare' (ibid. 240, cons. 5). 'Praesumptuosa
curiositas et singularitas in omni scientia causant de facili scissuram . . . per contrarium
unitas linguarum ecclesiasticum aedificium stabilivit' (ibid. 248, cons. 9).

N.B. the hitherto unnoticed radical reform proposal: 'Amplius deduceretur est istis
expedire unicum Studium esse theologiae generale in tota Ecclesia, aut saltem in tota
Gallia' (ibid.). See *Jean Gerson*, ed. Steven E. Ozment, Textus Minores 38, Leiden 1969,
82, n. 4.

On *singularitas* in its pejorative sense, see also Staupitz, *Libellus de exsecutione aeternae
praedestinationis* (see n. 43 above), cap. XXII §224.

[77] 'peius errant quam Pelagius ipse': *In 2 Sent.* dist. 26–8 q. 1 art. 2 (see n. 70), 61.26f.

[78] Greving's work, which was excellent for the time, is in need of revision sixty years later
to the extent that Eck's affinities with the Ockhamist school within nominalist theology are
now much more clearly discernable. On this topic see the work of Walter Moore cited
above in n. 13. For the rest, Greving lets himself be influenced too strongly by Eck's
modestia when he says: 'Eck pflichtet im Chrysopassus der Lehre von der doppelten
bedingten Prädestination bei . . . will aber seine Meinung andern nicht aufdrängen' (*CC* I
66, n. 5). Cf. also Greving, *Johann Eck als junger Gelehrter* (see n. 13), 69: 'Der Geist, in
dem Eck seinen Chrysopassus herausgab, ist also kurz dahin zu charakterisieren: er war eine
Verbindung von Selbstbewußtsein und Bescheidenheit.'

[79] C III 25, fol. G ii^vf. on the *causa reprobationis:* 'TERTIO sic [obiicit Thomas
Argentoracensis]: Si deus solum pro beneplacito voluntatis reprobaret aliquem, tunc deus
esset crudelis et iniustus. Consequens est impossibile. Sequela autem probatur: quia omnis
ille qui sine alia ratione quam beneplacitum voluntatis creaturam aliquam rationis capacem
et experientiae sensitivam deputat ad aeternam poenam et horibilissimam, ille utique
videtur crudelis. Nam crudelis est princeps et tyrannus, qui sitit sanguinem subditorum
suorum. Has rationes Thomae adduco tamquam persuasivas, non nescius quam faciliter
possint evacuari.'

2. Concerning predestination as election by grace, Eck agrees with Ockham and Biel in distinguishing two types: in extraordinary cases, for example that of the Virgin Mary, he feels there is an uncaused predestination 'in advance of foreseen merits.'[80]

3. The central principle of his doctrine of predestination, which he defends without any reservations – 'I do not see how any person who draws breath can deny it' – is contained in the formula 'do your best' (*facere quod in se est*). It is therefore within the realm of what human beings are able to do, to give in to the divine influence, and when one does so, one earns – of course only by meritorious effort – grace and consequently eternal glory.[81]

4. Finally, Eck expresses his position clearly when he says – again in debate with Gregory of Rimini – 'Gregory piles up a great many things concerning predestination, justification and baptism. But we cannot accept his conclusion that a person is justified *because* he is

---

[80] C II 94, fol. Fv[r]: 'CONCLUSIO. Misericordissimus deus aliquos sine ratione praedestinat; aliquos vero cum causa et ratione, non quidem necessitante, sed congruente et decente. Ista conclusio habet duas partes. Prima pars probatur sic: Quia aliqui ex speciali gratia sunt ordinati ad vitam aeternam ita quod sibi ipsis non sunt derelicti, sed praeveniuntur a gratia ne ponant obicem, ergo aliqui praedestinantur sine ratione praevia in eis praevisa aut reperta. Antecedens probatur . . . [reference to Mary with an appeal to Bernard according to Biel's interpretation, *III Sent.* dist. 3 q. 2 art. 1 concl. 1; cf. q. 1 art. 3 K; *Collectorium* (see n. 21), III 97.18 –98.K 1–96K 53]'; cf. C III 28, fol. G iii[r]. Cf. also Oberman, *Der Herbst der mittelalterlichen Theologie*, 181–203; *The Harvest of Medieval Theology*, 185–206. N.B. in the *conclusio:* 'aliquos vero cum *causa* et ratione' is a dangerous precedent that contradicts Eck's own principle that there is no *causa* except God, only a *ratio* (C III 17.21, fol. G[v]f.). *Causa* must be understood in this context in its nominalist sense: *de potentia ordinata*. Cf. for example Ockham, *II Sent.* q.3P, and Biel, *I Sent.* dist. 41 q. 1 art. 1 nota 2; *Collectorium* I 729.B1–17. Eck initially posed the question in quite general terms: 'utrum sit aliqua ratio vel causa praedestinationis . . .' (C I 3, fol. A[v]).

[81] C III 60, fol. H iiii[r]: 'QUINTUM corollarium. Quod voluntas nostra acquiescit motioni divinae est vera praedestinationis ratio ex parte praedestinati non de condigno, sed de congruo et decenti. Nam hoc faciendo facit quod in se est; et non video quomodo ullus hominum qui spirat possit huic refragari, nam non potest non esse in potestate hominis facere quod in se est. Faciendo autem quod in se est praeparat se de congruo ad gratiam et per consequens ad gloriam. Est ergo in ipso homine quo potest facere ut habeat vitam aeternam per meritum de congruo.' Cf. C III 51, fol. H ii[v] and C III, 52, ibid.: 'ergo est ratio ex parte voluntatis nostrae potentis facere dispositive saltem et de congruo ut sit praedestinata. Antecedens patet per beatum Augustinum in pluribus locis super Ioannem: Si non traheris, ora ut traheris; si non es praedestinatus, fac ut praedestineris.' Cf. also the definition of *facere quod in se est* in C IV 3, fol. K iiii[v] with reference to Gerson and Biel: 'Facere quod in se est est removere obicem et impedimentum gratiae . . .'

predestined; rather, the opposite is true.'[82] The distance between Eck (1514) and Staupitz (1517), the teacher of both Karlstadt and Luther, could not be clearer or more easily grasped!

It was no coincidence that Eck dragged Gregory's name into the debate in 1518. Not only did Wittenberg allow the reading of Gregory's works and teaching in his tradition (the *via Gregorii*), but the Wittenberg theologians also declared themselves to be 'Gregorians' – at least, that is what Eck heard. Karlstadt, as a teacher at the University of Wittenberg and a defender of Luther, who had openly distanced himself from Capreolus (*via Thomae*) and Scotus,[83] is directly implied by any mention of Gregory. Eck's references to Gregory as the representative of a particular school are much more heavily fraught with emotional content than his restrained portrayal of other theological positions that were, in his opinion, at least potentially admissible. The *Chrysopassus* was a thorough preparation for this dispute. It meant that Eck knew in advance where he stood and what he would say; Karlstadt also knew, as his answers demonstrate, what position Eck occupied in the vast labyrinth of medieval scholastic opinion. It is, however, of little concern whether Karlstadt actually accepted Eck's invitation to read the *Chrysopassus* in 1518 – or even earlier.[84] Even if he did not, he laboriously attempted

---

[82] C IV 6, fol. K v[r]: 'DUM IN TERTIA confirmatione multa accumulat Gregorius de praedestinatione, iustificatione, ac baptismo, Respondendum est non admittendo suam causalem: quia ille est praedestinatus, ideo est iustificatus; sed potius econtra.' Cf. Gregory, *In 2 Sent.* dist. 26–8 q. 2 art. 2 (see n. 70), 110.25–9.

[83] '[S]ectam et Capreolinam et Scotisticam manifesta interpretatione successive profitebar,' Kähler (see n. 64), 3.20.

[84] Luther cannot have read this treatise of Eck's younger years before 18 March 1518; otherwise, he would not have expressed such astonishment at the scholastic tenor of the *Obelisci*. Concerning Luther's knowledge of the *Chrysopassus*, the only evidence available is *WA* 2, 673.4–8: 'Satis indicavit hoc Lipsica disputatione, Indicant et libri eius de praedestinatione et mystica theologia: omnia fortissime et summa primo tentat, ita ut casum grandem illi misere metuam. Breviter, ipse tu nosti, dolia vacua esse sonantiora plenis.' In J. C. Mylius, *Memorabilia bibliothecae academiae Jenensis,* Jena-Weißenfels 1746, which also lists the books from the old Wittenberg university library (from before 1547), there is no listing for the *Chrysopassus.* However, there was at least one copy at Wittenberg, because it was burned, so Luther tells us, at the Elster Gate on 10 December 1520; see *WA* 2, 234. In his inaugural lecture at Wittenberg, delivered on 19 August 1518, Philip Melanchthon attacked Eck in the course of his general assault on scholastic dialectic, probably on account of Eck's commentary on Peter of Spain: *In summulas Petri Hispani . . . explanatio,* Augsburg (1543), ed. J. Metzler SJ, Münster 1930, LXXV; cf. Eck's treatise of

to free himself from his past; his debate with that past allowed him direct access to Eck's way of thinking, his 'system of coordinates'. The historian, however, who must attempt to get inside this confrontation across the gulf of the intervening centuries, cannot do without the *Chrysopassus* if he wishes to shed more light on the background to Leipzig.

Serious consequences for the unity of the reforming camp arose from the different paths taken to Leipzig by Luther (via Heidelberg and Augsburg) and Karlstadt. This should not, however, stop us from pursuing the trail marked out by Karl Bauer[85] – namely considering the Wittenberg circle as a whole, in order to do justice to a linguistic creation of Luther himself: to 'Wittenbergize' (*Wittenbergescere*). Despite the constant flux in the ranks of the Wittenberg theologians and their supporters, the fates of Luther and Karlstadt, with their shared, deeply-felt obligation to Staupitz, are intimately connected – so much so that there is no reason to imitate those observers (and there are many) who see the *via leucoriana* (the path of Wittenberg), which both men represented, from the perspective of their subsequent alienation and enmity. Luther was told almost simultaneously by Karlstadt that he had been proceeding in too slow and too conservative a fashion, and by Staupitz that he was going too fast and was too radical: demonstrating not only that these three had never really formed a common front, but also a certain disappointment over the realization that the path they had followed together at some places was not going to allow them to go any farther together.[86]

1507, ibid. LXXIIf. No. 1 (1) and 1 (2); 'De corrigendis adolescentiae studiis', in: *Melanchthons Werke in Auswahl*, III: *Humanistische Schriften*, ed. R. Nürnberger, Gütersloh 1961, 32.20. Eck's Vienna theses (cf. n. 29) and this commentary on Peter of Spain were doubtless among the 'Eckiana' burned at the Elster Gate.

[85] Karl Bauer, *Die Wittenberger Universitätstheologie und die Anfänge der Deutschen Reformation*, Tübingen 1928. Cf. Luther's emotional letter from Nuremberg, written three days before he arrived in Augsburg (7 October), his 'testament' to the Wittenberg circle (Karlstadt, Amsdorf, Melanchthon, Beckmann et al.): 'De Eckio nostro minor est fama, quam vellem. Creditur Nurmbergae non adeo bene Wittenbergescere, quin Theologis Vittenbergensibus inuidiam operari voluisse dicitur. Sautium mihi est cor erga eum, [cum] aliud didicer[im]' (*WAB* 12, 14.6–9; 4 October 1518).

[86] Even before the unrest at Wittenberg (1521–2), Luther was conscious of the differences between himself and the other Wittenberg theologians, though in the sense of 'diversity in unity'. Cf. his letter of 15 February 1518, to Spalatin: 'Mihi in indulgentiis hodie videri non esse nisi animarum illusionem et nihil prorsus utiles esse nisi stertentibus

Let us return, at the end, to our starting point. In 1518, under the single heading 'do your best' (*facere quod in se est*) and in the parallel debates between Karlstadt and Eck and Luther and Prierias, the two central points of contention of the 95 Theses were clearly developed. The historian may be permitted to regret, in retrospect, that Karlstadt's impulsive and aggressive love of a fight prematurely restricted mobility in questions of state and ecclesiastical policy and diminished the number of potential allies of the reform.

The theologian, however, can only confirm that this is how the battle on two fronts was carried out. Luther prepared the way for this battle when he turned away from his program of university reform and took on the project of reforming the Church in his historically powerful 95 Theses, which cannot be explained away as mere topics for academic discussion.

---

et pigris in via Christi. Et si hanc sententiam non tenet noster Carlstadius, certum est tamen mihi, quod eas nihil ducit' (*WAB* 1, 146.55–8). I do not see Luther's private statement on this matter as more radical than the *Tractatus de Indulgentiis,* in which he could judge indulgences in so positive (*forte*) a fashion as *suffragii* that 'today more than earlier' ('nunc . . . quam olim') 'multi intrant [in purgatorium] et pauci pro eis laborant, dum praecedentes et adhuc superstites utrinque segnes fuerunt et sunt, Papa eis isto saltem modo succurrit' (*WAB* 12, 8.143–9.148; 31 October 1517).

I am therefore unable to agree with Ernst Kähler's claim that Luther's statement at Leipzig 'fast sophistisch klingt': 'I have never denied that indulgences are useful; but they are no use to Christians, i.e. for those whose actions are ardent, who love and seek Christ as befits their [!] name ['non Christianis, hoc est fervide agentibus, Christum secundum nomen suum (!) amantibus et quaerentibus . . .']; these people do not wish to be freed of works (obligations), they want more works to be imposed on them' (*WA* 59, 557.3899f.; Kähler, 'Beobachtungen zum Problem von Schrift und Tradition in der Leipziger Disputation von 1519', in: *Hören und Handeln. Festschrift für Ernst Wolf,* ed. H. Gollwitzer and H. Traub, Munich 1962, 214–29; 229). Cf. the traditional statement in the *Tractatus de Indulgentiis:* 'Perfecte contritus evolat sine indulgentiis . . .'; and in the *conclusio:* 'Id itaque diligenter attendendum, ne indulgentiae, id est satisfactiones, fiant nobis cause securitatis et pigritiae et damnum interioris gratiae. Sed sedulo agamus, ut morbus naturae perfecte sanetur et ad Deum venire sitiamus prae amore eius. . .id est assidue sanantem gratiam eius quaeramus' (*WAB* 12, 7.66f.; 9.152–6).

Nor can I agree with Kähler's conclusion: 'Damit wird die Problematisierung der verpflichtenden Tradition von einer ganz anderen Seite her vollzogen, nämlich von der Frage her: Wem gilt sie? Ihm geht es um die christiani, mit ihnen allein [?] will er es zu haben haben. Die traditionelle Autorität wird entmächtigt, da die (wahren) Christen dessen nicht bedürfen, was die Kirche ihnen hier anbietet' (229). This, as I see it, 'converts' the Luther of Leipzig and 1519 into either a Joachimite *fraticellus* or a forerunner of the later antinomians.

Chapter 7

FROM PROTEST TO CONFESSION: THE CONFESSIO AUGUSTANA AS A CRITICAL TEST OF TRUE ECUMENISM

Why ought we to concern ourselves with the Confession of Augsburg? Let us first measure the distance that separates us from it before we try to cross the gap. What motivates us to attempt this jump into a narrow past? Certainly, it is narrow compared to current ambitions to think not in terms of single countries or continents, but globally; not in terms of denominations, but ecumenically. It is narrow because we are no longer driven by fear of the final cleansing fires, but by the prospect of a universal conflagration here and now.

Only one sentence from the entire Confessio Augustana is immediately applicable as a political program in our threatened world: 'Without violence, by the Word alone' – 'sine vi humana sed verbo'.[1] A non-violent reformation – that has an immediate appeal for us. But even this bridge to the past will not hold much weight. Compared to the genuine, verifiable history of the Reformation as it was experienced by contemporaries, this congenial slogan is merely one splinter of a party platform that served persuasive, not practical, purposes. The path from the posting of the 95 Theses at Wittenberg to the program of the Evangelicals at Augsburg leads across the battle field at Mühlhausen, where the peasants were cut down, row upon row, by the well-equipped princely armies.

We can do justice to the Confessio Augustana only if we are prepared for it to tell us things that do not correspond to the liberal ordering of our own world. We must resist the temptation to squeeze a few drops of (con-)temporary relevance from the Ausburg Confession, because its significance is to be found not at the beginning of the path of historical inquiry, but at the end.

---

[1] *Die Bekenntnisschriften der evangelisch-lutherischen Kirche*, Göttingen 1982⁹, 124.9.

1. The Non-violent Reformation

The Confessio Augustana was the answer of the Evangelicals to an imperial demand that they justify their Reformation. It started out as a status report of the Reformation *à la* Wittenberg already begun in various territories and cities of the Empire. Frequently reworked by Melanchthon, this accounting developed into a confession of faith, the Confessio. It was read out solemnly before the Imperial Diet at Augsburg, a city that had since Roman times been called *Augusta Vindelicorum:* hence the Confessio *Augustana.*

The Emperor's demand was doubly surprising. Nine years earlier, the Pope and the Emperor, the two most powerful rulers of Europe, had in a rare moment of agreement anathematized Luther as a heretic and thus condemned him – as a deadly danger to Church and Empire – to temporal and eternal death. Even though they could not lay hands on him, they attempted to carry out the spiritual death sentence. His writings were banned, could not be printed or sold, and were publicly burned. The first surprise is to be found in the despatches to Rome of the papal legates: in the years 1521 to 1530, the evangelical movement grew ceaselessly, despite the threats and obstacles placed in its path. Though Luther stood alone before the Emperor at Worms in his refusal to recant, the Confessio Augustana was signed by entire territories and by two cities, Nuremberg and Reutlingen.

The second surprise was that the Emperor's summons to the Imperial Diet declared that he was ready to listen 'in love and benevolence'[2] – hence seemingly above the parties – to both the Evangelicals and the adherents of the old Church. He saw himself, therefore (and this is the surprise) as the highest court of appeal in matters of belief.

---

[2] *Urkundenbuch zu der Geschichte des Reichstages zu Augsburg im Jahre 1530,* 2 vols., ed. K. E. Förstemann, Halle 1833–5 [Osnabrück 1966], vol. 1, 8. The Emperor was at first hesitant to appear in person at the Imperial Diet in Germany. The state of affairs in the Kingdom of Naples and the impending campaign against Florence made it seem more important that he stayed in Italy. That Charles finally decided to attend the Diet can be ascribed to the pressure exerted on him by his brother Ferdinand and by his chancellor, the Bishop of Trent. Cf. H. Rabe, 'Befunde und Überlegungen zur Religionspolitik Karls V. am Vorabend des Augsburger Reichstags 1530', in: *Confessio Augustana und Confutatio. Der Augsburger Reichstag 1530 und die Einheit der Kirche,* ed. E. Iserloh, Münster 1980, 101–12; 105f.

Charles stood between the established battle fronts in ecclesiastical politics. For almost four months, up to February of 1530, he lived beside the Medici Pope Clement VII in the Palazzo Pubblico of Bologna and pressed the Pope energetically to call a council right away. He failed – because the popes had learned to fear councils. German pressure for a council only intensified this fear, or as Pope Clement said in 1530: 'The Germans will turn the Council and the whole world upside-down.'[3]

As we now know, rather the opposite was true: the Curia turned the Church and with it, all of Germany and the rest of the world upside-down by preventing a council, which was the last chance to maintain the unity of the western Church.[4] After Luther's excommunication, this was perhaps the gravest error committed by the papacy *vis-à-vis* the Reformation. Only a tiny minority in the Empire would have been content with an unreformed Roman Church, and the Emperor certainly belonged to the majority in this regard.

If we consider other possibilities for reforming the Church and putting the religious dispute to rest, there was, aside from a general council, the alternative of a national council. The Pope did indeed prevent a general council, but the Emperor himself blocked a German national solution. He simply refused the urgent plea of his brother Ferdinand and of almost all the Imperial Estates to call a German national council at Speyer.[5]

A national council would have been a genuine opportunity for Europe and for the Church, because it would have laid the foundations for a national German Church. This notion was 'in the air' in Europe. Less than fifteen years earlier, the Pope had managed, by virtue of considerable diplomatic effort, to avert at the last possible moment the establishment of a national Church in France, with the Concordat of 1516. In this same year (1530), decisive steps were

---

[3] *Calendar of State Papers, Spain IV,* vol. 1, 822f., cited by H. Jedin, 'Die Päpste und das Konzil in der Politik Karls V.', in: *Karl V. Der Kaiser und seine Zeit,* ed. P. Rassow and F. Schalk, Cologne 1960, 104–17; 111.

[4] H. Jedin formulates the idea that such a council was impossible in more cautious terms: 'Es wäre vergebliches Bemühen, den Medicipapst für das Konzil zu gewinnen' (ibid.).

[5] Further details can be found in my book *Werden und Wertung der Reformation,* Tübingen 1979², 337f.; English tr.: *Masters of the Reformation,* Cambridge 1981, 267f.

taken toward the independence of the English Church. However, for the Habsburg world-empire, an independent German national Church would have posed a deadly threat and deprived it of its political foundation: the universal Habsburg Empire needed a universal Church. In the absence of a general or national council, the Emperor could do little but insist not only that he was the Protector of the Church (according to time-honored medieval custom), but also that his was the highest authority to decide questions of faith.[6] A medieval pope would never have taken this from an emperor, but Clement VII remained silent: a general council seemed far more dangerous.

One person who did not remain silent in 1530 was Martin Luther. His intervention leads us to a third, and this time lasting, surprise. *Not the Pope, but Luther dug in his heels against a new imposition of imperial control over the Church, against confusing an Imperial Diet with a council, against the confusion of Christ and the Emperor.* He develops the freedom of a Christian logically into the freedom of the Church of Christ.

In 1530, Luther criticized his own performance at the Imperial Diet of Worms in 1521, a performance that is generally depicted today as the glorious final chapter in the development of the 'young' Luther. Looking back at Worms, he now sees that he confused, in his confession of faith in 1521, the two kingdoms: that of this world with that of Christ,[7] that of politics with the kingdom of faith, to which we gain access only by being saved in baptism. But now, in the year 1530, he is convinced of the opposite: 'The Emperor has no authority in this matter of ours.'[8]

The slogan cited at the beginning, 'without violence, by the Word alone', now comes into its own in the political struggle, not in

---

[6] This understanding of his role appears not only in personal correspondence, but also in the justification for his refusal to allow the Confessio Augustana to be read publicly: '[A]uch das ausscreyben des reichstages hilthe in, das allein seyne M' iders opinion horen und darunder handeln wolle' (Valentin von Tetleben, *Protokoll des Augsburger Reichstages 1530*, ed. H. Grundmann, SVRG 177, Göttingen 1958, 75).

[7] The terms used to describe these kingdoms vary, but what they refer to is clear. In the *Small Catechism* of 1531 Luther speaks of 'Gottes und der welt reich' (*WA* 30I, 351.3f.).

[8] *WAB* 5, 470.5f.: '[C]ausam nostram non posse ferre Caesarem iudicem.'; see also 456.3–5: 'Vides autem causam nostram redire in similem eventum, quo et sub me Wormatiae fuit, scilicet ut Caesarem iudicem patiatur.' Cf. ibid., 455.57f.

Utopian dreams. The Emperor is fighting for the imperial Church and the empire of the Church; Luther's Reformation favors a dividing line between the two spheres to establish and preserve both the freedom of the Church and the secular character of the empire.

Seen from Luther's perspective, the festival we celebrate today [21 June, the anniversary of the Confession's public proclamation – trans.] does not commemorate the political recognition of the Reformation, because the 'Kingdom of this world' and the 'Kingdom of Faith' are governed in very different ways. The modern-day celebration commemorates what, for Luther, was a joyous occurrence: thanks to the reading of the Confession in the midst of the Imperial Diet's business, amidst icy, steely political maneuvering, the Gospel was proclaimed publicly. As Luther said, it was God's good counsel 'that broke down the Emperor's and Princes' door for our Confession of Faith . . .'.[9] Georg Spalatin, the first evangelical Christian to participate in high politics, and Luther's go-between with the Prince-Elector of Saxony, went so far as to claim that the hearts of their opponents were miraculously softened by God's intervention.[10] Luther did not believe that the Emperor experienced a sudden change of heart: God forced the door to allow the open proclamation of the Gospel. Luther's urgent advice was not to imitate his performance at Worms and thereby confuse an Imperial Diet with a council. *An Imperial Diet is always an Imperial Diet, and cannot become a council.* Charles V remained the German Emperor and did not become the head of a Church, an ecclesiastical lord. A Confession of Faith is not merely 'politics by other means'; it is not concerned with 'the art of the possible'. Negotiations for a concordat between Christ and the Emperor are useless, in fact dangerous; they are even impious.

After reading out the Augustana, Melanchthon and the Saxon theologians were ordered home by Luther: 'You have made your Confession, now come back . . . I absolve you from this Imperial Diet in the name of the Lord. Now home again, home again!'[11] Political reassurances are unnecessary, in fact they are sure signs of weak faith.

[9] *WAB* 5, 480.29f.

[10] See *WAB* 5, 472.1–6.

[11] 'Igitur absolvo vos in nomine Domini ab isto conventu. Immer wieder heim, immer heim!' (*WAB* 5, 480.21f.).

A peculiarity, indeed a characteristic, of the Gospel is that it is persecuted in the world; suppression is normal, not toleration. The concrete political context for the test of the Augustana is simply this: at the end of the summer of 1530, three pastors were dismissed from Augsburg, where the Confessio Augustana had just recently been pronounced, and a fourth pastor was thrown into jail with the Anabaptists who were already locked up there.[12]

Today we celebrate the Confessio Augustana openly and in safety. We do not even think about overcoming the fundamental differences between Church and state, nor especially of a reconciliation and union of throne and altar. We remember on the one hand God's merciful intervention that allows us to be evangelical Christians. On the other hand, we are thankful that we are privileged to be able to bear witness to our beliefs in the Federal Republic of Germany, protected by the *Grundgesetz* [Basic Law, the German constitution – trans.]. It is a great privilege, but a temporary one that ought not to lull us into a false sense of security or let us become smug and inattentive. We ought to use it to prepare ourselves for a time when confession of faith will once again be accompanied by the dangers of martyrdom. Finally, we ought to give thanks today that we enjoy this privilege while innumerable fellow Christians in many other parts of the world do not.

We have heard how Luther disapproved of Melanchthon staying at the Imperial Diet. Does his criticism have anything to do with Melanchthon's *opus,* the Confessio Augustana itself? Luther communicated to the Prince-Elector his agreement with the Confessio Augustana, yet he could not stop himself from adding: 'I cannot step so softly and quietly'.[13]

The first thing to consider is that this is an addition to the unreserved praise of the main clause: the Confessio 'pleases me greatly, and I don't know how I would improve or change it' (the Confessio 'gefellet mir fast [sehr] wol, und weis nichts dran ze bessern noch endern'). It makes no sense to interpret the adjoining prayer as a piously disguised criticism: 'Christ our Lord help that it bring forth much and great fruit, as we hope and pray.

---

[12] See *WAB* 5, 464 n. 2.
[13] 'Denn ich so sanfft und leise nicht tretten kan' (*WAB* 5, 319.7f.).

Amen.'[14] Scarcely two months later, Luther thanks God 'who hears our prayers' from the fullness of his heart: 'It fills me with unspeakable joy to have experienced this moment, when [Christ] was publicly proclaimed in this marvelous Confession.'[15] Luther's praise is clear, but he could not step as lightly as the Confessio Augustana. He would doubtless have formulated it in harsher terms. Along with free access to the Gospel, the walls of the papacy must fall. Along with justification by faith alone, the institutions of works-righteousness must be demolished. This demolition must include the rejection of Purgatory, masses for the dead and indulgences. The Confessio Augustana is cautious on these points. Melanchthon felt that clearly emphasizing the bishop's role as shepherd of the flock and servant of the Gospel would put the Pope in his place, even without harsh denunciations.

Luther pressures Melanchthon: 'dare to trust in the Gospel alone, without political alliances to the imperial court and papal throne' – alliances that are only temporary in any case. In a flood of letters, Luther entreated his representative to break off negotiations, not to turn the Confessio Augustana into a mere 'Augsburg program'. Political security is, so far as Luther is concerned, arbitrary interference in God's rule: 'We ought to behave like people, not like God.'[16] 'We need faith desperately if the cause of faith is not to become a cause without faith.'[17]

We are confronted here by positions of principle that we ought not to judge too readily. Melanchthon negotiates because he fears a religious war – that is, a civil war – that would throw Germany into

[14] 'Christus unser herr helffe, das sie viel und grosse frucht schaffe, wie wir hoffen und bitten, Amen' (*WAB* 5, 319.6 and 8f.). Cf. Luther's unstinting praise for the Confessio Augustana in its final form: 'Relegi heri tuam [scil Melanchthon] Apologiam diligenter totam, et placet vehementer' (ibid., 435.4f.). Even from the perspective of two years later, in 1532, Luther's view does not change: 'Der reichstag zu Augspurg ist mit keinem gelt nicht zu bezalen propter confessionem fidei et verbi Dei factam a nobis; den da haben sie bekent, das unser confession recht sei und ware' (*WAT* 2, no. 1481; cf. *WAT* 1, no. 486).

[15] 'Mihi vehementer placet vixisse in hanc horam qua Christus per suos tantos confessores in tanto consessu publice est praedicatus confessione plane pulcherrima' (*WAB* 5, 442.12–14). In his enthusiasm Luther practically gushes about the Emperor, whom he endows with almost Davidic traits.

[16] 'Wir sollen menschen und nicht Gott sein' (in a Latin letter dated 30 June 1530, and addressed to Spalatin via Melanchthon; *WAB* 5, 415.45).

[17] 'Tantum est opus fidei, ne causa fidei sit causa sine fide' (*WAB* 5, 414.30).

utter misery. In his negotiations he appeals to reform-minded powers in the Church and empire, and courts the educated in all camps and parties. Melanchthon was certainly wrong in imagining a third, politically formative power. Without being too timid,[18] he demonstrated a good nose for reality in his premonitions of war. He was right to warn all and sundry: 'The Church is threatened by disaster; not only Germany, but all of Europe is in the most appalling danger.'[19] This analysis of the situation dates from Augsburg (3 June, 1530); it was fully realized in the German civil war and the first European 'World War', which ended only in 1648 after many more than just thirty endless years.

Luther's works are also full of warnings against war and disastrous times. He shares Melanchthon's worries about the future without reservations. What he does about them is a different thing: we did not found the Church, we did not invent the Gospel, we did not discover the Reformation. The Church, the Gospel and the Reformation are all God's affair. This is what Luther means when he tries to impress on Melanchthon the negotiator: 'Do not give away more than you have.'[20]

---

[18] The concluding section of the lovely but unfortunately unfinished Luther book by H. Bornkamm is dedicated to his agreement on this topic with H. Rückert: H. Bornkamm, *Martin Luther in der Mitte seines Lebens. Das Jahrzehnt zwischen dem Wormser und dem Augsburger Reichstag,* Göttingen 1979, 603, n. 94; cf. 599, n. 77. According to Rückert's interpretation, Luther was not criticizing the Confessio Augustana but Melanchthon's existential *Angst.* Cf. H. Rückert, 'Luther und der Reichstag zu Augsburg. Glossen zu drei Briefen Luthers von der Coburg', in: *Deutsche Theologie* 3 (1936), 67–96; 76f. Reprinted in Rückert, *Vorträge und Aufsätze zur historischen Theologie,* Tübingen 1972, 108–36; 116f. Luther's central critique, however, is directed at that which causes Melanchthon's *Angst,* briefly stated in a letter from the Coburg on 27 June: 'Philosophia tua ita te vexat, non theologia . . .' (*WAB* 5, 399.16f.). This warning concerning the philosophy of worldly politics and calculation expresses Luther's feeling that Melanchthon misses the point about the two kingdoms. Rückert's interpretation is correct to the extent that Luther emphasizes the *vexare.* In passing: I know of no analysis of Melanchthon's 'fate' more penetrating than Rückert's, published in the same volume for the first time. It is a speech presented at Tübingen on the occasion of the anniversary festivities for Melanchthon held on 28 June 1960: 'Philipp Melanchthon', in: *Vorträge und Aufsätze,* 137–44.

[19] '[A]nimadverti ex multis signis vestram Celsitudinem maxime affici calamitate ecclesiae et periculo non solum totius Germaniae, sed omnino totius Europae' (*Melanchthons Werke in Auswahl,* vol. VII,2, Gütersloh 1975, 163.30–164.4; a letter addressed to Archbishop Albrecht of Mainz).

[20] '[G]ebt nicht mehr, denn Ihr habt, ne cogamini denuo ad difficilius et periculosius bellum pro evangelio defendendo' (*WAB* 5, 578.36f.).

Both before and after the reading of the Augustana, Luther warns Melanchthon in the sternest terms not to 'philosophize',[21] not to stick his nose into God's business: 'Is it a lie, then, that God gave his Son for us?', his son 'to whom all power is given on earth and in heaven. Better to fall with Christ than to stand with the Emperor.'[22] Melanchthon should throw this in his opponents' face: 'Be as defiant and obstinate as you like under your Emperor, we will defy you in the name of ours and see who wins.'[23]

It is now clear that Luther was quite right, even in political terms. We know what was actually going on at Augsburg because we have access to Cardinal Campeggio's nunciature reports to Rome; we can read the instructions from Rome, the official documents of the Imperial Diet and some of the imperial correspondence.

Even though negotiations with Melanchthon continued through June and July, the papal legate Campeggio had long been under instructions from Rome to make no concessions.[24] The Emperor had long ago given up his promised neutrality, and allowed the *Confutatio* – the refutation of the Confession of Augsburg – to be issued in his own name on 3 August.[25] Luther, however, had not been arguing politically. Politicians are supposed to take care of politics; the Church should stand by its Confession.

---

[21] 'Sed frustra haec scribo, quia tu secundum philosophiam vestram has res ratione regere, hoc est . . . cum ratione insanire, pergis, et occidis te ipsum, nec vides prorsus, extra manum tuam et consilium positam causam etiam extra curam tuam velle agi' (*WAB* 5, 412.51ff.).

[22] 'Soll's denn erlogen sein, daß Gott seinen Sohn für uns gegeben hat . . .' and 'scilicet ille regnator mundi. Et esto, ruat, malo ego cum Christo ruere, quam cum Caesare stare' (*WAB* 5, 411.13f.; 412.27f.).

[23] 'Trotzt nur getrost auf Euern Kaiser, so wollen wir auf unsern auch trotzen, und sehen, wer das Feld behält' (*WAB* 5, 412.46–8). Cf. Melanchthon's outwardly completely different, though essentially identical, formulation: n. 35 below.

[24] Salviati to Campeggio; Rome, 13 July 1530 (*Nuntiaturberichte aus Deutschland nebst ergänzenden Aktenstücken*, 1st section: 1533–1559, 1st supplement: 1530–1, ed. G. Müller, Tübingen 1963, no. 21, 81). It is not difficult to agree with G. Müller: 'Den transalpinen Vorgängen im rauhen und barbarischen Norden widmete Rom nur wenig Aufmerksamkeit. Das Weltgeschehen war entscheidend. Und "Welt" war für Clemens VII. zuerst einmal Italien' (*Die römische Kurie und die Reformation 1523–34. Kirche und Politik während des Pontifikats Clemens' VII*, Quellen und Forschungen zur Reformationsgeschichte 38, Gütersloh 1969, 93).

[25] *Die Confutatio der Confessio Augustana vom 3. August 1530*, ed. H. Immenkötter, Corpus Catholicorum 33, Münster 1979, 76.14–17; 204f.).

Now it becomes clear all at once that the formula 'without violence and by the Word alone' is not a pleasant slogan or a comfortable motto. It signifies the risk of faith – in all its consequences – and the willingness to live *without* a state Church apparatus, *without* a political safety net. The maintenance of the Church is to be entrusted to *God,* who makes its reformation *his own* business. He will protect the Church with *his* power by means of the Word, until the end of time.

2. Not Roman, but Catholic!

We have examined the historical *Sitz im Leben* (context) of the Augsburg Confession. The colossal superstructure of the medieval Church, which had grown up over the centuries, was being flattened, but a smooth modern building free of cracks did not just appear in its place. For this reason we must ask how we are to read the Confessio 450 years later, in a changed world and with a very different idea of what the world is: what survives to our own age that we can recognize as valid truths? The message of the Confessio is contained in its interpretation of faith, and consists of four points:

1. Christian faith is in accordance with the Scriptures.
2. Christian faith is catholic.
3. Christian faith is protestant.
4. Christian faith is evangelical.

These points determine and explain each other, one after the other, such that they will provide us with a full appreciation of what it means to be evangelical only after we have worked through all of them.

1. Christian faith is in accordance with the Scriptures

The final sentence of the Confession is highly significant: 'Should anything be missing from this Confession, we are ready, God willing, to give more information in accordance with Holy Scripture.'[26] The Confessio Augustana does not replace Scripture, rather it presupposes

---

[26] 'Si quid in hac confessione desiderabitur, parati sumus latiorem informationem, Deo volente, iuxta scripturas exhibere' (*Bekenntnisschriften,* 134.35–135.3). In Melanchthon's draft the formula 'God willing' (*deo volente*) pertains more clearly to the success of exegesis: '[D]urch Gottes Gnad aus heiliger göttlicher Schrift . . .' (*Bekenntnisschriften,* 136.24f.).

Scripture and forces us back to Scripture. The evangelical Confession is open to answering new questions on the basis of Scripture – though not for new structures to satisfy religious needs. The Confessio Augustana obliges us to provide more information only in accordance with Scripture. We are obliged to assume and fulfil this task along with our neighbors in faith. The scriptural principle is not presented in the Confessio Augustana as an isolated article; rather, it prepares the way for all further – and from today's perspective, all future – Christian confessions because it is founded on agreement with Scripture and because it can be revised only by reference to Scripture. At the end it says: 'Among us, nothing will have any validity, neither in doctrine nor in our ceremonies, that is contrary to Holy Scripture or the universal Christian Church.'[27] This 'universal Church' is the listening Church, which listens to Scripture, as Luther succinctly put it with a 'certain' play on words: 'The Church is holy and certain in Christ's Word. Outside Christ's Word she is certainly in error, a poor sinner, yet not damned, for the sake of Christ in whom she believes.'[28] The last sentence 'yet not damned, for the sake of Christ' is meant to console and express acceptance of all members of the divided Church.

2. Christian faith is catholic

The sentence just cited also touches on the second point: Christian faith is catholic. It confesses *with* the whole Church and *for* the whole Church because it embraces the entire truth of Christ. This catholicity is firmly anchored in the Confessio Augustana and is not to be confused with Roman Catholicism.

Roman Catholicism later distanced itself from the Reformation, at the Council of Trent, and thus from evangelical catholicism as defined and contained in the Confessio Augustana. Since the First Vatican Council, confirmed by the Second, 'catholic' has been so firmly identified with 'Roman' that, so far as Rome is concerned, any

---

[27] '[D]aß bei uns nichts, weder mit Lehre noch mit Ceremonien, angenommen ist, das entweder der heiligen Schrift oder gemeiner christlichen Kirchen zuentgegen wäre' (*Bekenntnisschriften*, n. 1 above, 134.21–5).

[28] 'In Christus wort ist sie heilig und gewis, Ausser Christus wort ist sie gewis eine jrrige, arme sunderin, doch unverdampt umb Christus willen, an den sie gleubt' (*WA* 30III, 342.14–17).

doctrinal reformation is to be condemned as compromising the truth. Reformation is therefore always a dispute over true catholicism.

Given that such far-reaching issues are at stake, it is very difficult to comprehend the Confession's lapidary summation: 'The whole dispute concerns only a few abuses.'[29] Melanchthon repeats ten times after reading the Augustana that the whole thing rests on a few abuses, then adds for emphasis: 'Not one single dogma separates us from the Roman Church.'[30] That is certainly no longer true; the Confessio Augustana has in this regard been superseded by subsequent church history. But was it possible to claim such doctrinal closeness even in 1530 without stretching the truth? Two points of view deserve to be emphasized in our answer to this question.

First, the celebrated phrase, 'the whole dispute concerns only a few abuses' has two functions – a fact that has been consistently overlooked. The double function becomes clear only when we note that this sentence occurs at the end of the first part. It announces that the second part of the Confessio will treat a few abuses, but also reaffirms that complete unanimity reigns concerning the first part.

The first part of the Augustana formulates the dogma, *the teaching of the undivided catholic Church: the dogma concerning the catholic church is dictated to and demanded from the Roman Church.* The Roman Church has been split by abuses from which it must be freed so that it can return to catholicity. The necessary process of liberation began in Saxony. The phrase 'a few abuses' is not toadyism, but instruction, entreaty and a serious warning. *Dogma,* that is, God's Revelation and the salvation of humanity, is not subject to negotiation.

The Confessio Augustana enjoins the dogma of catholicism on the Roman Church. This injunction relies on the effect and impact of the Gospel to 'get inside' the abuses and unmask them as shallow and empty. The Gospel itself is no dogma, but the basis, cause and interpretive framework of dogma. The Gospel of justification,

---

[29] 'Tota dissensio est de paucis quibusdam abusibus . . .' (*Bekenntnisschriften,* 83c.14f.; 83d.12–14). In the notes of Bornkamm's German translation of the Confessio Augustana, *Das Augsburger Bekenntnis* (Gütersloher Taschenbücher/Siebenstern 257, Gütersloh 1978[2]), this passage is attacked by Bornkamm – as is usual in the literature – as an attempt to minimize the differences between the two confessions in an unacceptable way *(Das Augsburger Bekenntnis,* 79, n. 48).

[30] 'Dogma nullum habemus diversum ab Ecclesia Romana' (*CR* 2,170; *Melanchthons Werke in Auswahl,* vol. VII, 2, 196.21f.).

understood in accordance with the Confessio Augustana, is the life-force of the believing Church, the capacity to understand dogma (the truth about God and humanity), to live it, to make it come to life. Living experience repeats the dogma of the old Church, not to prove its own orthodoxy but to strengthen the foundations of the besieged medieval Church. In this regard, the Confessio Augustana is simultaneously catholic and unsurpassably modern. There can be no withdrawal into a particular denominational world. The Confession is heard in the entire Church as it really is, abuses and all.

From the perspective of Augsburg, the medieval Church is our mother Church. But the doctrinal positions taken by the modern papacy are also our concern, along with the case of Hans Küng, because *our* catholicity is also at stake here.

The second point of view to be emphasized is that the power of the Confessio Augustana on this point is timeless; it is also bound to a specific time because it originated at a specific juncture of church history. Seen in historical context, it is an example of *strategy* in the service of faith. Far from all Protestant self-congratulation, the Confessio Augustana confesses the uttermost catholic faith, such that when it is rejected by Rome, the separation of the Roman from the catholic Church must necessarily follow. In order to make Augsburg comprehensible as a moment suspended between epochs, I will suggest a risky comparison of Melanchthon's enterprise in 1530 with Chamberlain's policy of appeasement and his peace mission to Munich in 1938 (29 September). The efforts he made at Munich provoke disagreement to this very day, but this at least cannot be denied: that the alliance of democracies was able to shed the last inhibitions of pacifism in the fall of 1939, when war broke out, was in part due to the knowledge that they had done their utmost to prevent war at Munich. The Confessio Augustana documents strategy in the service of faith in that its proponents also did *their* utmost at Augsburg.

Luther demonstrates more sympathy for Melanchthon's position than some modern scholars do, even when he remarks: 'I am afraid that we cannot agree quite so completely now, in 1531, as we could at Augsburg.' In those days we were still willing, Luther continues, to recognize episcopal official power and authority, so long as we were allowed clerical marriage, the cup for the laity, the reform of holy services and the Mass[31] – thus summing up the 'few abuses', the reform of which Melanchthon insisted was not 'negotiable'.

The Reformation was forced by the Emperor and by the Pope to go its own way after 1530. That modern Protestantism has consigned dogma to oblivion and neglects the sacraments appears in the clear and cold light shed by the Confessio Augustana. This state of affairs demonstrates how difficult and thorny a path we have trodden. The challenge presented by the Confessio Augustana is to return to the lived experience of catholicity – a challenge that has long since ceased to apply to Rome alone.

3. Christian faith is protestant

In 1529, one year before the solemn pronouncement of the Confessio Augustana, a minority of the Imperial Estates protested against the decision made by the Imperial Diet of Speyer to suppress the Reformation by force. The reason given for this protest was that 'where God's honor and the salvation of our souls are concerned, each person must stand alone before God and give an accounting of himself . . .'.[32] The Augsburg Confession is the fulfillment of this protestation. At that time, the protest was designed to defend the imperial rights of the evangelical Estates. The Confessio Augustana is an accounting of faith at the imperial level that in turn served legal interests at the imperial level, interests that are no longer relevant.

The Confessio Augustana bears noticeable marks from Lutheran participation in the politics of the empire: its unmistakable disapproval (*improbant*) of the Reformed tradition and its harsh condemnation (*damnant*) of the free Churches. The clear differences between the Lutherans, the Reformed (Sacramentarians) and Anabaptists (*Schwärmer*) can all be laid out in sober theological argument – even more explicitly than the Confessio Augustana does. But aside from sincere efforts to demonstrate the common ground shared with the Roman Church despite their deep differences, no

[31] 'Ich habe sorg, das wir nimer mehr so nahent zw samen khumen werden als zw Augspurg' (*WAT* 4, no. 4780; 495.7–9). Cf. *WAT* 1, no. 898; *WAT* 2, no. 2325b; *WAT* 4, no. 4731.

[32] '. . . in den Sachen Gottes Ehre und unser Seelen Heil und Seligkeit belangend [muß] ein jeglicher für sich selbst vor Gott stehen und rechenschaft geben . . .': *Deutsche Reichstagsakten,* Jüngere Reihe, vol. VII,2, Stuttgart 1935, 1277.29–31.

clear attempt is made to include the Lutherans' more radical adversaries within the sphere of catholicity. The Reformed tradition is chastised for its peculiar teachings on the Lord's Supper, but the Anabaptists are proscribed because they are seen exclusively in light of the miserable events surrounding Thomas Müntzer and the Peasants' War – which accounts for their unacceptably distorted portrait in the Confessio Augustana.

The historian must pass judgement: things could not have turned out otherwise. The Anabaptists excited attention at that time not so much for their beliefs (as a function of faith) as for their activities in the realm of politics: they were rebellious conspirators, dangerous to the common good, who, quite simply, compromised the cause of the Lutheran Reformation. The Protestant Estates could not afford to be seen as rebels and schismatics – like the Anabaptists – under pain of death. In 1530, moreover, commitment to the unity of the Church was inseparable from the struggle for the unity of the empire. The world-wide appeal of the Reformation soon transcended the bounds of the empire – which originally protected this movement, but soon afterward hindered it. Only when the sacred dream of the Holy Roman Empire of the German nation had been dreamed to an end could the internal and external foes of the Reformation – whether in Strasbourg or Zurich – come back into clear focus. Only when the Anabaptists had proven themselves to be capable of building communities and behaving in a socially responsible way – outside the territory of the empire, on much larger continents – could their truly profound theological divergences be discussed without the threat of excommunication.

The link between the Protestation of 1529 (and with it the term 'Protestant') and the idea of 'Protestants' within the empire is only one side of the story, and a temporary one at that. The permanent effect of the Speyer Protestation of 1529 is that where God's honor and the salvation of our souls are concerned, each person must stand alone before God. At that time, imperial law protected the right of the evangelical Estates to make this declaration. Not long after, this objection became the 'Protestant principle' that applies to all believers. Despite a positive attitude toward this world and despite its largely conservative concepts of order, the basic motivation behind the Confessio Augustana reappears repeatedly: the resolve to obey God in preference to men.

The Confessio Augustana also demands that we do our utmost to ensure that the Church – as far as possible – respects, affirms and supports the secular order. The unmistakably protestant responsibility that each person has before God constitutes a fixed border which we are not allowed to cross. Often decried as an individualistic undermining of society, this tradition actually bred tolerance and contributed to the development of democratic ideals, including the protection of minorities.

The negative side of the concept 'protestantism' becomes a positive affirmation of life 'in the shadow of the Cross' when the congregation of the faithful is persecuted and the authorities deny it protection. This principle is already formulated in the Protestation of Speyer and included in the Augsburg Confession. Duke, later Prince-Elector, Johann Friedrich of Saxony, a signatory of the Confessio Augustana, made this reservation concerning one's responsibility before God into the charter of Christian state ethics. In a letter to the chief of the House of Orange-Nassau he closes, officially for himself and in principle for all Christians: 'better an unmerciful Emperor than an unmerciful God'.[33] Johann Friedrich had to pay an unmerciful Emperor the highest price that could be exacted from him: the electoral dignity. The last signatories of the Confessio Augustana, the Mayor and Council of Reutlingen, opted – against all political reason, surrounded as they were by Habsburg territories – for a merciful God. In this regard, Protestantism was both untimely and outside time.

4. Christian faith is evangelical

The fundamental reason for Christians to appeal (legitimately) to the Confessio Augustana is its testimony that Christian faith is based on the Gospel alone. We have no choice but to lay bare this sensitive point. It provides a perspective that allows us to describe the Christian faith as scriptural, catholic and protestant. The base line that runs through all the articles is formulated thus at the end of the Confessio: 'The most important article of the Gospel will always be that we receive God's grace through faith in Christ without any merit

[33] 'lieber einen ungnädigen Kaiser als einen ungnädigen Gott' (*Johann Friedrich der Grossmütige 1503–54*, ed. G. Mentz, Jena 1903, section 1, 136, n. 21; addressed to Count William of Nassau and dated 24 October 1530).

of our own.'[34] The Confessio Augustana is not proclaiming a new Reformation dogma that has to be believed. The central point is the vital force of the Church and justification.

Justification is the basis of the relationship between God and the individual human being. The process of justification changes the relationship between the Church and the world. The world is no longer made worthy only by the Church and by God's grace, but is recognized for its own merits, its dignity and value, as a gift of God. This recognition demands first of all that the most serious disease of the time be healed: the Prince-Bishop must be neutralized, and the evangelical bishop is to practice discipline without human violence, with God's Word alone. This phrase signals the end of an important part of the Middle Ages. Political and ecclesiastical rule are bent back into shape and restored, each to its own divinely-appointed sphere of activity.

This means on the one hand the withdrawal of the Church from secular power politics. On the other, Christians return to the world strengthened and free to create a space purged of political ideologies, in which the worldly needs of our neighbor are the legitimate and highest standard of political decisions. Where the kingdoms are separated and bent back into their proper shape, the Augustana's doctrine of justification is not only ecclesiastically enjoined, but set free to do good in the world.

Let me end with an anecdote that originates, in all probability, in a historical event. During the Imperial Diet at Augsburg, a rich citizen invited the leading theologians from both sides to eat with him, among them Melanchthon and one of his most vehement adversaries, Johannes Cochlaeus. After the food was served, Melanchthon said grace. The Old Believers were surprised that Lutherans could pray too. Melanchthon replied to them: 'The Papists don't even know what prayer is, they should learn it from us.' Finally Cochlaeus was unable, at the end of the debate that ensues, to say anything else other than his own confession of faith: 'However that might be, he would stick to their Mother, the holy Christian Church.' Philip

---

[34] 'Dann es muß je der furnehme Artikel des Evangeliums erhalten werden, daß wir die Gnad Gotts durch den Glauben an Christum ohn unser Verdienst erlangen...' (*Bekenntnisschriften*, n. 1 above, 129.4–7).

Melanchthon answered: 'Well then, we'll stay with our Father and see who is more likely to go to the Devil.'[35]

The historian cannot tell who was right about the quickest way to Hell, but is forced to admit: Roman Catholicism is remarkably closed. The price of its confessional unity, however, has been the constant extension of the Church's arbitrary authority, right up to the infallibility of the pope. The evangelical party, free of these hierarchical constraints, has been able to react to the changing pressures of the times with more sensitivity to the condition of the world – and has of course paid for this freedom with a corresponding loss of substance. The Confessio Augustana calls us back today to a full life in faith: to live *in accordance with Scripture,* listening to the Word; to live a *catholic* life in confessing for the entire Church; to live a *protestant* life in the principle of resistance based on love for our neighbor; and to live an *evangelical* life, trusting in the Father.

We are Mother Church with all those who have gone before us in faith – capable of error, in need of correction; without any guarantee that there will not be catastrophes and disasters along the way. But we live in hope that we will reach the end safe, saved, in accordance with God's promise.

[35] 'Zuletzt . . . hebt Cocleus ahn und spricht, sie mochten sagen, was sie wolten, er wolte bey der mutter bleyben, bey der heiligen christlichen kirchen. Do hat Philip geantwort: Ey, so wollen wir bey dem vater bleiben, und wil zusehen, wer do ehr wirt zum Teuffel faren!' (*WAT* 4, XLII).

Chapter 8

TRUTH AND FICTION:
THE REFORMATION IN THE LIGHT
OF THE CONFUTATIO

1. Truth and Fiction

'O how I wish they would publish their *confutatio*.'[1] Martin Luther did not live to see the publication of this imperially-mandated reaction to the Confessio Augustana in the name of the Roman Church. The papal legate Campeggio intervened[2] after the Confutatio was delivered on 3 August 1530, to ensure that the Evangelicals did not receive a transcript. The text was not printed until 1559, at Cologne and Mainz, then in an unrevised second edition at Cologne in 1573.[3]

In consequence, during the decisive phases in the spread of the Reformation and its struggle for legitimacy at the imperial level (up to the Religious Peace of Augsburg, 1555), the Confutatio made a public appearance at an Imperial Diet and left its mark in the documents but, unlike the Confessio Augustana, its theological content played no noticeable historical role. As Luther was told,[4] the original version, known as the *Catholica et quasi extemporalis responsio* (Catholic and, as it were, extemporaneous response), was toned down considerably and shortened at the Emperor's command. The 'confutators' were the imperial spokesmen.[5] The *Catholica responsio*

---

[1] 'O quam optarem, ut ipsorum confutatio in lucem prodiret' (*WA* 30III, 389.11f.). The Weimar edition dates this fragment to 1531, yet there is no reason not to date it as early as fall of 1530. The earliest parallel to Luther's pride in the Confessio Augustana documented here ('Ita nostra confessio et Apologia in summa gloria est edita', ibid., 389.9f.) can be found in the letter to Conrad Cordatus (dated at the Coburg on 6 July 1530; *WAB* 5, 442.12–14).

[2] See J. Ficker, *Die Confutatio des Augsburger Bekenntnisses. Ihre erste Gestalt und ihre Geschichte*, Leipzig 1891, 87f.

[3] Cf. H. Immenkötter, *Die Confutatio der Confessio Augustana vom 3. August 1530*, Münster 1979, 52f. (= Conf.).

[4] *WAB* 5, 533.21f.; in a letter from Justus Jonas dated 6 August 1530.

[5] See Ficker (n. 2), 58–61.

was much harsher and, with its careful refutations of Luther's theses in particular, much more than a stop-gap effort to answer the Confessio Augustana. It was much more substantive in every regard than the Confutatio.

No matter how 'eirenic' the Confutatio seemed, Luther at least could not fail to understand it – like the *Catholica responsio* – as a clear rejection of any attempt at an evangelical Reformation of the Church. On 30 April 1531, Luther states clearly in retrospect that, already at Augsburg, the Pope had suppressed the liberation of the conscience by faith alone.[6] Scholarship still agrees with Luther that behind the outward differences, particularly those concerning baptism, the Mass and the invocation of saints,[7] there lurked a fundamental ecclesiological disagreement: does the Church continue forever in its apostolic mission, unwaveringly and legitimately, simply because it is the Church, or is its infallibility based on something outside its control, not contained in its structure, but authorized, protected and upheld by the Word alone? Luther referred to the events at Augsburg in a sermon about a year later. He went straight to the heart of the matter, to the notion of the unerring Church: 'As they claimed at Augsburg . . . the Church *is* pious because it *must* be holy on account of the inspiration of the Holy Spirit. Christ recognizes no such inspiration except by the Word alone; he will not allow the Holy Spirit to be separated from the Word.'[8]

Melanchthon remained optimistic until the last moment in negotiations with the papal legate at Augsburg, but his judgement, delivered at the time and on the spot, was no less unequivocal than

---

[6] 'Istam [doctrinam] papa hat unterdrucket et iam Augustae damnata' (*WA* 34I, 360.2; cf. *WA* 30II, 303.23; 30III, 283.25f.; 298.22f.).

[7] See on confession: *WA* 34I, 307.5ff.; on the Mass: *WA* 50, 204.10ff.; on the invocation of saints: *WA* 30III, 312.14ff.

[8] 'Wie sie zu Augsburg unter dem Reichstage in dem Edict furgaben: die Kirche ist from, darumb mus sie aus einsprechung des heiligen Geistes heilig sein [reden]. Solch Einsprechen wil Christus nicht haben, bindet allein an das wort [denn allein aus dem wort], er wil den heiligen Geist nicht abgesondert haben von seinem Wort' (*WA* 33, 274.3–11; weekly sermon on John 6–8, read between 5 November 1530 and 9 March 1532 at Wittenberg; the passage in question must date to the year 1531). Cf. *WAB* 5, 590.11–14.

Luther's: 'I believe that all sincere men have become more certain of the cause after hearing this childish Confutatio.'[9]

In the introduction to his edition of the Confutatio, Herbert Immenkötter described its rejection by the theologians surrounding Luther as generally 'smug and unthinking'.[10] Even if one hesitates to agree entirely with his dismissive evaluation – 'sure of victory' or even 'triumphal' would be closer to the mark – the evangelical reaction to the Confutatio was unanimous.

A glance at the first responses to the Confutatio from the evangelical camp help explain how this modern editor formed his opinion. Georg Spalatin's crushing retort to the Roman–imperial refusal to give the evangelical party a transcript of the Confutatio is characteristic: If they give us their rebuttal, as they ought to, they will have the worst of it. If they don't, it only reflects badly on their honor, and is a sure sign that they are ashamed of their actions.[11]

The dismissive reaction of the Evangelicals only seems 'reflexive', or rather 'overly critical' if we agree with Immenkötter's high praise of the Confutatio: it was in no way a bagatelle; rather, 'it clearly indicated the position of the Old Church on this matter'.[12] This presents us with a second, more far-reaching issue. Immenkötter himself elsewhere characterizes the immediately preceding period as evincing a 'frightening lack of theological clarity and dogmatic certainty'.[13] If we compare Immenkötter's two positions, his praise of the Confutatio and his critique of late medieval theology, we are forced to the astonishing conclusion that the Roman Church

---

[9] 'Viri boni et sapientes omnes visi sunt mihi erectiore animo esse, audita illa pueriliter scripta confutatione' (*WAB* 5, 537.26–8). Melanchthon expressed a similar sentiment on the same day in a letter to an unnamed correspondent: 'Omnes boni viri videntur mihi, audita illa, in nostris partibus facti firmiores, et adversarii, si qui sunt saniores, dicuntur stomachari, quod has ineptias obtruserint optimo Principi Caesari' (*CR* 2, 252; cf. *Melanchthons Briefwechsel, Kritische und kommentierte Gesamtausgabe*, ed. H. Scheible, vol. 1: Regesten 1–1109 (1514–30), Stuttgart 1977, 421, no. 1015). Cf. Melanchthon's reference to the 'publica testimonia multorum bonorum virorum' in the preface to the Apology. *Die Bekenntnisschriften der evangelisch-lutherischen Kirche*, Göttingen 1982⁹, 144.30–8. See also n. 53.

[10] 'selbstzufrieden und unkritisch': Conf., 49.

[11] *Annales reformationis*, ed. E. S. Cyprian, Leipzig 1718, 149; cited by Ficker (n. 2), 89. See also *WAB* 5, 538, n. 3.

[12] Conf., 48.

[13] H. Immenkötter, *Um die Einheit im Glauben. Die Unions-verhandlungen des Augsburger Reichstages im August und September 1530*, Münster 1973, n. 3.

underwent a miraculous conversion at Augsburg! How else can we explain so unprecedented a revolution – the Confutatio suddenly achieved the clarity that had been so lacking in the late Middle Ages?

Immenkötter is certainly not alone in his denigration of the late Middle Ages. Joseph Lortz blamed this lack of clarity on late medieval nominalism, which he censured as 'not (fully) Catholic' or even 'fundamentally un-Catholic'.[14] This laid the foundation for the positions of Erwin Iserloh,[15] and, more recently, Vinzenz Pfnür,[16] who dismiss Luther's critique of late medieval theology and the late medieval Church as merely 'relative', that is, only partially correct. Finally, Immenkötter goes so far as to decry this alleged theological confusion as characteristic of the late Middle Ages in general.

The sources indeed allow scholars to extend such a battle-front over an entire epoch by referring to a theological school, even through the work of a single theologian; but in a completely different way than Immenkötter does. Luther did not simply – as Pfnür claims – contradict one single, isolated theologian, the Tübingen professor Gabriel Biel (+1495), but attacked and refuted an entire normative theology that enjoyed widespread pre-eminence, had not been 'corrected' by the theological authorities of the Church (*Magisterium*) for nearly 200 years and grew directly out of ecclesiastical practice. Are we to believe that Luther's polemic bolts of the Reformation's early years – generally condemned by his present-day critics in the Catholic camp as 'the exaggerations of 1520 and 1521'[17] – provoked a 'clarification', a (in the truest sense of the word) miraculous Catholic conversion? If this were the case we would have no trouble agreeing on the healing power of Luther's theology – its power to keep the Church together and help build it up, and the power of the doctrine of justification, which propelled Luther's adversaries toward so-called 'full' catholicity.

---

[14] 'nicht (mehr voll-) katholisch' and 'wurzelhaft un-katholisch': J. Lortz, *Die Reformation in Deutschland,* vol. 1: *Voraussetzungen, Aufbruch, erste Entscheidung,* Freiburg 1962 [1939], 176, 173.

[15] Summarized in the *Handbuch der Kirchengeschichte,* ed. H. Jedin, vol. 4, Freiburg 1967, 42f., 51ff.

[16] Cf. V. Pfnür, *Einig in der Rechtfertigungslehre? Die Rechtfertigungslehre der Confessio Augustana (1530) und die Stellungnahme der katholischen Kontroverstheologen zwischen 1530 und 1535,* Wiesbaden 1970, 386f.

[17] Cf. Pfnür (n. 16), 188, 390, 392f.

Peter Manns has provided us with eloquent, well-documented and well-founded arguments against striving for ecumenism at Luther's expense by over-emphasizing the Confessio Augustana in hope of papal recognition.[18] Might it be possible to escape the dangers Manns pointed out by taking the Confutatio more seriously, thus revealing Luther's *catholic* mission and casting him as a prophetic savior of the Church? How much of this is mere projection, ecumenical wishful thinking, or even enthusiastic fiction – and how much is sober, possibly even sobering historical truth?

2. Reformation in the Light of the Confutatio

How did the authors of the Confutatio justify their role? Were they so indifferent to the program of the 'Wittenburg Movement', which in 1531 was spreading throughout Germany, that the Reformers had good reason to suspect they had been stricken with 'Satanic blindness'?[19]

The Confutatio nowhere suggests that the Church is in need of reformation. Apart from the general allusions to reform in the Emperor's epilogue,[20] there is a single exception concerning the abuses of the Mass denounced in the Confessio Augustana (Article 24).[21] The Confession of Augsburg is not concerned with abuses *per se* – for instance, the endless multiplication of private masses, which are then sold. Instead it pillories the deception of the faithful, who are led to believe that they can achieve justification by doing 'good works' – that is, endowing masses – rather than through faith alone. Whereas the central critical point of the Confessio Augustana is that such abuses have been allowed by the Church for centuries, the Confutatio merely admits: 'Every reasonable person wants such abuses to be

---

[18] Cf. P. Manns, 'Zum Vorhaben einer "katholischen Anerkennung der Confessio Augustana": Okumene auf Kosten Martin Luthers?', in: *Ökumenische Rundschau* 26 (1977), 426–50. Pfnür uses the thesis of 'the polemically exaggerated statements made by Luther' – though with the addition of the phrase 'and by other reformers of his time' – to explain the harsh condemnations pronounced at the Council of Trent (V. Pfnür, 'Anerkennung der Confessio Augustana durch die katholische Kirche?', in: *Internationale katholische Zeitschrift 'communio'* 4 (1975), 298–307; 5 (1976), 374–81; 477–8; reprinted in *Katholische Anerkennung des Augsburgischen Bekenntnisses?*, ed. H. Meyer et al., Frankfurt 1977, 60–81; 69).

[19] '. . . sapientissimi et humanissimi . . . sunt sub captivitate Sathanae.' *WA* 32, 176.24.

[20] Conf., 205–7.

[21] Conf., 203.7–17; *Bekenntnisschriften*, 92.10–19.

abolished.'[22] But it devotes not a single word to the question in principle: had the Church really been in error for so many centuries?

There is no indication that the confession of guilt made by the papal legate Francesco Chieregati (in January of 1523, in the name of Pope Adrian VI at the second Imperial Diet at Nuremberg) had any role to play, let alone that it might play a part in the Confutatio. The Confutatio is silent on the question of guilt – not surprisingly, since it was not intended as a confession, but as a refutation.[23] Refutations generally do not contain an admission of guilt; rather, they seek to justify one's own position. This explains the almost simultaneous appearance, with the concept *catholica,* of another term used by the Roman Church to refer to itself: *ecclesia orthodoxa* or *fides orthodoxa.*[24]

The birth of orthodoxy, therefore, dates not to the second half of the sixteenth century and not to the internal Protestant dispute over Luther's legacy, as is generally assumed, but to Augsburg in 1530. The imperial epilogue proclaims extensive agreement with the Confessio Augustana, but at the same time, demands that the Evangelicals adapt themselves (*conformare*), in questions that were 'perhaps' (*fortasse!*)[25] still disputed, to what had previously been defined as the 'orthodox' faith of 'the holy, common and Roman Church'.[26]

This insistence that unimpeachable orthodoxy can exist only within the Roman and Catholic Church recognized by the Emperor is the common denominator of all the articles in the Confutatio. Its authors thereby delineated quite sharply the limits to Rome's desire for peace.

In formal terms we must distinguish between two strands of argument that sketch out the profile of evangelical heterodoxy as seen

---

[22] '. . . nemo est eorum, qui recte sentiunt, qui abusus sublatos esse non percupiat.' Conf., 161.16f.

[23] In the Emperor's epilogue the Confutatio is described nonetheless as a 'confessio ac responsio' (Conf., 205.2).

[24] Conf., e.g. 77.19; 125.11; 159.8.

[25] Conf., 204.13; 205.8.

[26] 'der heyligen, gemeinen und romischen kyrchen' (Conf., 204.14f.). Concerning the development leading from the 'catholic' to the 'Roman Catholic' church, see for instance the new pastors' oath (*Pfaffeneid*) demanded by Vicar General Johann Fabri of Constance of all the pastors in his bishopric. Cf. my book *Werden und Wertung der Reformation,* 308f.; English tr.: *Masters of the Reformation,* 243f.

by the Confutatio. For one, the Evangelicals stand accused of reviving ancient doctrines long since condemned as erroneous. Second, the inconsistencies and disagreements in the evangelical camp brand the Reformation with the mark of heresy, which by definition contradicts itself. Although the professional polemical theologians of the Roman Church, after the bull threatening Luther with excommunication ('Exsurge Domine', of 15 June 1521), generally accepted the view that the Reformation was a rekindling of long-banned heresies, modern ecumenical dialogue has backed away from such charges – probably as the theology of the reformers becomes better known.

The second argument, concerning the differences within the evangelical camp, was at that time secondary, but now plays a significant role. However, the idea that doctrinal consistency is a guarantee of truth does not bode well for the future of ecumenism. At the time of the Reformation, differences in the interpretation of Holy Scripture between Wittenberg, Strasbourg, Zurich or Geneva were at first a great shock to the reformers, and then a grave menace – which they did overcome *without* sacrificing their obedient 'listening' to Scripture for the sake of maintaining the unity of their movement.

In order to establish how the Confutatio viewed the Reformation not only in structural terms, but also in terms of content, we need look no farther – aside from ecclesiology – than the articles concerning baptism (11), penance (12) and the Mass (24). The doctrine of justification turns out, not surprisingly, to be a shared theme in all these areas. The features of the doctrine of justification woven into these three articles can be grasped easily. 'Catholic orthodoxy' is characterized as the *via media,* the golden mean, between Pelagianism and Manicheism.

The authors of the Confutatio do not argue that the Confession of Augsburg went significantly beyond this standard of Catholic orthodoxy. On the contrary, it reaffirms the evangelical rejection of Pelagianism.[27] But it does hesitate to drive home the point that it would be Manichean to deny that merits are earned 'through the assistance of divine grace'.[28] The Confutatio consistently understands

[27] See Conf., 85.2–4.
[28] 'durch beystandt der gotlichen genaden'; 'per assistentiam gratiae divinae . . .' (Conf., 84.15; 85.11f.). As a citation of 'another' biblical authority, the redactor added this fundamental conclusion: 'Ubi enim est merces, ibi est meritum' (ibid., 87.1f.).

justification as sanctification ('making righteous'[29]) and rejects the position articulated in the Confessio Augustana that justification is due to faith alone.[30] Article 28 of the Augustana, 'On free will', is accepted, yet accepted in a specific sense: 'A true Christian should and must walk the middle way, so that he does not allow of too much to free will, as the Pelagians do, and so that he does not deny freedom of the will, as the godless Manichees have done . . .'.[31] The Augustana's distinction between servitude in regard to God (*coram Deo*) and freedom in regard to one's fellows (*coram hominibus*) is replaced by the golden mean, the path that leads between Pelagius and Mani.

If we were to draw a line here and conclude our discussion, we would of necessity arrive at results that are not only in accord with the Emperor's urgent call for peace, but also fit seamlessly into the modern ecumenical dialogue. The Confutatio evidently confirms what has been said in the past few years on the question of ecclesiastical unity from the perspective of the Confessio Augustana. The remaining differences concerning the doctrine of justification – and this has recently been confirmed by the evangelical side as well – 'need not be regarded as divisive with respect to the Church'.[32] But if such an accord is made of the straw of wishes and built on the sand of ahistorical enthusiasm, it will not last; indeed it can only cause damage. For this reason, we must subject this alleged consensus to rigorous testing against the 'spirit of the times' to determine how firm it really is. This does not absolve us of the necessity to do justice to the historical situation at Augsburg in 1530. The 'spirit' of this age is by no means new to the sixteenth century. It is unmistakably similar to the imperial desire for a united Europe capable of defending itself against incursions from the East.

[29] See Conf., 90.18; 92.1.

[30] 'cum id pertineat ad gratiam et caritatem' (Conf., 93.1f.).

[31] 'Dan also muß und soll ein rechter christ den mittelweg wandern, das er mit den Pelagianern dem freien willen nit zu vil zugebe, ime auch nit neme alle freyhait, wie dan die gotlosen Manicheer gethon haben . . .' (Conf., 116.16–18).

[32] '[brauchen nicht] als kirchentrennend bewertet zu werden, weil sie die Übereinstimmung in der Grundstruktur der Rechtfertigungsbotschaft nicht in frage stellen' (Dr. G. Gaßmann, President of the Lutherisches Kirchenamt, 'Die Rechtfertigungslehre in der Perspektive der Confessio Augustana und des lutherisch-katholischen Gesprächs heute', in: *Luther* 50 (1979), 49–59; 59). Gaßmann's position is based on a false dichotomy between what he sees as the central concern of the reformers, namely the doctrine of justification, and what he sees as our central modern concerns, namely the Lord's Supper and, above all, doctrinal points of ecclesiology (ibid., 49). For Luther's view, see notes 8 and 55.

3. Evangelical Recognition of the Confutatio?

We will start with Melanchthon's opinion that, except for a few 'scurvy vilifications' (*faule calumniae*) in the Confutatio, 'our Articles in themselves are all conceded'.[33] If the Confutatio really does concede the substance of the Confession of Augsburg, we are justified in asking whether – as a direct parallel to the proposal that Rome recognize the Confessio – the Confutatio can now be seen from the evangelical perspective as an acceptable element of a broader accord.

If we 'bracket out' the limitation expressed in Melanchthon's words 'in themselves' (*an ihnen selb*) – to which we will return – significant doubts emerge when we examine more closely the Confutatio's statements cited above concerning evangelical teaching on justification. On the surface, the condemnation of the Pelagians looks encouraging. But in fact, the Confutatio rejects a Pelagianism that never existed in that form, and that was never expressed in this way by Pelagius himself. The Confutatio reproves those Pelagians who teach that 'human beings can earn eternal life by their own efforts, without any help from God's grace (*seclusa gratia!*)'.[34]

The history of the concepts 'Pelagian' and 'Pelagianism' in the Middle Ages demonstrates that from our perspective, those who used and spread so extreme a definition of Pelagianism were Pelagians themselves. In their terms, the doctrine of justification seemed practically Augustinian, 'orthodox' in the language of the Confutatio, compared to the straw man of 'excessive Pelagianism'. Agreeing to the condemnation of a fictitious Pelagianism to be found somewhere in the history of *dogma* therefore did not eradicate actual Pelagianism within the context of *ecclesiastical* history. On the contrary, Augustine's genuine disciples are very clear on this point: the formulation of the Confutatio would alarm them and set off an immediate counter-offensive.

[33] 'Von der Lahr acht ich werde der Kaiser nicht disputieren. So sind unsre Artikel an ihnen selb alle concedirt in der Confutatio, allein sind etliche viele calumniae daran gehängt' (*CR* 2, 269). For the variant reading *faule* for *viele* see Pfnür, *Rechtfertigungslehre* (see n. 16), 250. A parallel to Melanchthon's judgement can be found in his *Gutachten* for Prince-Elector Johann of Saxony of 3/4 August (*CR* 2, 258); see *Melanchthons Briefwechsel* 1 (see n. 9), 419, n. 1009.

[34] Conf., 84.3f. Cf. the Latin version: 'Pelagiani damnantur, qui arbitrati sunt hominem propriis viribus seclusa gratia dei posse mereri vitam aeternam . . .' (ibid., 85.2f.).

The Confutatio claims that the *assistentia gratiae* (the help provided by grace) precedes all earned merit. This does nothing to clarify the situation. In terms of the late medieval debate, it is naïve and therefore revealing. No medieval theologian, not even Gabriel Biel, denied the existence of such 'assistance'.[35] The *Catholica responsio,* which was the lineal ancestor of the Confutatio, did provide the necessary reassurance that this auxiliary grace ought to 'precede, accompany and follow' merits.[36] But immediately following this admission, its authors felt obliged to be more precise and to make the telling distinction between *meritum de congruo* and *meritum de condigno.*[37] Given this distinction, all medieval Pelagians, semi-Pelagians or neo-Pelagians – I am not concerned here with precise nuances – could easily agree with this conclusion: 'Our works are of themselves in no way meritorious, but rather God's grace makes them worthy (*digna*) to earn eternal life.'[38]

The editor of the Confutatio criticizes Johannes Ficker for his facile commentary on the *Catholica responsio.*[39] Immenkötter deserves our thanks for his many references to Counter-Reformation works of the sixteenth century. If he had also sought out parallels in the late medieval literature, however (which he unfortunately felt he could not accomplish[40]), he would doubtless, in his first glance through the

[35] Conf., 84.15.

[36] 'Nam gratiam oportet prevenire, comitari ac subsequi' (Ficker (n. 2), 15.8f.).

[37] 'Errat itaque impie Luther, errat Rieger [Rhegius], qui temere dixerunt Paulum confodere omnia theologorum somnia de merito congrui et (con)digni' (Ficker (see n. 2), 18.13–19.1). In his last effort to reach a compromise, Luther imbued the *meritum de congruo* with a certain soteriological and historical importance, comparing it to the patient waiting of Israel for the fulfilment of the *promissio,* the incarnation of the Messiah, as he wrote in 1515. See *WA* 4, 262.4–11. In the farthest-reaching Roman Catholic attempt to come to an understanding on this question, thirty years later, Johannes Gropper based his view of *meritum de congruo* (as a good work *ex concedentia*) in the *promissio* in a similar, but ultimately very different way: 'Die promissio dei erlaubt es dem Sünder, nach Erfüllung der Voraussetzungen [sic] die Einlösung des Versprechens zu erwarten' (R. Braunisch, *Die Theologie der Rechtfertigung im 'Enchiridion' (1538) des Johannes Gropper,* Münster 1974, 236, cf. n. 210). The Council of Trent also condemns Pelagians, but does not touch *meritum de congruo.* See my study 'Das tridentinische Rechtfertigungsdekret im Lichte spätmittelalterlicher Theologie', in: *ZThK* 61 (1964), 251–82; reprinted, with responses to questions raised by H. Rückert, in: *Concilium Tridentinum,* ed. R. Bäumer, Darmstadt 1979, 301–40.

[38] 'opera nostra ex se nullius esse meriti, sed gratia dei facit illa digna esse vitae aeternae' (Conf., 87.11f.).

[39] Conf., 37, n. 12.

[40] Cf. Conf., 71.

material, have come across the main work by the most important author of the Confutatio, the *Chrysopassus* of John Eck. Eck – the first German counter-reformer and later main author of the Confutatio – was certain that the golden 'middle way' between Pelagius and Mani meant that instead of *God's election by grace, Man's choice of God* constituted the first step on the path to salvation, as Walter L. Moore has demonstrated.[41] God's grace, according to this view, does not free us to believe, but guarantees our right to self-determination, which in principle can be achieved by all, and is not cancelled by sin.

Therefore, the authors of the Confutatio did not undergo a 'miraculous conversion'[42] (*miraculum conversionis*) so far as the doctrine of justification is concerned, that might justify a retrospective evangelical recognition of the Confutatio. The permanent element, from the late Middle Ages to the Diet of Augsburg in 1530 and beyond, certainly is not 'a lack of theological clarity'. The *Chrysopassus* and the Confutatio are clearly intended – without contradicting Paul and Augustine, but without taking them too seriously either – to safeguard the moral preoccupation of Pelagians at all times: 'Who e'er aspiring, struggles on, / For him there is salvation.'[43] You can, because you should![44]

---

[41] See W. L. Moore, Jr., *Between Mani and Pelagius. Predestination and Justification in the Early Writings of John Eck*, diss. Harvard, Cambridge, MA 1967, 57f.; cf. his edition *In primum librum Sententiarum annotatiunculae D. Johanne Eckio praelectore anno ab Christo nato 1542*, Leiden 1976.

[42] The answer of Bartholomäus von Usingen, an Augustinian from Erfurt and one of the Augsburg 'confutators', to Melanchthon's apologia for the Confessio Augustana (1531/2) shows just how little of a 'miraculous conversion' there was. Bartholomäus proposes a distinction between the fulfilment of the law *quoad substantiam actus* (on the basis of one's own natural ability) and *quoad intentionem praecipientis* (in a state of grace). This distinction has the same function as that between human *merita de congruo* and *merita de condigno*, namely to ensure the freedom of human will to choose good or evil and to understand such choices as relevant to the salvation of our souls: 'Nostra autem legis impletio non est immunda, simpliciter loquendo, ita quod sit peccaminosa. Quia si impletio illa fit extra gratiam, est impletio quoad substantiam actus, et illa est actus neutralis, qui medius dicitur inter meritum et demeritum. Si autem fit ex gratia, est impletio ad intentionem praecipientis et est meritoria gloriae' (*Bartholomaei Arnoldi de Usingen O.S.A., Responsio contra Apologiam Philippi Melanchthonis*, ed. P. Simoniti, Würzburg 1978, 139.846–140.852; cf. 141.909–142.914).

[43] Johann Wolfgang von Goethe, *Faust, Parts One and Two*, translated from the German by G. M. Priest, New York 1969 (1941), 341; 'Der Mensch, der immer strebend sich bemüht, den können wir erlösen' (Goethe, *Faust* 2, Act 5, 11936f.).

[44] Cf. I. Kant: Man judges 'daß er etwas kann, darum weil er sich bewußt ist, daß er es soll, und erkennt in sich die Freiheit, die ihm sonst ohne das moralische Gesetz unbekannt

4. Gospel or Orthodoxy

Finally, let us turn to the limitations contained in Melanchthon's judgement concerning the Confutatio: the articles of the Augustana are conceded 'in themselves' (*an ihnen selb*). The context suggests that he wanted to distinguish within the Confutatio between its formal approval – or rather, non-refusal – of evangelical theology and the evidence drawn from the history of the Church by its authors, which seemed to him historically so bungled and foolish[45] that all observers free of prejudice are now certain they (and therefore 'we') are right. In this connection, Melanchthon – the reformer who more than all other evangelical theologians had delved into the *Testimonia Patrum*[46] (the testimony of the Church Fathers) and compiled a thorough knowledge of the witness borne by the primitive Church – was thinking specifically of the claim made by his opponents for the unerring and reliable orthodoxy of the Church, unchanged from the beginning right up to the sixteenth century. What looked at first glance to be merely a question of style, on account of the 'vilifications' (*calumniae*), now on closer examination proves to be nothing less than a fundamental disagreement concerning ecclesiology.

---

geblieben wäre' (*Kritik der praktischen Vernunft*, 1. T. 1. B 1. H. §6 (II 39)); 'He [sc. man] judges, therefore, that he can do a certain thing because he is conscious that he ought, and he recognizes that he is free – a fact which but for the moral law he would never have known' (T. K. Abbott, *Kant's Critique of Practical Reason and other works on the Theory of Ethics*, London 1909[6], 119). Kant is using none other than the classic, 'biblical' argument of Pelagianism, which had been examined by Gregory of Rimini (+1358) and rejected with reference to Augustine's position: '[H]omini praecipitur a deo, ut ista bona opera agat, sicut patet per totam sacram scripturam, igitur possibile est homini agere talia opera. Alioquin deus praecipisset homini impossibilia sibi . . .' (*In 2 Sent.* dist. 26–28, q.1; *Gregorii Ariminensis OESA, Lectura super Primum et Secundum Sententiarum*, vol. VI, ed. D. Trapp and V. Marcolino, Berlin 1980, 23.6–8; cf. 17.25–7). Gregory's counterargument: 'Ex his (scil. verbis Augustini) colligitur quod utique homo pro statu isto debet et tenetur esse sine peccato, nec tamen potest per se tantum sine adiutorio divinae gratiae esse sine peccato . . . Et ideo non sequitur ut possit ex solis naturalibus bene agere' (ibid., art. 3; 77.1–6).

[45] See n. 9, above. The envoys of Nuremberg also noted the inadequacy of this argument in their report to the council and officials of their city: 'die großen Hauptartikel, die Priesterehe, das Sacrament unter beider Gestalt zu nehmen, und das die Meß kein Opfer sey, deßgleichen daß die Klöstergelübde nicht zu halten seyn, [sind] gänzlich verworfen und für unchristlich geachtet worden, und mit seltsamen Argumenten beschützt und verantwortet' (*CR* 2, 250 (4 August 1530)).

[46] Cf. P. Fraenkel, *Testimonia Patrum. The Function of the Patristic Argument in the Theology of Philip Melanchthon*, Geneva 1961, esp. 52–109.

Melanchthon has been accused down to the present day of not understanding this disagreement, in part because he wrote to the papal legate only a month before the Confutatio was read out: 'We respect the Pope and the entire order of the Church, so long as the Pope does not repudiate us.'[47] Many historians have interpreted and still interpret this as a betrayal of Luther, as pussy-footing and as a deviation from the 'reforming' cause. In answer to these charges, I would like to draw the reader's attention to a statement made by Luther in 1533, a statement that has not been accorded much notice by scholarship, in which he takes the words right out of Melanchthon's mouth:

> We have always until now, particularly at the Imperial Diet of Augsburg, made it clear to the Pope and bishops in the humblest of terms that we do not want to destroy the rights and power of their Church, but, as long as they do not force us to accept unchristian principles, help them to exercise these rights and this power of theirs.[48]

Luther had already explained (1531) how he conceived of the integration of the Evangelicals into the papal Church: 'I have sent out a diligent and loyal admonition to the clergy at this Imperial Diet in Augsburg[49] and asked most urgently that they do not let this Diet –

---

[47] 'Ad haec Romani pontificis auctoritatem et universam politiam ecclesiasticam reverenter colimus, modo nos non abiiciat Romanus Pontifex' (*CR* 2, 170). Melanchthon himself admitted that he was rather too concerned with peace and concord at Augsburg: 'Ego non dissimulo me, propterea quod nostros noram, fuisse pacis cupidiorem Augustae' (*CR* 2, 632; in a letter to Hieronymous Baumgartner in Nuremberg, 15 February 1531); for this dating (not 1533 as the *CR* would have it) see Scheible, *Melanchthons Briefwechsel*, vol. 2: Regesten 1110–2335 (1531–9), Stuttgart 1978, 21, no. 1124. Yet Melanchthon correctly identified the Confessio Augustana with Luther's most deeply-held convictions and program, when he wrote in the preface to the second volume of the Wittenberg edition: 'Et quid retineri voluerit (scil. Lutherus), et quam formam doctrinae et administrationis Sacramentorum probaverit, liquet ex confessione, quam Dux Saxoniae Elector Iohannes, et Princeps Philippus Landgravius Cattorum etc. in conventu Augustano Imp. Carolo V. anno 1530. exhibuerunt' (*CR* 6, 163.)

[48] 'Wir haben uns bis da her allezeit, und sonderlich auff dem Reichstage zu Augspurg, gar demütiglich erboten, dem Bapst und Bisschoven, das wir nicht wolten ir Kirchen rechte und gewalt zu reissen, sondern, wo sie uns nicht zu unchristlichen Artikeln zwüngen, gern von inen geweihet und regirt sein, und auch helffen handhaben solch ir recht und gewalt' (*WA* 38, 195.17–22). Cf. *WA* 30III, 284.17–19 (1531). Even the rejection of papal authority does not automatically mean the rejection of episcopal authority. In a letter formulated by Luther, episcopal authority is actually recognized and given full support. See *WAB* 8, 310.12–18 (Luther's letter for Nikolaus Hausmann to the Bishop of Meissen, dated 28 October 1538); cf. *WAT* 4, 456.20–4, no. 4731 (1539).

[49] *An die gantze geistlichkeit zu Augsburg versamlet auff den Reichstag Anno 1530. Vermanung Martini Luther*, *WA* 30II, 268–356.

in which the whole world places such heartfelt hope, which keeps the whole world panting with great longing – end without results, but try to achieve this much: [1.] that peace be made, [2.] all and sundry give up their abominable abuses, and [3.] room be made for the Gospel.'[50]

Luther and Melanchthon believed for a long time, right up to the Imperial Diet at Augsburg, in allowing the Gospel free rein, in trusting in the effects of the Word to change and renew even historically established structures, the pope and the institutions of papal doctrine.

The dispute at Augsburg made a double break in Reformation history. The Augustana is a caesura for the Protestants because it broke free from the battle against the Roman Church and moved the Evangelicals past conflict and polemical exchanges to their own confession of catholicity. The Confutatio is a turning point because it takes up the battle and coordinates the polemical effort to mobilize papal orthodoxy against the evangelical confession.

In order to avoid distorting the view held in common by all the reformers, we must insist that the acceptance of the Confessio Augustana by the Catholic Church, which considers its judgements on Scripture to be infallible, actually marks a deep divide between the two camps. The Augustana had already been recognized, namely in the Confutatio: 'in themselves', but without the 'liberation' of the Gospel. In Luther's language, and in condensed form, this means: The Confessio Augustana was recognized in the framework of the *captivitas augustana*[51]

---

[50] 'Ich hab an die geistlichen auff diesem Reichstage zu Augspurg mein vleissig und trewes vermanen lassen offentlich ausgehen und aufs höhest gebeten, das sie ja nicht den Reichstag, da alle welt so hertzlich auff hoffet und gaffet mit grossem sehnen, sollten on ende zurgehen lassen, sondern dahin handeln, das friede gemacht, etliche ire grewel geendert und dem Evangelio raum gegeben würde' *WA* 30III, 276.3–9. W. Günter provides a brief sketch of Luther's idea of a national church independent from Rome, but closes with the claim that this plan failed due to the vital power of the old, universal church: *Martin Luthers Vorstellung von der Reichsverfassung*, Münster 1976, 105; cf. 98ff.

[51] Cf. nn. 6 and 19 above. To Luther, making room for the Gospel was the great success of Augsburg in the face of the raging and foaming of the Papists: 'Der Reichstag zu Augsburg, Anno 1530, ist alles Lobens werth; denn da ist das Evangelium auch unter die Leute kommen in andere Nation und Lande, wider beide, des Kaisers und des Papsts Willen und Versehen. Drüm was da verzehret ist, das soll Niemand nicht reuen . . . Die Papisten hatten den Kaiser beredt, daß unsere Lehre ungereimt sollte seyn, und wenn er käme, da würde er sie alle heißen schweigen, daß Niemand kein Wort würde dürfen sagen. Aber es hat sich viel anders begeben. Denn die Unsern haben da das Evangelium offentlich fürm Kaiser und ganzem Reich frei bekannt, und haben die Widersacher, die papisten, aufm selbigen Reichstage aufs Höchste zu Schanden gemacht' (*WAT* 2, 45.5–8, 17–21; no. 1323 (1532)).

(the 'Captivity of Augsburg'), that is, without the Gospel being set free in the Church of Rome.

Now we see in evangelical theology that not only canon law, rejected at the Elster Gate in 1520, but also the Church of Rome – the pope and bishops – is left behind by the evangelical expansion of the true catholic Church. From the two ecclesiastical parties two confessions were born, meaning two Churches, each bound to its respective Confession. On the conditions of free proclamation of the Gospel, the pope and papal government would have been acceptable to the Evangelicals – but only *iure humano* (by human law). But when 'orthodoxy', defined as a tradition sanctioned by the pope, is declared to be the decisive norm and rule of faith,[52] there can be no grounds for an accord, no matter how many individual articles are agreed on. Luther experienced this dilemma as well, and often referred to it in his *Table Talk*. Melanchthon felt precisely the same way. And today a growing number of genuine Catholics would agree, on the basis of the Gospel.

From the perspective of our time, some formulations of the Confutatio seem reasonable as they are written; it takes a great deal of scholarly effort to convince even 'educated people'[53] that the condemnation of a factitious Pelagianism does not prove anything about the doctrine of justification. The decisive point is that the Gospel is the highest authority and court of appeal in matters of faith,

[52] This is the case even where articles that occasioned no dissent are concerned. See Conf., 79.3; 83.7.

[53] When Melanchthon first got his hands on a copy of the Confutatio, he was upset not because it was an unequivocal condemnation, but precisely on account of its ambiguity: 'Sed vidi nuper Confutationem, et animadverti, adeo insidiose et calumniose scriptam esse, ut fallere etiam cautos in certis locis posset . . . Non delecta nos discordia . . . Sed non possumus abiicere manifestam veritatem et Ecclesiae necessariam' (Preface to Melanchthon's Apologia of the Confessio Augustana (mid-April, 1531), *CR* 2, 497); cf. Scheible, *Melanchthons Briefwechsel* 2 (n. 47), 30, no. 1148; *Bekenntnisschriften,* 143.14–16. It is unworthy of a scholar to defend tyranny against his own better judgement and knowledge: 'Deinde hanc tantam turpitudinem artificiose excusant, fingunt prodesse, ut conservaretur auctoritas et ἀξί ωμα eorum, qui praesunt . . . Indignissimum est autem, praecipue doctis viris, tamquam satellites esse tyrannorum, et quidem Deo bellum inferentium, ac eorum confirmare furorem, et incendere saevitiam. Quid cogitari turpius hac servitute potest? Praesertim in illis, qui ad consilia regum, qui ad Ecclesiae gubernacula propter eruditionem evehuntur, ut sint religionis verae monstratores et custodes, non ut iniustis dominorum cupiditatibus adulentur' (Preface to Melanchthon's *De ecclesiae autoritate* . . . (1539), *CR* 3, 723f.); cf. Scheible, *Melanchthons Briefwechsel* 2, 445, no. 2227.

even higher than the pope[54] and councils. This authority allows us to fill time-honored declarations of councils and impressive formulae of concord anew with spiritual content, or even, if necessary, to leave them behind because they are inseparable from their time. The pilgrim Church – and it alone really thirsts for reformation – is freed from the prison of orthodoxy and obedience only by returning to the primitive Christian challenge and risk of interpreting Scripture according to the times.

The central points of Roman Catholic dogmatic development up to 1870 and, in my opinion, even including the constitution *Lumen gentium* proclaimed at the Second Vatican Council, were already clear to Luther in 1531:

> Those who invent the fiction in their heart that the Holy Church is entirely holy and has no sin or error are very coarse theologians and blind teachers. This is a figment of their imagination, on which they base so many articles of faith. Scripture, however, disagrees, as everyone has heard. No-one ought to believe the Church if it acts or speaks without and outside the Word of Christ.

Luther grasps the essence of the truly evangelical Church with a 'certain' play on words: '[The Church] is holy and certain in Christ. Outside the Word of Christ, [the Church] is certainly a poor erring sinner, but not damned – for the sake of Christ, in whom she believes.'[55] The last clause ('but not damned – for the sake of Christ . . .') is both a consolation and a promise for *all* members of the divided Church.

---

[54] See G. Müller, 'Martin Luther und das Papsttum', in: *Das Papsttum in der Diskussion,* ed. G. Denzler, Regensburg 1974, 73–101; esp. 90–4.

[55] 'Es sind gar grobe Theologi und blinde lerer, die jnn jhrem hertzen tichten, das die heilig kirche sey gantz heilig und habe keine sunde noch jrthum. Solchs ist jhrs kopffs getichte, darauff sie so viel artickel des glaubens bawen. Die schrifft sagt aber anders davon, wie gehöret ist. Und sol auch der kirchen selbs niemand gleuben, wo sie on und ausser Christus wort thut odder redet' and 'Inn Christus wort ist sie [die Kirche] heilig und gewis. Ausser Christus wort ist sie gewis eine irrige, arme sunderin, doch unverdampt umb Christus willen, an den sie gleubt' ('Glosse auf das vermeinte kaiserliche Edikt' (1531), *WA* 30III, 342.9–17). The certainty of the final half-sentence is based on the *testamentum Dei,* which Luther had highlighted in his first lectures on the Psalms. Cf. *WA* 3, 288.30–289.10.

In Faber's *Psalterium Quincuplex* Luther notes, with reference to Ps. 88.29 ['Et pactum meum fidele erit ei'], concerning verse 31 ['Si autem derelinquerint filii eius legem meam']: 'Magnum hoc verbum, quod facile omnes hereses frangat, qui scil. pactum Christi non irritum fiet propter peccata nostra, sicut nec stat aut incepit propter peccata nostra' (*WA* 4, 510.1–3.)

Chapter 9

ZWINGLI'S REFORMATION BETWEEN
SUCCESS AND FAILURE

1. Cantonization and Parochialism

Is Zwingli's Reformation anything more than an episode between
Luther and Calvin? To claim that it had a world-wide or even a
European influence seems presumptuous in the light of recent
Reformation history, which assigns Zwingli's Zurich to the 'city
Reformation' and characterizes this phenomenon in sociological
terms as a process of 'communalization'.

If communalization means the emancipation of the city, which
dates back to the late Middle Ages, and in conjunction with this, the
'localization' of the Reformation – as compared to the territorial
Reformation of the princes – then the events at Zurich in the years
1519–31 are reduced *de facto* to an internal Swiss affair touching
hardly more than the area of the canton. The image of the parochial
Leutpriester (secular 'people's priest', that is, pastor) of the local
church at Zurich fits this interpretation well. Zwingli was able to
unite the religious and the political emancipation of the city with
such consummate skill that he even ended his life on the battlefield as
an *Antistes* (here: chief pastor) without clerical robes, as a cleric in
arms, as a member of the citizen militia. Despite the defeat at Kappel
in 1531, the Reformation had taken root and been 'naturalized'
politically at Zurich to such an extent – according to this view – that
Zwingli's legacy was in no danger within the city walls, at least.

This 'bourgeois' interpretation of Zwingli has to be tested critically.
There is no doubt that Zwingli was not accorded a comprehensive
and balanced interpretation for centuries because he was constantly
represented as somehow inadequate when compared to Luther, or as
dependent on the Wittenberg reformer. The lasting contribution of
the celebrated Zwingli specialist, Gottfried W. Locher, consists in

having understood Zwingli on Zwingli's own terms, thus freeing him from the anathema pronounced on him by the Gnesio-Lutherans. The extent and boundaries of Zwingli's influence, however, cannot be ascertained without comparing the reformer of Zurich with Martin Luther,[1] nor without fitting Zwingli into the framework formed by the Strasbourg reformer Martin Bucer, Zwingli's independent successor Heinrich Bullinger and the Genevan pastor of pastors, John Calvin. In the absence of a larger evangelical context, the historian is forced to resort to the equivocal concept of 'Zwinglianism' – which, as the literature demonstrates, can make no claim to precision.[2] To describe Bucer and Bullinger as 'Zwinglians' is a kind of forced baptism. Their association and shared characteristics become clear only when they are compared to Luther, which I will undertake in the third part of this chapter.

2. Zurich: The Prototypical City Reformation

The term 'communalization of the Reformation'[3] contains an important element of truth, just as the image of Zwingli as a cleric in arms on the battlefield furnishes evidence for the radical and logically consistent redefinition of clerics as citizens, a redefinition which stripped them of their special privileges. This term delineates the field in which Zwingli became a reformer and Zurich an evangelical city. But we ought to recognize the limits set by this urban interpretive framework. The perfect interlocking fit, the smooth co-operation between Zwingli and Zurich postulated in recent trends, but only aspired to by Zwingli, is not borne out by the evidence in the sources. Above all, limiting the sphere of our investigation to the urban

---

[1] See Ulrich Gäbler, 'Luthers Beziehungen zu den Oberdeutschen und Schweizern von 1526 bis 1530/31', in: *Leben und Werk Martin Luthers von 1526 bis 1546*, ed. H. Junghans, Göttingen 1983, 481–96, 885–91; and M. Brecht, 'Luthers Beziehungen zu den Oberdeutschen und Schweizern von 1530/31 bis 1546', ibid., 497–517, 891–4.

[2] The monumental study of G. W. Locher, *Die Zwinglische Reformation im Rahmen der europäischen Kirchengeschichte*, Göttingen 1979, even distinguishes between 'late Zwinglianism' – the 'Nachfolger-Tradition' founded by Heinrich Bullinger (584ff.) – and the 'form and legacy' of Zwingli's work, which produce only theological echoes (671ff.). Locher had to define the concept 'Zwinglianism' in a very broad way in order to describe Martin Bucer as a 'Zwinglian'. See Locher's excellent sketch of John Calvin in *Protestantische Profile. Lebensbilder aus fünf Jahrhunderten*, ed. K. Scholder and D. Kleinmann, Königstein/Ts 1983, 78–93.

[3] See P. Blickle, *Die Reformation im Reich*, Stuttgart 1982, 92; 158.

theater means losing all ability to perceive and understand Zwingli's regional, indeed his European, importance.

I will concentrate on 'taking inventory' for three decisive years: 1522–3, the year of the evangelical breakthrough; 1527–8, the year of alliances; and the year of crisis, 1530–1, which saw the Kappel War and Zwingli's death.

1. 1522–3: The Introduction of the Reformation

It is quite simply an error to imagine that Zwingli was harmoniously integrated into the political power structures of Zurich in the early twenties, and therefore grew 'organically' into the position of political 'helmsman'. This integrationist model is linked in a very unfortunate way to what only seem to be unequivocal key-words: 'biblical theocracy', or Zwingli as the mighty 'prophet', who represents correct belief and the right politics. To the extent that the historian's task is to describe reality, not ideals, these are distortions. They are based on a highly inflated estimate of how firm a consensus and how lasting an understanding were possible between Zwingli and the leading citizens in the council at Zurich. We are obliged to consider Zurich's internal situation briefly if we are to understand Zwingli's political positions and status in the city. The proper place to start is not the Zurich Disputation of 29 January 1523, but the defeat of Marignano (1515) and its critical *domestic* effects on the political structure and power relations in Zurich.

After Marignano, the representatives of the guilds demanded and received greater political responsibility. The city council was forced to commit itself to a policy that allowed no more experiments in foreign policy. Service in foreign armies and the granting of pensions were strictly limited by breaking off all alliances with foreign powers – except the alliance with the Pope, which had been sealed on 9 December 1514.

In 1518, Zwingli's call to Zurich was supported by the papal party, which had grown much stronger since the battle of Marignano. They doubtless knew that their candidate had accompanied the Glarus military contingent in 1513 and 1515 to protect the Pontifical State and that he had left Glarus after the shocking defeat which brought the French party to power.

In the summer of 1521, Zurich once again marched into Italy to secure Parma and Piacenza for the Holy Father. It was to be Zurich's last mercenary expedition. On 11 January 1522, Zurich prohibited mercenary service for foreign powers forever and without exception.[4] The passage of this long-overdue prohibition is often explained with reference to the influence of Zwingli's protests: he had, after all, publicly attacked the rich cardinals who employed Swiss youth and, if necessary, their blood in order to rage unchecked as 'wolves'. However, the decision made on 11 January was based not on Zwingli's attack on *curial* militarism, but on the council's policy of frustrating *French* attempts to hire Zurich mercenaries.

When the expedition to Piacenza was debated in the previous year, the council decided to send mercenary troops to Italy *despite* Zwingli's active opposition: 'agreements must be fulfilled' (*pacta sunt servanda*). The influence of the *Leutpriester* did not extend very far into the chambers of the city council.

Lent of 1522 saw the 'Lenten scandal' at the Froschauer house. This immediately set off an episcopal visitation, which was in turn supported by the Zurich council – *in spite of* Zwingli's public declarations and the appearance of his first evangelical treatise. Further violation of the Lenten fast was prohibited. 'No-one may eat meat on such days and at such times as have in the past been prohibited, except from necessity.'[5] The council once again took a position opposed to the *Leutpriester*.

The disputations have been cited repeatedly as proof of the close political co-operation between Zwingli and the council. However, they actually hide another series of conflicts.

Zwingli engaged in a 'private' disputation with the wandering Franciscan preacher Franz Lambert. This exchange was set off by Zwingli, who heckled Lambert's sermon at the *Fraumünster* (Cathedral of Our Lady) on 15 July 1520: 'Brother, you are wrong there.'[6] This method of interrupting sermons had already been used successfully by Zwingli's right-hand man, Leo Jud, on numerous

[4] See E. Egli, *Schweizerische Reformationsgeschichte*, vol. 1, ed. G. Finsler, Zurich 1910, 57.

[5] '. . . dass niemas zuo solichen vorhar verbottnen ziten und tagen on notdurfft sölle fleisch essen' (*Ratsmandat* (city council decree) of 26 February 1523; E. Egli, *Aktensammlung zur Geschichte der Zürcher Reformation in den Jahren 1519–33*, Zurich 1879 [Nieuwkoop 1973], 118, n. 339); cf. the first Lenten decree of 9 April 1522, which is the same in substance.

[6] 'Bruder, da irrest du' (G. Finsler, *Die Chronik des Bernhard Wyss 1519–1530*, Basel 1901, 16).

occasions, and was quite simply a violation of the policy of 'calm and order' (*Ruhe und Ordnung*) pursued carefully and consistently by the city council. One week later, the opposing parties – Zwingli and the lectors of the three mendicant orders – were summoned before a committee of the Small Council. The Chapter of the *Grossmünster* was included, as well as the two other *Leutpriester* and Konrad Schmid, Bachelor of Theology, probably as an expert witness (*peritus*). Six months before the clergy of the city and surrounding countryside under Zurich's control were summoned as a group, the council tried to defuse the explosive situation by putting Zwingli into contact with the élite of the old Church. No matter how much this improved Zwingli's status as the representative of his party, the council's decision to allow only preaching in accord with Scripture was still that of a non-partisan authority. Even the disputation that took place six months later, generally known in Zwingli studies as the 'first Zurich disputation', still was not *Zwingli's* disputation, but remained – against his expectations – an affair of the city council.

The city council not only approved these disputations, it organized them. In both cases the council judged the outcome of the disputation – the 'hearing against each other' (*Verhör gegeneinander*). As in 1523, the council ordered, for the sake of 'liberating the city', that preaching *not* be argumentative: 'You are to treat each other in a friendly way.'[7] The authorities still hoped to drain this swamp of poisonous quarrels.

The three events, from the 'Lenten scandal' (April 1522) through the disputation with the monastic dignitaries (21 July 1522) to the great disputation before the council (29 January 1523), mark three steps on the path that led from eliminating the spiritual authority of the Bishop of Constance to establishing the religious jurisdiction of the Zurich council as the final court of appeal.

There is no doubt that Zwingli's influence was growing during this period. When the episcopal delegation from Constance arrived in April 1522 to conduct a visitation on account of the Lenten 'sausage-eating' episode, Zwingli had a hard time getting a hearing from the council.[8] He was summoned before a council committee in July.

---

[7] Finsler, *Chronik*, 19.

[8] Cf. *Acta Tiguri*, Zwingli's description of the events from 7–9 April 1522, addressed to Erasmus Fabricius, in: *Huldreich Zwinglis sämtliche Werke* (= *ZW*) I, 144.5–11; cf. the introduction, 137f.

Bürgermeister Marx Röist now took the initiative and tried at first to settle the dispute in as private a way as possible. He felt he could prevent further escalation of tensions by ordering Zwingli and the mendicants to preach along the same lines. Although he was responsible for public order, he wanted to refer the substantive judgement of the theologian's controversy to the Cathedral Chapter of Zurich. When Zwingli protested[9] and his partisans in the council started to bother the *Bürgermeister,* however, the council ordered that all preaching be based on Scripture alone: 'Indeed, you masters of the mendicant orders, it is my lords' intention that you should only preach the Holy Gospel from now on, St. Paul and the prophets, which is Holy Writ, and leave Scotus and Thomas and such things alone.'[10]

What is unique and lasting about the subsequent disputation before the council of 29 January 1523, the so-called 'first Zurich disputation'? It is no longer possible to insist that this disputation made Holy Scripture the standard for preaching. Even the formulation of the *Abschied* (the declaration which enjoins scriptural preaching) is no innovation. Nor was it a novelty to hold a disputation before the council: it was merely a stage on the road to urban emancipation from episcopal jurisdiction. Since scholars have read the *Abschied* from Zwingli's perspective and have, therefore, interpreted it as a victory for him, only one phrase has become well-known: that allowing the *Leutpriester* to continue 'as in the past' (*wie bisher*). Although his preaching and theology are thereby acknowledged as 'scriptural' this phrase does not grant Zwingli the exclusive rights nor the spiritual monopoly that he thought it did.

In accordance with the political aims of the Small Council, particularly of *Bürgermeister* Marx Röist, *both* parties were dismissed with the order not to call each other heretics nor to insult each other,[11]

[9] 'Ich bin in diser statt Zürich bischof und pfarrer und mir ist die seelsorg bevolen; ich han darum geschworen und die münch nit; si sond uf mich acht han und ich nit uf si; dann so dick si predigend, das erlogen ist, so will ich's widerfechten . . .' (Finsler, *Chronik,* 19.)

[10] 'Ja, ir herren von örden, das ist miner herren meinung, daß ir sollend nun fürohin predigen das heilig evangelium, den heiligen Paulum und die propheten, daß die heilige gechrift ist, und lassend den Scotum und Thomam und sollig ding ligen' (ibid.). Zwingli himself reports to Beatus Rhenanus: 'Mandatum erat, ut relictis Thomabus, Scotis reliquisque id farinae doctoribus unis sacris literis nitantur, quae scilicet intra biblia contineantur' (Zurich, 30 July 1522, *ZW* VII, 549.3–5).

[11] 'einanderen hinfür dheins wegs schmützen, ketzeren, noch andere schmachwortt zureden' (*ZW* I, 471.7f.).

under pain of severe punishment. Only when a majority of the Small Council insisted on maintaining their policy of pacification *after* the end of the disputation held in October of 1523 did the Great Council decide to exercise control over not only basic legislation governing preaching, but also over the practical regulations and ordinances concerning correct, licit preaching. Until this time at least, there was no such thing as 'Zwingli's Zurich'. In 1523 – while the magistrature was still decisively under the influence of the Small Council in religious matters – there is reason to speak of Zwingli's influence as a preacher, but not of his power as a politician.

One seemingly tiny detail is a clear sign of Zwingli's distance from the council. It has been overlooked in the past, probably because it does not fit into the common image of 'Zwingli's Zurich'. On 20 January 1523, the eminent Swiss humanist Glarean (+1563) complained in a letter from Basel that Zwingli told him the wrong date for the disputation – nine days early: 'Your letter, in which you wrote that the disputation would take place on January 20th, led us completely astray, because I eagerly showed it to my friends everywhere; everyone who read it and has gone to Zurich for no reason will now be angry with me . . .'[12]

Zwingli's letter to Glarean contained yet another error. The *Leutpriester* assumed that he would preside himself after the fashion of a medieval university professor who, according to the university statutes, presides over the disputation concerning the theses he has composed and published. But everything happened differently in this case. The council took such a large part in planning the disputation that Zwingli was not even consulted by the council concerning the date. And not only the *date,* but also the *form* of the disputation was a complete surprise to Zwingli: whereas he had been preparing for *his* disputation, right down to the traditional series of academic theses, *Bürgermeister* Marx Röist and the Small Council pushed their plan through for a 'hearing' of the two sides. Zwingli and the council simply did not co-operate on this matter.

---

[12] 'Mirum in modum fefellit nos charta tua, in qua scripseras XIII. Kalendas Februarias venturam disputationem. Eam cum ubique sedulus apud amicos circumferrem, quidam viderunt ac Tigurum iverunt, fortassis mihi infensi, cum celeritas tua et te et me fefellerit' (*ZW* VIII, 9.1–4).

Nevertheless, the disputation held before the council does have two faces. For one, the summons and the *Abschied* fit seamlessly into the policy of peaceable order pursued by the Small Council and directed against Zwingli as well as his adversaries. It was due to Zwingli's theological interpretation and significance that this local event, embedded in city politics, became a spiritual event that reached far beyond the walls and canton of Zurich. The renewal of theology and of the Church was initiated in Zurich on the basis of Holy Scripture; this decision for renewal settled the question once and for all and by proxy, as it were, for all of Christendom: the Holy Spirit does not say one thing today and another tomorrow.[13] That particular roomful of people, therefore, was a Christian assembly.[14] The 'council disputation' became Zwingli's *Council,* representing the entire Church. The council of Zurich merely called a hearing; Zwingli discovered in it the first evangelical General Synod. This redefinition of a hearing as a 'Christian assembly' has epochal significance for the history of the universal Protestant Church. *The event itself is as 'local' as its meaning is 'universal'.* Zwingli speaks of Zurich's 'authority by proxy', but the power of the Reformation in Zurich was not yet that complete.

2. 1527: The Confederacy of the Evangelicals

Just as it seemed as though the political leadership and the city's pastor might be 'of one heart and soul', the perspectives and strategies of the council and the reformer threatened to split irreconcilably once again.

By necessity Zurich's internal policy sought to resolve tensions within the walls and to avoid all strife with the mercantile class engaged in foreign trade, and with those guilds that had anything to do with the outside – particularly the 'Butchers', who depended on a steady supply of men from the inner cantons of Switzerland to maintain their numbers. All alliances that might involve Zurich in broader conflicts had been abrogated and were to be avoided. Zwingli, however, was keen on new alliances; he saw Zurich merely as the beginning, as a starting point and prototype for the much-needed pacification of Christendom that accompanies obedience to God's Word.

[13] *ZW* I, 514.9f.
[14] *ZW* I, 495.10f.

One document merits particular attention because it has preserved Zwingli's all-encompassing view of the Reformation: his plea for an alliance, in the summer of 1527, that would be able to face up to the pan-European expansionism of the Habsburgs. Since Zwingli had failed completely in this attempt by 1529/30, German historians have not been able to refrain from concluding that this idea was nothing but the enthusiastic and naïve plan of an amateur politician hampered by the particular disadvantage of Swiss blinders, without the ability to see beyond the Swiss border. His correspondence with Philip of Hesse, written in a secret code, has even been dismissed as 'a game of cowboys and Indians'. This judgement has been made all the easier by the condemnation of Philip's bigamy common among moralizing historians, a judgement which has tended to eclipse the sharp political vision of Zwingli's correspondent in Hesse, the man who would later be the leader and *spiritus rector* (guiding influence) of the Schmalkaldic Alliance.

Swiss historians have not been so confused in their judgement, and have recognized Zwingli's all-encompassing political ambitions. This judgement is correct. The introduction of the Reformation at Berne (1528) meant much more to him than just another canton won over; it was a decisive step on the way toward a 'true confederacy' (*eine wahre Eidgenossenschaft*). But even this interpretation falls short of the mark. The reformer of Zurich doubtless wanted not just a loose co-operation between Swiss towns and cities at *Tagsatzungen* (federal Diets), but a firmly established Swiss nation (*natio helvetica*). This was achieved both despite and thanks to the Second War of Kappel.

His broader vision, which transcended national boundaries, has not yet been mentioned. On two folio pages, dated by Walther Köhler (+1946) to the summer of 1527, Zwingli set out his political program. It is an impressive sketch for a trans-national confederacy.[15]

In order to place this plan in proper perspective, we must resort to comparisons with modern alliance patterns, such as the ambitious though as-yet unrealized plan, born of the Second World War, to establish an independent European defensive alliance with the goal of guaranteeing European unity, security and independence. The title subsequently added to Zwingli's plan *Why we ought to unite with*

[15] *ZW* VI 1, 197–201.

Constance, Lindau, Strasbourg etc. – that is, with the upper Rhine, Lake Constance and Alsace – *under one law* does not immediately reveal everything Zwingli expected of the city's leaders: Zurich ought to think and act not merely with reference to all of Switzerland, but with reference to all of Europe.

Constance and Lindau had been Emperor Maximilian's strategic bases of operations in the Swabian War of 1499, the memory of which was still fresh and terrifying. Nonetheless, these cities should not be thought of as 'hostile foreign parts', Zwingli felt, but rather included in a broadly-based defensive alliance after all unhappy memories and resentment had been put to rest. Like the Landgrave of Hesse, the 'shepherd of Zurich' was capable of thinking on a European scale and opposing to the Habsburg dream of universal empire the alternative vision of a confederate evangelical alliance.

What then, was Zwingli's goal? It was 'one people and one alliance'[16] from Switzerland to Strasbourg. We can add that this confederacy would have constituted precisely the barricade – a kind of *cordon évangélique* – between Burgundy and Austria, between Habsburg and Habsburg, that Emperor Maximilian had tried to prevent by founding the Swabian Alliance (*Schwäbischer Bund*). The new confederacy would push its way into the power vacuum left by the crumbling Swabian Alliance – but *against* the Emperor. In retrospect, the success of such an alliance would have brought forward the Schmalkaldic War of 1547 by about twenty years – to a time much more favorable in military terms for the evangelical side.

This document is of interest for two reasons. First, it demonstrates yet again how much more Zwingli was than a mere 'City Pastor' (*Stadtpfarrer*). Of equal importance are the theological grounds and arguments with which Zwingli prefaced his plan: although the cause of the Reformation can survive only 'by the power of God' (*uss der kraft gottes*), God generally does not intervene directly in the course of events on earth but makes use of people to provide (his) people with 'help and protection' (*hilff und schirm*). Since God allows this treaty of alliance to be concluded, 'it is clear that he wants to use it for good purposes.'[17]

In the third part of this chapter, we will return to this basic position for the purpose of comparing Zwingli to Luther. Zwingli sums up his

---

[16] That 'ein volck und pündtnus wurde . . .' (*ZW* VI 1, 201.17).

[17] '[es] ist . . . offembar, das er inn zuo guotem bruchen wil' (*ZW* VI 1, 200.9).

entire theology in this single sentence. God directs the history of humanity with consummate power and skill toward the time when human and divine righteousness will grow into unity. God clearly approves of Zwingli's proposed treaty, because it would lead to 'peace, order, equity and justice' ('friden, ruwen, billichkeit und gerechtigkeit'). The all-powerful, just director of history guarantees the efficacy of the Reformation in establishing justice. It is therefore the task of all believers to advance the Reformation with all their might, in the certain knowledge of God's support and of victory. Zwingli's political theology starts from this principle, which in turn makes *Realpolitik* the execution of God's righteous justice, trusting to God's omnipotence.

This fundamental principle does not, however, have anything to do with Zwingli's own experience – quite the contrary! Helmut Meyer has been able to demonstrate, by means of painstaking research, just how closely Zwingli was involved in the deliberations of the city council[18] – even in those of the *Geheimer Rat,* the 'privy council'. However, Zwingli's constant participation in political affairs in the last years of his life and his advancement to the most important committees of Zurich's governmental élite do not refute the thesis that his influence was limited; rather, his overt political 'success' at Zurich minimizes, indeed hides, the extent to which he was isolated in the last years. The Marburg Colloquy (October 1529) was the precondition to a far-reaching evangelical accord with Electoral Saxony and Hesse. Its failure was topped in the following year by the decision of the imperial cities Constance and Strasbourg – without, perhaps even against, Zurich – along with Lindau and Memmingen, to present the Emperor with their own Confession at Augsburg, the *Tetrapolitana.* Zwingli's far-sighted European plan had failed.

His efforts to unite the Swiss 'nation' did seem more successful, to the extent that the five cantons of inner Switzerland (Lucerne, Uri, Schwytz, Unterwalden and Zug) had allowed free preaching of the Gospel. But the victory of the First War of Kappel did not bear fruit, because Zurich decided to join the double-edged Bernese strategic boycott. From Zwingli's perspective, the city of Zurich had refused to seize the opportunity which God had provided.

[18] H. Meyer, *Der zweite Kappeler Krieg. Die Krise der Schweizerischen Reformation,* Zurich 1976, 316–23.

3. 1531: The Catastrophe of Kappel

Johann Stumpf remarked in his *Chronica* how strongly Zwingli felt he had been left in the lurch by the political élite of Zurich. On 26 July 1531, the reformer announced his resignation and intent to leave Zurich with the explanation that 'the *pensioner* [people drawing pensions] of the Five Cantons are taking the upper hand in Zurich as well'.[19] Threatening to resign strengthened Zwingli's support at first. Stumpf's chronicle (which is not sufficiently appreciated today; it has been labelled 'too partisan') continues: 'This threat frightened many, such that many eyes overflowed with tears.' Three days later the council itself begged him 'to stay with them until death'.[20]

Which is exactly what happened. But it makes absolutely no sense to conclude on this account that Zwingli fell at Kappel as an obedient burgher in the service of the city council. On 9 October, when the Five Cantons were already mobilizing, Zwingli painted in his last sermon a grimly realistic portrait of his hopeless political isolation. Zurich was chained to the Five Cantons by financial interests; all warnings were too late:

> But no loyal warning made to you helps; everything is in vain. The pensioners of the five cantons have too much *ruggen* [backing] in this city. There is a chain, from which I have in the past torn many rings, and broken it, but it is whole now. [Stumpf explains: meaning the secret oligarchy of the well-wishers of the five cantons in Zurich.] This chain will strangle me and many a pious Zuricher. I am finished. You will deliver me into their hands, but you will still knock horns with me.[21]

Zwingli answers in advance – and correctly – the question as to why mighty Zurich put only 3,500 men in the field on 11 October against an opposing force twice as strong. His answer is more convincing than those of modern observers, with their doubtless correct

[19] Johann Stumpf, *Chronic vom Leben und Werk des Ulrich Zwingli*, ed. L. Weiss, Zurich 1932², 166. On Stumpf's chronicle, see P. Wernle, 'Das Verhältnis der schweizerischen zur deutschen Reformation', in: *Basler Zeitschrift für Geschichte und Altertumskunde* 17 (1918), 227–315, 248–50.

[20] 'Ab dieser red erschrack mencklich, also daß vielen die ougen übergiengend'; they asked him 'by inen zu blyben, bis in den todt' (Stumpf, *Chronica*, 166).

[21] 'Aber es hilft kein getrüwe warnung an üch, sonder ist alles vergebens. Die pensionär der fünf Orten habend zuviel ruggens in diser statt. Es ist ein ketten gemacht, uß der ich bishar mengen ring gerissen und sy oft gebrochen hab, aber jetzund ist sy ganz. (Verstand die heymlich oligarchy der fünf orten gönner Zürich.) Dise kette wirt mir und mengen frommen Zürcher den hals abziehen. Es ist um mich zuthon. Ihr werdend mich ihnen in die händ bringen, aber ihr werdend ein hörnli mit mir abstoßen' (Stumpf, *Chronica*, 169).

references to the short time available for mobilization and inadequate military tactics and strategy. The defeat was, in fact, a foregone conclusion; as Zwingli predicted, the chain had been made whole again. Five hundred men of Zurich fell in less than an hour.

Zwingli's view of history – that the almighty God would lead the Reformation to its final victory – explains the catastrophic defeat at Kappel. The catastrophe consisted not in military weakness and tactical errors, but in God's refusal to smash the 'chain' of Zurich's opponents.

The consequences of the Second Kappel War prepared the future course of the Swiss Confederacy, a course that Germany first discovered with the Religious Peace of Augsburg in 1555, reaching its end only after much bloodshed in 1648. The practical political principle that is to this day considered to be a German invention is in fact a product of rational Swiss politics, set out in the Second Peace of Kappel at Deinikon on 16 November 1531: 'Cuius regio, eius religio' (the religion of a territory is determined by its lord).

3. Luther and Zwingli

The defeat at Kappel made waves far beyond the narrow confines of the canton and the Swiss Confederacy. A flood of reproaches descended on the fallen chaplain. The harshest reactions came, not surprisingly, from Wittenberg. As late as 1544, Luther thundered that [Zwingli's downfall at] Kappel is the fate of all sects and zealots, 'the terrifying judgement of God, where Zwingli met such a wretched death'.[22] Is this merely Saxon self-righteousness, Luther's stiff-necked certainty that he was right, expressed in terms just as strong and as dogged as ever, thirteen years after Zwingli's death?

These two great reformers were born hardly seven weeks apart – yet they are separated by the space of an entire epoch. In short, Luther was experiencing the End Time; Zwingli lived in modern times. The gap that separated them in theology and piety, in the doctrine of the sacraments and 'Christian' politics had far-reaching consequences. To measure the distance between these epochs, we must go beyond details to the basic question posed by our analysis of Zwingli's influence and activities as *Leutpriester* in Zurich and as a political

---

[22] 'das schreckliche urteil Gottes, da der Zwingel so jemerlich ward erschlagen' (*WA* 54, 154.17f.).

theologian with European ambitions: the question of God's righteousness and omnipotence.

God's omnipotence is a pressing concern in all Christian thought, and occupies a central position in evangelical theology as well. Luther and Zwingli both interpret God's omnipotence according to a specific and particular paradigm. When Luther speaks of God's omnipotence, he throws his view of the Devil into sharp relief, with considerable consequences for his interpretation of history: human history is not the era, the time of God's omnipotence, but of his powerlessness; the history of the Church is the era of the persecuted Church, vulnerable to Satan's fury, a fury that will end only with the end of the world.[23]

For the sake of comparison, we will now turn our attention to the reformer of Zurich. I will concentrate on a scholarly-exegetical text: Zwingli's reading of Isaiah, which he presented in the pedagogically innovative form of learned 'prophecy' in 1527 and made public the following year in his preaching. Isaiah 42.8 clearly 'reveals' God alone in his almighty majesty: 'My glory I will not give to another'. This single text, Zwingli argues, smashes all Wittenberg's theology concerning the Lord's Supper. The real presence of the historical Christ on the altar is not biblical, because it requires that Christ be present physically all over the world – *ubique* – at the same time. 'Ubiquity', however, is a characteristic of eternal God, therefore it touches only Christ's divine – not his bodily, human – nature. Christ's human nature is neither eternal, infinite, nor everywhere (*ubique*) present: God does not give his majesty to any human being.[24]

Scholarly depictions of the controversy over the Lord's Supper have not taken Zwingli's exegesis of Isaiah into account, because of its relative lateness and because it offers nothing new in this area toward distinguishing Zwingli from Luther. This text does, however, express a program that lends it paradigmatic importance for our understanding of the *philosophical* presuppositions of Zwingli's theology. Zwingli breaks God's nature down into its component parts with the logical persuasiveness characteristic of the medieval *via antiqua* (scholastic theology). Rather than present the entire sequence of his argument, I will emphasize only this principle: Ubiquity is an

[23] See ch. 3 above, 'Martin Luther: Between the Middle Ages and Modern Times'.
[24] *ZW* XIV, 336.32–337.15.

inalienable and non-transferable characteristic of God alone. On this rests his omnipotence: 'However, to be everywhere is a hidden property belonging only to spiritual beings. Indeed, this is where his omnipotence originates.'[25]

Not only can it be proven that God exists, but it can be shown what he logically must be like. God must be ubiquitous, because it is a necessary corollary of his omnipotence. The entire argument is sustained by reasoned, necessary connections, which are revealed in his introductory formulae: 'it is necessary' (*necesse est*), 'therefore' (*ergo*), 'from this, then' (*hinc enim*) and 'it cannot' (*non potest*), along with all the features of a 'proof' in the rationalistic theology that was called the *via antiqua* in the Middle Ages, and which has held Protestant theology captive since the time of Hegel and German Idealism. The *via antiqua* is 'logical' in the sense of a chain of cause and effect that can be followed logically by a thinking person. The *via moderna* broke this chain.

Two key passages from William of Ockham (the *Venerabilis Inceptor*) confirm this: 'It cannot be proved that God is omnipotent, but grasped and held by faith alone.'[26] The 'rational and logical' analysis of God's nature and characteristics comes up against an impenetrable barrier in the form of God's peculiar and particular way of being and perceiving, divine activities which are not structured according to the standards of human logic: 'God's mind is of a different sort than our minds'[27] – impossible for us to grasp.

Here Luther is entirely within the tradition of the *via moderna,* in that he accepts a radical separation between God's wisdom and human thought, and proposes the omnipotence of God as an article of faith. Luther's conclusions lead far beyond Ockham: omnipotent God will lead history to final victory; this can be and is to be believed despite the evidence of reason and of one's conscience, despite the visible and tangible power of the Devil, by faith alone. God's

---

[25] 'Ubique autem esse, intima ac sola numinis est proprietas. Hinc enim dimanat omnipotentia' (*ZW* XIV, 337.9–11).

[26] 'Non potest demonstrari quod Deus sit omnipotens, sed sola fide tenetur' (Quodlibet I, q.1 ad 7; *Guillelmi de Ockham. Quodlibeta septem,* ed. J. C. Wey CSB, *Opera Theologica* IX, St. Bonaventure, NY 1980, 11.230f.).

[27] '[I]ntellectio Dei est alterius rationis a nostris intellectionibus' (Quodlibet III, q. 1 ad 3; ibid., 207.202f.).

omnipotence is hidden. It functions in history 'by means of its opposite' (*sub contrario*). His power rests, disguised, in the Cross.

In Zwingli's theology, the Devil has already been deposed and overcome; he has been, as it were, de-mythologized. Luther believes that the Devil rules over his world-wide empire with all his might and violence until the last day of the End Time: the Devil is the *rex saeculi*, the king of this world. From Luther's perspective, Zwingli was ensnared in the causal chain of philosophical theology long before he was fettered by the conspiracy of the Zurich pensioners. I would like to close this comparison of Luther and Zwingli with two reflections: a glance backwards and a glance into what might be a less narrow future.

First: Luther's doctrine of the Lord's Supper was not a sudden and inconsistent relapse into the Middle Ages[28] set off by Zwingli; rather, it is based on fundamental decisions which represent a deep gulf between Luther and Zwingli. Therefore we are justified in claiming that the dispute over the doctrine of ubiquity, which was at the center of the Reformation from 1525 on, could have been conducted in a much more fruitful and promising fashion on the basis of the doctrine of divine omnipotence or providence. Ockham's use of the term *sola fide* disentangles theology from the causal web of logical metaphysics. Luther adopted this insight in so far as he believed that God can be perceived only via Scripture – reason can only stand by and gape in amazement. Scripture therefore puts 'believing reason' in its proper place: radical exegesis resists logical necessity. The 'scriptural principle' – believed with great certainty by all involved to be the common basis of the Reformation – was mortgaged from the very beginning to the all-encompassing dispute over the Lord's Supper.

Second: Zwingli's 'evangelical discovery' was characterized by obedient listening to God's biblical call to penance: 'Repent!', reform yourselves. His evangelical ethics grew out of obedient submission to God's omnipotent will to enforce true righteousness in history over against injustice and opposition. In this respect, Zwingli's Reformation had world-wide consequences. Zwingli's death and the catastrophe of Kappel allowed the urban Reformation to expand the

---

[28] See also: Oberman, *Werden und Wertung der Reformation*, Tübingen 1979², 368; English trans.: *Masters of the Reformation*, Cambridge, 1981, 288.

evangelical legacy beyond the walls of cities and thereby to move across Europe. In consequence, the Reformation eventually surpassed Zwingli's visionary plan of 1527 by much more than he could ever have hoped.

Zwingli listened to Scripture in a new way, with a sharpened sense of social justice that made the Reformation modern. Luther also listened to Scripture in a new way, but experienced the Reformation eschatologically. His belief in the Devil made him look medieval from the perspective of the Enlightenment, which then set very narrow boundaries to his sphere of influence. The differences between Luther and Zwingli could be papered over by their agreement on the Lord's Supper (the *Abendmahlskonkordie*), but not overcome. The healing of Protestantism throughout the world and the evangelical contribution to the unity of the entire, genuinely catholic ecumenical Church depend on whether or not it is possible to break through the double chain forged by individual reason and individual dogmatism which Luther and Zwingli attacked, each in his own way, with the weapons of the Gospel.

To conclude: Zwingli won Zurich for the Reformation, but gambled with the local Reformation to attempt the Reformation of all Christendom. For this reason alone, Zwingli defies definition as a mere city reformer. The 'counter-reformer' Fabri called him a 'second Luther', 'only more dangerous'. Fabri came from Constance, so he knew all about the political ferment engendered by 'that Swiss reformer' and the threat it posed to Habsburg designs on Europe. Fabri was wrong, however: Zwingli's policy of alliances had no lasting effect. Zwingli became really 'dangerous' to Roman plans to regain control over Europe only after Kappel. Odd as it may seem, this defeat allowed Zurich to exert a powerful influence on the subsequent history of the Christian world.

Chapter 10

ONE EPOCH – THREE REFORMATIONS

1. The Reformation: A Theological Revolution

Marxist historians traditionally have seen the German Peasants' War of 1524/5 as the first in a series of revolutions. But now even 'bourgeois' (mainstream) German historians evince a certain pride in the 'German Revolution'. The Reformation is now billed both within the Marxist camp and without as a revolution; or at least, as a 'proto-revolution', which is how I too am inclined to understand it. On the other hand, scholars have reached no consensus concerning the relative importance of religious motivations during the Reformation. At most, some will 'stretch the point' to concede that Thomas Müntzer proposed and worked toward a fully theological revolution. Stretch the point, indeed! Our understanding of the Reformation will be broadened considerably if we go beyond this narrow concentration on Müntzer and consider Reformation theology in general in order to reveal its explosive potential as a revolutionary force capable of acting on all aspects of society.

It would be easy to get lost in a maze of definitions before even attempting the main task as sketched above. Yet the three terms in the title of this subsection are in need of clear and precise definition. This applies not only to the word 'revolution', but also to 'Reformation' and even to the adjective 'theological'. We will begin with the central concept of 'revolution' because it is the key to an integrated definition of all three terms. However, we would do well to remember that as recently as twenty years ago, the term 'revolution' was used to condemn the Reformation and was immediately recognizable as a polemical gambit borrowed from the anti-Protestant vocabulary of Roman Catholic theological polemic. 'Revolution' in this context meant *insubordination,* a brash refusal of obedience to Mother

Church. In this view, the pattern of disobedience can be traced to the very beginnings of the Reformation. It all began with Luther's 'Nein!', his refusal in October of 1518 to obey Cardinal Cajetan's well-known order: he could not bring himself to pronounce the six letters that make up the word *revoco* (I recant). Six months later he would repeat his act of 'rebellion', this time before the Emperor at Worms – that is, against secular authority as well.

To the extent that recent generations have been able to move the study of the Reformation beyond the confines of denominational debate and to concentrate in a more sober and professional manner on historical, theological and intellectual issues, we have been able to tune in the words of the *dramatis personae* a little more clearly. Behind the revolutionary refusal to recant we are now able to discern the reformers' intention to pledge and affirm their obedience to what they understood to be the true Church.

The Reformation, therefore, can be seen as a 'revolution' only, and at the very most, with regard to the struggle against the Church embodied in the Papal State, and against the hierarchical Church as the supreme authority and court of appeal in secular as well as religious affairs. This battle raged throughout the Middle Ages over the power claimed by Rome *super gentes et regna* (over nations and kingdoms), from the time of the Investiture Contest to the Fifth Lateran Council of 1516.

Equally unconvincing is the idea that the Reformation was a 'revolution' against the secular authorities. The Reformation was the product of and itself produced a broad range of attitudes toward the authorities. In point of fact, these attitudes overall were very clearly *anti-revolutionary.* The only exceptions are to be found in Müntzer's later writings, starting with his *Sermon to the Princes* of 1524/5, and in the foundation (ten years later) of the Kingdom of God at Münster, in 1534/5, an event that was in any case catastrophically behind the times. Müntzer and Münster are exceptions in the sixteenth century; they certainly cannot justify the application of the term 'Radical Reformation' (in the sense of a radical upheaval) to the entire left wing of the Reformation.

Müntzer and Münster did serve at the time as an excuse to label the Reformation a revolutionary movement and to condemn it as such. Yet modern historical debate cannot afford to elevate this transparent propagandistic pretext to the level of historical fact. The effects of propaganda are, no doubt, facts in their own right, but these effects are not limited to promoting the Peasants' War as 'the revolution of the sixteenth century'.

Calvin, for example, was disturbed by Münster far more than he was by Müntzer. Calvin and the other reformers saw revolutionary reformation as an illegitimate phenomenon *always* attendant on the preaching of the Gospel. His conclusion, at which he arrived in the 1530s during the composition of his commentary on Romans, remained unchanged for the rest of his life: 'For there are always inflammatory and rebellious spirits who believe that the Kingdom of Christ cannot be established properly unless all worldly powers have been abolished and destroyed . . .'; only 'scatterbrained fools' imagine that the freedom Christ has afforded us smashes every yoke imposed on us by human authority (*servitutis iugum*).[1] No modern historian is brash enough to follow Calvin's judgement in this matter, but we are obliged to heed his warning not to confuse the fascinating exceptions of the Reformation era with its main characters.

The de-confessionalization of Reformation history has brought forth more balanced judgements, but there is also a price to pay. The events of the first half of the sixteenth century are no longer subjected to narrowly dogmatic interpretation, but theological interpretation has also been banished. The 'scatterbrained fools' denounced so sharply by Calvin are frequently proclaimed as the 'true reformers', that is, those not motivated by theological considerations. They are often presented as the 'real' agents, seen from the social perspective, behind the progressive, forward-looking decisions and events of the Reformation. Yet this point of view does make some sense – if only because there is every reason to ask whether the Reformation actually set more in motion, perhaps even *much* more, than was intended.

Before we approach this question, however, we must insist that despite all the value of interpreting history in the light of subsequent experience, none of the ecclesiastical parties of the time and no individual, whether 'left-wing' or 'right-wing', 'radical' or 'magisterial', 'populist' or 'educationally élitist', would have

---

[1] 'Sunt enim semper tumultuosi spiritus, qui regnum Christi non bene extolli credunt, nisi aboleantur omnes terrenae potestates' (*Iohannis Calvini Commentarius in Epistolam Pauli ad Romanos,* ed. T. H. L. Parker, Leiden 1981, 281.9–12; on Romans 13.1).

understood or agreed with the ideals of the French or Russian revolution. For all these groups, there was no question of a 'revolution from below', nor of achieving respect for human rights, but only of establishing God's law and justice, legitimated entirely from on high. This includes both the 'scatterbrained fools' and Calvin. If we want to listen closely to contemporary voices, we must also cultivate a desire and an ability to engage in debate about theological questions with the 'common man' in the taverns and with the learned town councillors at City Hall.

The radical rejection of theological factors in explanatory models – a hopelessly ahistorical position – has been greatly favored and even accelerated by a host of external circumstances. Two of these, for instance, are the marked personal and psychological distance of many historians from the Reformation itself and the growing inability to understand the Latin sources, especially those written in the technical language of theology, a specialized language which even experts decipher only with considerable effort.

We must also recognize that the history of theology dominated Reformation history in all confessional camps for so long, and with such pale and narrow interpretive results, that the reaction was both necessary and well-deserved. This reaction is exemplified and at the same time justified by the aggressive challenge posed in the word 'revolution'.

Long before the time of Jacob Burckhardt, the Reformation and Renaissance appeared to be a single epoch because both seemed to demonstrate the visible, concrete consequences of ideas and purely intellectual discoveries. The term 'revolution', however, evokes questions of social power and upheavals, in clear opposition to the notion that education and rational understanding grow and expand in an organic fashion, a notion best represented in our terms by the word 'evolution'. The formerly dominant belief that ideas are constitutive of reality had to be questioned and changed to allow historians to return to the noise and debates of the streets. Yet the danger of overreaction is quite clear: scholars have shifted the main focus of their research from the 'thought of the reformers' to 'what the reformers did'; the question is no longer 'What did they think?'; but 'What did they accomplish?'

This has meant, in terms of method, a shift from interest in individuals to concern for groups, from biography to prosopography, from treatises to tax rolls, from Collected Works to collections of documents. In short, research into the ideals and religious values of the time has given way to the determination of social and political 'factors' and 'chains of events'. This reorientation becomes a distorting overreaction when it projects modern experiences onto the past and brushes aside religious statements and arguments as the incidental linguistic trimmings characteristic of a time we have left far behind. This excessive zeal for new perspectives blocks all access to a period when God and the Devil, not banks and bombs, were Great Powers.

The future belongs, or so we can hope, to those historians of the Reformation who are ready to study historical programs for change in conjunction with the results obtained. The lofty 'vantage point' from which historians are required to pass judgement is not identical with subsequent history: that would be fraud, pure and simple. This 'vantage point', rather, is created from a synthetic view of the whole. This means that we cannot be satisfied with Calvin's dismissal on theological grounds of the 'scatterbrained fools'; we must also mount guard against those historians who would isolate the political and social circumstances as the single determinative and causal factors in history.

To arrive at a synthetic, integrated explanation of the importance and the limits of the Reformation, we must accord an equally serious examination to political, social and religious factors, understood as potentially fruitful 'sounding-boards' (*Resonanzpotential*) to test explanatory theses concerning the widespread effects of the Reformation.[2]

This means that we must come down from the empyrean heights both of our predecessors' history of ideas and of 'enlightened' history *ex post facto*. The modern debate about 'revolution' would not have been understood, or would have been misunderstood, in the sixteenth century. The only meaning of the word *revolutio* that might have been current to contemporaries is that of the earth's orbit around the sun, or vice-versa. Even when the Puritan historian Edward Haie applied the word *revolutio* to the Reformation — so far as I can tell, for

[2] See the foreword to the first edition of my book *Werden und Wertung der Reformation*, Tübingen 1979[2], ixf.; this foreword is not reproduced in the English translation *Masters of the Reformation*, Cambridge 1981.

the first time, and one hundred years earlier than has generally been thought – in 1583, he remained indebted to the astronomical image of planetary movement: revolution is '[the] course of God's word and religion, which from the beginning hath moved from the East, toward and at last unto the West . . .'.[3] The Reformation is a revolution understood as the mobilization and departure of the Gospel on a global voyage of discovery, on the way to 'God's own country'.

What we mean today by revolution was expressed during the Reformation era, including Haie's time, by very different Latin and German terms, ranging from *res novae* (nonsensical novelties) through *mutatio* (illicit changes) to *rebellio* (disobedience); from *Aufruhr* (illegal uprising) to *schwytzern* (acting like the Swiss). In the magisterial tradition of Luther, Melanchthon, Zwingli, Bucer and Calvin, *rebellio* is rejected unanimously as subversion, hateful to God. If resistance was required, in this line of thought, it was considered legitimate only as resistance *to* revolution, as battle on the side of the traditional order and traditional law, both of which were good precisely because they were traditional. The resistance of the reformers was therefore directed against the power of the Church, against papal pomp, masses for the souls of the dead and the cult of the saints. These 'papal innovations' were, judged by their ideological content, the *res novae* (nonsensical novelties) which had in the past overturned the traditional and divinely-willed order in the Church and in society.

Nonetheless, these *res novae* were already hundreds of years old, and truly rooted in the daily life of both the 'common man' and the 'big shots'. To do away with these 'innovations' was entirely contrary not only to the official teachings of the Church, but also to the experiential content of popular piety. The introduction of the 'old order' (*alte Ordnungen*) affected all of public life in revolutionary ways. Resistance to 'revolution' actually functioned as a revolution.

The concept 'revolution' has certain uses, but they are not all obvious: the introduction by the public authorities of the 'old order' in the sphere of theology and the Church caused upheavals that cannot be 'brushed off' or disregarded in favor of the 'real'

[3] Cited by H. Jantz, 'The Myths about America: Origins and Extensions', in: *Deutschlands literarisches Amerikabild*, ed. A. Ritter, Hildesheim 1977, 37–49; 43.

developments in the social and political realm. Theology was no longer kept under lock and key in academic institutions, but had become the *cause célèbre* of a new public awareness. If the Reformation deliberately attacked oppression, deception and stultification, it was because theology, seen as both knowledge of faith and practical wisdom applicable to the problems of life, was to be brought out of the monasteries and universities into the streets and city halls. The phenomenon of Reformation pamphlets cannot be understood if these 'shock troops of the Reformation' are seen as mere 'media', as messengers for a program. Rather, they are themselves a program, living theology as read and understood in the council meeting rooms and popular watering holes.

Given the estimate that Martin Luther was responsible for over half of pamphlet printing before mid-century, his program cannot have failed to make its mark: theology is a public accounting of scholarly discoveries that demand internal and external changes. A second conclusion is also unavoidable: given the massive sales of Luther's works, it is not too bold a statement to say that he succeeded in freeing scholarly theology from the Babylonian captivity of secret and secretive academic debate.

Whether the changes that were demanded and carried out were 'revolutionary'[4] in the modern sense can be determined only if revolutionary consciousness *and* its achievements are considered together. There is no use in listing theological principles if we forget to ask to whom these principles appealed and why.

The use of violence is not the necessary criterion for 'revolution'.[5] Innovations that have been accorded a certain legitimacy and are then carried out at the correct time no longer lead inexorably to *rebellio* (unrest). *For this reason, a successful revolution often disguises itself as an evolution.* Such successful disguises explain why scholars searching for 'revolutions' in the Reformation era often find nothing but the

---

[4] See C. Brinkmann, *Soziologische Theorie der Revolution,* Göttingen 1948; K. Griewank, *Der neuzeitliche Revolutionsbegriff. Entstehung und Entwicklung,* Weimar 1955.

[5] See Max Bäumer's highly informative article, which seems to hesitate on this point. Nevertheless, he is unwilling to deny that the bloodless introduction of the Reformation in Braunschweig was revolutionary in character: 'Sozialkritische und revolutionäre Literatur der Reformationszeit', in: *Internationales Archiv für Sozialgeschichte der deutschen Literatur* 5 (1980), 169–233; 219.

Peasants' War. This blinkered perspective is favored by the ideological links or even fetters that bind it to the great modern revolutions; but it is also an unpaid and now overdue bill for jumping to the conclusion that the Reformation as a whole is identical with Luther's Reformation, and for limiting the Reformation to the first decades of the sixteenth century. The main reason for this distortion, which identifies revolution with violence, is the silencing of theological and religious motives as powerful factors tending toward *Enderung* (change, re-formation).

2. Three Disguised Reformations

Concentration on 1525 as the year of the revolution blurs the outlines of the general state of things in Europe north of the Alps. In this area there were at least three 'disguised revolutions', in the sense just sketched, between 1400 and 1600.

1. The first is the powerful conciliar movement, an ecclesiastical parallel to the development in the constitutional sphere of proto-parliamentary government. Research into the dramatic events and developments along the axis formed by the Councils of Pisa, Constance, Basel and Pisa (1409–1511) has fallen strangely silent. Historians of the Reformation can object with some justification that they have more important tasks to which they must attend. And in any case, had not the entire movement been compromised by Hus and Wyclif, outmaneuvered by the concordates obtained by the popes, from Martin V to Leo X, and finally, within the reforming camp itself, disowned and condemned by Luther? Conciliarism, it might seem, was an intermezzo without far-reaching consequences, nothing more than a passing irritant to papal claims to sovereignty.[6] Sovereignty over all of Christendom had been demanded by Pope Boniface VIII (*Unam sanctam*, 1302); it was also claimed on the eve of the Reformation, with the full approval of his council, by Leo X (*Pastor aeternus*, 1516); and it was confirmed

---

[6] The extent to which conciliarism and its centrally important goals have come to be seen as an intermezzo has been demonstrated by a well-known historian, John Keegan, who recently stated, in a bland matter-of-fact way, that 'the popes had, of course, never claimed political sovereignty over Christendom . . .' (*New York Times, Book Review* 89 (1984), no. 11, 33).

publicly as an article of faith in order to avert the threat of an independent Gallican Church.

Had papal councils reduced conciliarism *ad absurdum?* A surprising answer rang out in England fifteen years later. The danger which the pope had just managed to avert in France with the collaboration of Francis I could no longer be kept at bay in England. Henry VIII refused to follow curial injunctions concerning his marital affairs. The idea of a national Church, born of conciliarism, became a reality. This was evidently more than just the confused dream of a few disappointed partisans of the conciliar principle. Given the historical power and concrete consequences of the conciliar idea, it is irresponsible to ignore, in studies on the history of the Reformation, one highly-charged moment: on St. Martin's Day (11 November) 1524, the Holy Roman Empire of the German nation might have established a German national Church, an *Ecclesia Germanica.* Assured of the support of all the Estates, this plan would have been realized had Emperor Charles V not opposed it with all his might. The Reformation is frequently lamented as a German tragedy – often in connection with the defeat of the peasants. However, the definitive frustration of hopes for a national Church in Germany is to a much greater extent the crucial point at which Germany missed a historic chance to discover itself as a nation.

Conciliar or Gallican ideas were not, therefore, devoid of influence, even though a constitutional revolution in the Church was prevented. The development of the right to resistance drew in its turn on conciliar ideas. In Germany, the election of the emperor was interpreted as a constitutional contract with the Prince-Electors, which contributed to the legitimation of defensive alliances between princes. This legal construct had been borrowed by the conciliarists from Roman law a century earlier in order to restrain the *plenitudo potestatis* (claim to absolute power) of the papacy. This solution was adopted by the constitutional experts of Electoral Saxony and presented to a hesitant Martin Luther. The principle of the constitutional contract was used to justify the right to resist an emperor who breaks the contract and opposes the common good, thereby losing automatically the rights of lordship conceded to him by contract.

Gallican ideas lived on in French jurisprudence and tended toward *popular* sovereignty and the rewriting of the *right* to resist as the *duty* to resist tyranny. The legitimation of resistance gained currency and strength in the sixteenth century from the humanists' rediscovery of Roman law. The praise commonly accorded the 'democratic' or parliamentary progress implicit in Calvinist constitutional thought overlooks the pre-Calvinist conciliar tradition.

Conciliarism is indispensable as the interpretive background to early modern parliamentarianism. Theodore Beza, Calvin's successor and trustee, placed the parliamentary institution higher than the office of the king. However, the parliament remains, in his view, a potential control mechanism, whose *plenitudo potestatis* is activated only in an emergency: if the king turns out to be a tyrant and thus forfeits his power, the parliament automatically becomes the highest constitutional body. One modern commentator has ridiculed Beza's solution: in such cases, a tyrant will no doubt be able to prevent parliament from meeting; this parliamentary theory is, therefore, nothing but a fiction.[7] However, Beza is in fact on firm ground with the theoretical practice and political experience of the conciliarists, who took the daring steps that led to the decretum *Frequens* (1417). This far-sighted decision of the Council of Constance removed the calling of church councils – at least for a time – from arbitrary papal power. This 'fiction' had thus already passed a crucial 'reality test' 150 years before Beza's time.

Socially, the main proponents of conciliarism belonged to the high aristocracy. They were great lords and great landlords. Their revolution was neutralized within the Church, at least in France and Germany, after the debacle of the Council of Basel. The conciliar idea, however, and the concomitant legitimation of the right to resist, based on Roman law, was still alive and kicking. These inheritances from the heyday of conciliarism were to help blaze the trail of the Reformation. They were adaptable enough to be used with great precision and effect by the Huguenots, starting in mid-century.

2. The second Reformation, which was able to disguise itself as an 'evolution', at least for as long as it was successful, was the

[7] R. E. Giesey, 'The Monarchomach Triumvirs: Hotmann, Beza and Mornay', in: *Bibliothèque d'Humanisme et Renaissance* 32 (1970), 41–56; 44. Giesey's work is cited with approval (but with incorrect page numbers) in the unclear article of his student R. R. Benert, 'Lutheran Resistance Theory and the Imperial Constitution', in: *Il Pensiero Politico* 6 (1973), 17–36; 33.

emancipation of the urban bourgeoisie and the establishment of urban élites that were to determine internal and external policy via the institution of the Small or Lesser Council. In our review we can cut corners, because it is here that modern research has made the greatest progress.

The burghers' relationship to the bishop, initially distant and later often hostile, the establishment of urban preacherships and Latin schools, the naming of urban administrators from their own ranks to oversee monasteries and convents, hospitals and poor relief: all these late medieval developments contribute to the composite image of urban emancipation from ecclesiastical jurisdiction within a climate of pious criticism of the Church and pointed attacks on the clergy.

The unrest (*tumultus*) so greatly feared in all places and by all urban magistrates, as noted in council minutes, was for a long time considered to be a threat posed by the urban 'common man' who did not belong to a guild and who was seen as particularly susceptible to discontent and protest movements. It is easy to overlook a second source of tension, namely the social broadening of the class of burghers eligible to serve on the city council. This led to disputes over the distribution and limitation of political responsibilities and power, and thus intensified the power struggle between the Small and Great Councils. As the prosopographical research of Thomas A. Brady, Jr., has shown for Strasbourg,[8] these tensions could be minimized, controlled and papered over, except in the crisis years 1525 and 1548, by means of precise and deliberate patrician policies concerning family alliances and elections. However, such strategies in no way resolved these tensions.

In Zurich as well, the rapid succession of events at the beginning of the Reformation – between the summer of 1522 and the autumn of 1523 – can be explained only in the light of the structurally predetermined conflict of interests between the Great and Small Councils. Until the Great Council decided in January of 1524 to appropriate control over religious policy from the Small Council, *Bürgermeister* Röist and the Small Council had pursued a patrician policy aimed at maintaining calm and order, a policy which later interpreters were rather too quick to term 'evangelical'. Only after

[8] *Ruling Class, Regime and Reformation at Strasbourg, 1520–55*, Leiden 1978.

Zwingli was able to mobilize his supporters in the Great Council did the Reformation begin in earnest at Zurich.[9]

The important point is not the tendency of priests to become citizens, a development characteristic of the late Middle Ages, but that master cobblers, butchers and bakers become officials with responsibilities in both civil and religious communities. Zwingli desired, pushed for and solidified this development. The priesthood of everyone eligible to serve on the council was the disguised revolution carried out by the Reformation at Zurich.

3. The constant power struggle between the Small and the Great Councils[10] has been presented using the case of Zurich because this perspective provides a natural transition to the third revolution to come under our scrutiny: the infiltration of city councils' policies by urban concerns and perspectives. There is at present a clear tendency in scholarly research to emphasize the 'communalisation' that went hand-in-hand with the introduction of the Reformation; in the case of Zurich, scholars even speak of a 'localization'. The sources also support this view, as the urban reformers indeed wanted to realize the 'horizontal' relationships of the Gospel for the sake of the common good in each of their cities.

Yet an unavoidable conflict of interests breaks out at this point: the 'evangelically' ordered commonwealth does not stop at the city walls, in the view of these reformers. Their goal is 'universalization', not 'localization'. The reformation of the city is merely an interim project, not the final goal of evangelical preaching. It is impossible to overlook the seeds of future conflict even with an élite that has been won over to the Reformation. Expressions like 'Zwingli's Zurich' or 'Zwingli's theocracy' are misleading for the simple reason that they conceal just how short the tense period of so-called symbiosis actually was, even with the newly-restructured power élite. Zwingli was

[9] *Werden und Wertung der Reformation*, 256–8, English trans.: *Masters of the Reformation*, 200–2; cf. chapter 9, 'Zwingli's Reformation Between Success and Failure', *supra*.

[10] The compendious study of O. Mörke has broadened our horizons to include north-western Germany. Mörke orients his work toward the demarcation lines between those eligible and those not eligible to serve on the council. *Rat und Bürger in der Reformation. Soziale Gruppen und kirchlicher Wandel in den welfischen Hansestädten Lüneburg, Braunschweig und Göttingen*, Hildesheim 1983. Mörke's well thought-out formulations constantly lead back toward our topic; see his p. 305, n. 41.

counselled by his own left wing as early as 1525/6 to keep a bit more distance between himself and the council. He was to compromise himself in the next year: against local and national interests and against the opinion of both the Small and Great Councils, he favored the inclusion of Zurich's hereditary enemy, Swabia, in a broad evangelical confederacy, and the swearing of an oath with the other members to undertake together a 'pre-emptive strike' against the enemies of the Gospel.[11]

As Zwingli bitterly foretold in his last sermon, he was abandoned to his fate shortly thereafter in the Second Kappel War by a tightly-forged 'chain' of powerful interests belonging to the old Zurich aristocracy. The 'peoples' pastor' was isolated and saw his end approaching.[12]

Zwingli's death in arms might serve as a paradigm of the cleric-turned-burgher, and as a personification of the bourgeois Reformation. However, this perspective blocks our view of his program for far-reaching reformation including other cities and beyond: his convictions broke out of the narrowly circumscribed sphere of urban interests and achieved an orbit the center of which was not determined by commercial interests and military security. The authorities' strategy, based as it was on an overriding concern for the calm and good order of the city, was thereby endangered in every conceivable way.

The urban Reformation reached its limits by 1530/1. The defeat of Kappel spelled the end of this brand of Reformation politics. Zwingli's plan to 'de-localize' the political and religious policies of the city council failed entirely. The urban community for a short time had set the pace of the Reformation and provided a bridgehead for it in many cities. The reformed city lost its function as the standard-bearer of Christian society reformed by God, as well as its view of itself as a model for other communities.

After Kappel and Zwingli's death in arms, reproachful obituaries poured in from all sides. Initially, Zwingli's personal failings and

---

[11] W. Bender has pointed to Zwingli's vision of a great *civitas christiana: Zwinglis Reformationsbündnisse. Untersuchungen zur Rechts- und Sozialgeschichte der Burgrechtsvertäge eidgenössischer und oberdeutscher Städte zur Ausbreitung und Sicherung der Reformation Huldrych Zwinglis,* Zurich 1970, 177f.

[12] Johann Stumpf, *Chronica vom Leben und Wirken des Ulrich Zwingli,* Zurich 1932², 169.

behavior inspired the most stinging rebukes. But when Martin Bucer condemns the Second Kappel War, his critique concerns more fundamental issues. His three short, hard words are unequivocal: 'Evangelium cruce vincit': not the sword and armies win the Gospel's battles, but the Cross alone. The 'bishop' of Zurich, Bucer charges, went to war on his own initiative, without first bothering to find out what God wanted.[13] A week later, Leo Jud informed him that all of Zurich might well be lost to the Reformation.[14]

The military defeat was a God-send, however, for the next Reformation, the heavily persecuted Reformation of the refugees. Calvin understood the message of Kappel; he also learned from Bucer at Strasbourg (1538–41) that in order to succeed, 'Reformation' needs its *own* ecclesiastical organization, so that the cause of the Gospel is not subject to the authority of the city council. On the eve of the Second World War, Hans Baron published his first article to appear in the New World. He too was a refugee without a permanent home – a scholar 'formerly of the University of Berlin', and now in the diaspora. The article, 'Calvinist Republicanism and its Historical Roots', has been attacked repeatedly in scholarship, but I agree entirely with Baron's conclusions: the Imperial City of Strasbourg was the rich seed-bed in which the shoots of republican Calvinism took root and blossomed.[15] The most recent research on the topic suggests that we ought to stick to the path Baron marked out. As the outlines of the third Reformation come into focus, I would like to introduce a variation on our theme: *the city hall of the urban Reformation was to serve as an armory to the Reformation of the refugees.*

We have now arrived at a dividing line, which also serves to introduce the next phase of the Reformation. It is at this juncture that Calvin as a reformer achieves an independence fraught with consequences for subsequent history, not just in Europe but around the world. Only as a result of these developments were the refugees, who were put to flight by the Interim after the defeat of the

[13] Bucer writes in a letter to Ambrosius Blarer that Zwingli acted 'inconsulto domino' (14 November 1531; *Briefwechsel der Brüder Ambrosius und Thomas Blaurer 1509–1548*, vol. I: 1509–June 1538, ed. T. Schiess, Freiburg im Breisgau 1908, 286).

[14] 'In his male veretur, ne omne evangelium apud Tigurinos excidat', in a letter to Ambrosius Blarer dated 29 November 1531 (Schiess, *Briefwechsel* I, 292).

[15] In: *Church History* 8 (1939), 30–42; 42.

Schmalkaldic League, able to survive the severe test of faith imposed on them by the disappearance of official protection. Without the shelter provided by city councils, the refugees were forced to place their trust in God alone, without regard for military victories and defeats. I am willing, therefore, to adopt Robert Kingdon's thesis without modifications: '[T]he changes in Geneva between 1526 and 1559 constitute a genuine revolution.'[16] Kingdon considers the Genevan reform to be the most extreme variety of Reformation. The rejection of papal authority, the secularization of the monasteries and convents and the annulment of canon law constitute an anti-clerical thrust so powerful that we have every reason to call it a revolution.[17] The third Reformation also preserved its disguise for as long as it was successful.

Yet we might say exactly the same things about Zurich. In what respect was Geneva actually more radical? Three points are characteristic of Calvin's Reformation:

(1) The articles of the church's constitutional incorporation are written in such a way as to guarantee freedom from interference by the city authorities. The constitution of the Genevan Church is essentially a counterblow aimed at the late medieval inter-penetration of Church and City Hall, originally a concession wrung from the bishop.

(2) The Genevan Consistory introduced ecclesiastically-controlled moral discipline in contradistinction to the Zurich system, in which the Marriage Court exercised a kind of public or civic discipline overseen by the Council. From the perspective of the Genevan aristocracy, this moral discipline was a restoration of pre-communal conditions, a relapse into the medieval world of ecclesiastical law. The Genevan oligarchy attempted to domesticate the Reformation as part of a 'communalized' political regime, but ran up against Calvin's determined opposition and failed; Calvin not only won the battle but overcame the communal hierarchy.

(3) Zwingli's thought and actions in the framework of his policy of alliances had already transcended the confines of locality and region.

---

[16] R. M. Kingdon, 'Was the Protestant Reformation a Revolution? The Case of Geneva', in: *Church, Society and Politics*, ed. D. Baker, Studies in Church History 12, Oxford 1975, 203–22; 219.

[17] Kingdon, 220, 222.

Furthermore, his thesis that 'the kingdom of Christ is also external
and visible',[18] was directed against Luther, from within the center of
the power structure bound and symbolized by the city walls. Here we
find a legitimate use of the expression 'communalization' – to the
extent that Zwingli saw the city reformed by its own Council as the
pattern by which all Christendom should be reformed.

In Calvin's view, the 'kingdom of Christ' was developing at
Geneva, but in a completely new and different way. The city of
Geneva is not the 'Christian corporation' (*corpus Christianum*) –
according to his political testament, set down a year before his death[19]
– but rather a bridgehead for the expansion of the kingdom of Christ.
The walls of the city do not protect a piece of Paradise from the harsh
post-lapsarian reality outside, nor do they fence in the civic
monastery, where God's will is carried out and where holiness guides
daily life. The walls do not surround monks with the security of the
cloister, but mark the exterior boundaries of a theological armory, in
which the main arteries leading out of the city are more important
than the defensive towers. In short: whereas Zwingli reformed
Zurich, Calvin reformed *from* Geneva. Calvin characteristically closes
his sermons with this prayer: 'Let him work this miracle of grace not
only here and for us, but for all the peoples and nations on earth . . .'
('Que non seulement il nous face ceste grace, mais a tous les peuples
et nations de la terre . . .').

In the tradition of Bucer, Calvin, Vermigli and Beza, debates and
treatises on the state, the constitution and resistance always refer to
the political institutions and constitutional organs of the 'lesser
magistracies' (*magistratus inferiores*). This formulation encompasses
not only the princes, at the level of the empire, or the Small and Great
Councils at the level of civic administration, but also – in Beza's
words – 'the middling [officials], and as is commonly said, the
subaltern [functionaries] between the highest jurisdiction or
authority and the people'. These new legal officials are 'subaltern', but

---

[18] '[R]egnum Christi etiam est externum . . .'; see the historical judgement of H. R.
Lavater, 'Regnum Christi etiam externum – Huldrych Zwinglis Brief vom 4. Mai 1528 an
Ambrosius Blarer in Konstanz', in: *Zwingliana* 15 (1981), 338–81.
[19] His sermon of 29 June 1562 on 2 Sam. 5; *Supplementa Calviniana I: Sermones de
altero libro Regum*, ed. H. Rückert, Neukirchen 1936–1961, esp. 104f. See also my article
'The "Extra" Dimension in the Theology of Calvin', in Oberman, *The Dawn of the
Reformation*, Edinburgh 1981, 237f.

not to the king; rather, to the state. As in ancient Rome, they serve the common good not only as as 'consuls, praetors and city prefects', but even as 'governors of provinces'.[20]

The seemingly unimportant transition from 'city prefects' to 'governors of provinces' is by French standards no innovation, but it does mark a new beginning in the history of the Reformation: the city is swallowed up by a larger community in a process that displaces the urban ideology of the early Reformation. The walls of the city are levelled. The *exodus from the city* characterizes the transition from the urban Reformation to the Reformation of the refugees; or after Luther's Reformation, from the second to the third Reformation.

Hans Baron once spoke of the 'vigorous anti-monarchic spirit of political Calvinism'.[21] However, the anti-monarchical thrust he correctly emphasized needs to be examined in more depth. At the same time and with the same thoroughness, we must consider the Calvinist triumph over the city and its institutions. Calvin made an end of the Reformation as 'communalization' even before Calvinism was able to break out of the 'territorialization' brought about by the Reformation.

3. The Reformation of the Refugees

To begin my summation, I would like to point out that we have for far too long now concentrated our attention and resources on the urban Reformation due to an unfortunate and misleading accumulation of historically-determined research agendas and interests. The urban Reformation lasted only a quarter of a century, from 1522 to 1548. After the first ten years (in 1530/1), it had already lost most of its political momentum in the ebb and flow of statecraft and territorial politics. The third Reformation adopted some important elements from its predecessor, adapting them to fit the times and endowing them with such renewed force that they in turn were to affect the course of history not only beyond the city

---

[20] '[I]ntermedii et, ut vulgus loquitur, subalterni inter summum magistratum et populum' (Theodore Beza, *De iure Magistratuum*, ed. K. Sturm, Neukirchen 1965, *quaestio* 6, 41). Cf. the French text in Kingdon's edition, Théodore de Bèze, *Du droit des magistrats,* Geneva 1970, 18.

[21] 'Calvinist Republicanism' (see n. 15). On Calvinist resistance in the Netherlands, see Q. Skinner, *The Foundations of Modern Political Thought,* vol. 2: *The Age of Reformation,* Cambridge 1978, 215f.

walls, but far beyond Europe north of the Alps. This third Reformation can be described as a revolution because it collected and concentrated the revolutionary force and potential of all three fields of conflict described above: this 'revolution' adopted the conciliar-parliamentarian rejection of papal and monarchical absolutism, it presupposed the city council's liberation from episcopal control, and it incorporated anti-oligarchic opposition to the urban élite of 'libertines' and 'eudemonists' – in the propagandistic terms Calvin loved so well. Finally, and most strikingly, the third Reformation completed the movement away from the integrated civic Reformation tamed by urban institutions and interests.

The Reformation of the refugees appears to be nothing more than the third phase of a unitary movement if we apply the traditional criteria of the threefold reforming *sola: sola gratia* (by grace alone), *sola fide* (by faith alone) and *sola scriptura* (by Scripture alone) are the continuous program of the Reformation that ties all three stages together. However, a closer examination shows up considerable differences within this unity: the urban Reformation and the Reformation of the refugees oppose Luther at two crucial points.[22] The seeming harmony between the camps concerning the three *solae* hides their entirely different understanding of the principle 'by Scripture alone' (*sola scriptura*). Throughout the areas touched by the Reformation in southern Germany and even in Geneva, Scripture is the new law. Scripture promulgates God's law not only for the Christian community, but for city and state; it replaces human and canon law. This understanding of Scripture corresponds to a specific program for Reformation (which is also in complete opposition to that of Luther[23]): the Reformation finally allows Christians to exercise a new obedience founded in biblical law.

In various ways, the third Reformation followed new paths that differentiated it from both the first and second Reformations. This is particularly true in three areas: the Calvinists' view of the Jews, the doctrine of resistance and the understanding of predestination. These three central concerns grew out of the refugees' novel experience of (forced) exodus from the sacral space of the cities to the promised

---

[22] See the typology I have developed in *Werden und Wertung der Reformation*, 371–6; English trans.: *Masters of the Reformation*, 290–4.

[23] See chapter 2, 'Martin Luther: Forerunner of the Reformation', above.

land beyond all territories and principalities: God bursts the bonds of borders and guides the fugitives to the 'New World'.

These three characteristics of the Reformation of the refugees require some further clarification:

(1) The disaster at Kappel prepared the reform party for even harder times, which materialized in the Interim. The deportees now read Scripture in the new light of their own experience. The 'argumentum Augustinianum' (Augustine's argument) against the Jews, which had lost none of its power right up to the sixteenth century, was no longer valid: now homelessness and exile could hardly be seen as signs of an irate God's rejection of his people.[24] A new relationship with the Jews thus became possible.

(2) Predestination was to Luther and Zwingli a self-evident corollary to the doctrine of justification. In the third Reformation, it also announces the mystery of the divinely-ordained progress of the Gospel from the city to the territory, and then from country to country, and finally to a new and different world. Predestination is the eternal and certain summons of God that calls 'us' – as it once called Abraham – away from the cities and the countryside, whether under the protection or despite the resistance of the authorities.

(3) The third Reformation based its subsequent development of the doctrine of resistance on experiences that Bucer revealed in a letter he wrote on 13 May 1549, while in flight from Strasbourg on the way into exile in England. Unbelief, gutless unbelief, led to the decision at Strasbourg to hold a general referendum in the city as to whether the Gospel ought to be given up to win favor with the Emperor. A fundamental decision of this kind cannot be left to the whims of unqualified citizens, majority or not. Such decisions are reserved to the *pars sanior,* the true believers.[25] It may interest the reader that the 'true believers', as at the election of a Benedictine abbot, are not the quantitative, but the qualitative majority. But what is important here is that resistance requires no democratic legitimation: even the vocabulary of the urban Reformation has to be modified to fit new circumstances!

---

[24] Cf. my book *Die Wurzeln des Antisemitismus,* Berlin 1983², 185–92; English trans.: *The Roots of Anti-Semitism,* Philadelphia 1984, 138–43.

[25] Bucer to Jakob Sturm; J. Rott, 'Un receuil de correspondances strasbourgeoises du XVIᵉ siècle à la bibliothèque de Copenhague (ms. Thott 497,2º)', in: *Bulletin philologique et historique* (1968), 749–818; 809–13.

The beginnings of the third Reformation are to be found in Bucer's writings; the refugee Church 'beneath the Cross' was born during the Interim in a diaspora that had been forced on the refugees politically, but which they would learn to interpret in theological terms and finally to embrace. Those who did not take the long road into exile, but stayed at home and cultivated the by now very old dream of the sacral space within the city walls, were abandoned as mere fossils in the subsequent course of the Reformation. The city councilmen who loyally obeyed the Emperor's religious mandate were caught up once again in the medieval imperial dream of the Free Imperial City. Yet under the ominous umbrella of territorial absolutism, they would become mere vassals, their unimportant towns now subject to territorial lords.

If we interpret the Reformation as a revolution, we will be able to perceive the real upheavals of the time only to the extent that we are able to refrain from applying the (modern) theory of revolutions to history. The only route appropriate to our task and goals lies along the path of observation, and perhaps even of participation. We must register the amazingly rapid succession of events, evaluate them as a contemporary would have done, and only then, in the garb of modern historians, are we justified in formulating an integrated and overarching analysis of the social, political and religious forces at work in our period and in our sources. If we shy away from these three investigative tasks, the three Reformations in question will remain veiled beneath their respective disguises, and so will the individual impact each had on subsequent history. The history of Europe north of the Alps, an area constantly divided and redivided, is in no way elucidated by the thesis that the Reformation was a revolution. It was the threefold Reformation that was to acquire historical influence and force. Each phase was able to enter into coalitions with different – disguised – revolutions. Martin Luther, however, was and remains an exception. He is claimed by different parties for different purposes, whether as the precursor of a national awakening, of urban liberties or as the herald of the imminent Kingdom of God. Luther himself eschewed coalitions, and preferred to await Reformation 'in these last days'. This is his 'final' and expansive, explosive significance.

PUBLISHING INFORMATION

The essays in this collection were originally published as:

1. Werden und Wertung der Reformation: Thesen und Tatsachen, in:
    *Reformatio Ecclesiae. Beiträge zu kirchlichen Reformbemühungen
    von der Alten Kirche bis zur Neuzeit. Festgabe für Erwin Iserloh,* ed.
    R. Bäumer, Paderborn 1980, 486–503.

2. Martin Luther: Vorläufer der Reformation, in:
    Verifikationen. Festschrift für Gerhard Ebeling zum 70. Geburtstag,
    ed. E. Jüngel, J. Wallmann, W. Werbeck, Tübingen 1982,
    91–119.

3. Martin Luther: Zwischen Mittelalter und Neuzeit
    A speech given on 5 November 1983, on the occasion of the
    Luther anniversary celebrated by the Evangelical Faculty of
    Theology at the Eberhard-Karls-Universität, Tübingen, in: *'Gott
    kumm mir zu hilf.' Martin Luther in der Zeitenwende,* Berliner
    Forschungen und Beiträge zur Reformationsgeschichte, ed. H.-D.
    Loock, Jahrbuch für Berlin-Brandenburgische Kirchengeschichte,
    Sonderband, Berlin 1984, 9–26.

4. Die Bedeutung der Mystik von Meister Eckhart bis Luther, in:
    Von Eckhart bis Luther. Über mystischen Glauben, ed. W. Böhme,
    Herrenalber Texte 31, Karlsruhe 1981, 9–20.

5. Wir sein pettler. Hoc est verum. Bund und Gnade in der
    Theologie des Mittelalters und der Reformation, in:
    Zeitschrift für Kirchengeschichte 78 (1967), 232–52.

6. Wittenbergs Zweifrontenkrieg gegen Prierias und Eck, in: *Zeitschrift für Kirchengeschichte* 80 (1969), 331–58.

7. Vom Protest zum Bekenntnis. Die Confessio Augustana: Kritischer Maßstab wahrer Ökumene
   A speech given on 21 June 1980, on the occasion of the Reutlinger Festwoche zum Jubiläum des Augsburger Bekenntnisses, in: *Blätter für württembergische Kirchengeschichte* 80/81 (1980/1981), 24–37.

8. Dichtung und Wahrheit. Das Wesen der Reformation aus der Sicht der Confutatio, in:
   Confessio Augustana und Confutatio. Der Augsburger Reichstag 1530 und die Einheit der Kirche. Internationales Symposion der Gesellschaft zur Herausgabe des Corpus Catholicorum in Augsburg vom 3.–7. September 1979, ed. E. Iserloh, Münster/Westphalia 1980, 217–31.

9. Zwinglis Reformation zwischen Erfolg und Scheitern: Zürichs Beitrag zur Weltgeschichte
   A speech given at Zurich on 11 January 1984, on the occasion of the Zwinglifeier in 1984.

10. Eine Epoche – Drei Reformationen, in:
    Zwingli und Europa. Referate und Protokoll des Internationalen Kongresses aus Anlaß des 500. Geburtstages von Huldrych Zwingli vom 26. bis 30. März 1984, ed. P. Blickle, A. Lindt, A. Schindler, Göttingen 1985, 11–26.

These essays were also published in *Die Reformation. Von Wittenberg nach Genf,* Göttingen 1986.

INDEX OF PERSONS

INDEX OF MODERN AUTHORS

INDEX VERBORUM LATINORUM